Viktor Schreckengost and 20th-Century Design

Viktor Schreckengost

and 20th-Century Design

Henry Adams

The Cleveland Museum of Art Distributed by the University of Washington Press, Seattle

For Gene Schreckengost,
without whom this book could not
have been written.

And to the memory of Bob Bergman,
who got this project started
but did not live to see it happen.

Board of Trustees

Contents

The exhibition is made possible by Hahn Loeser & Parks LLP and the John P. Murphy Foundation, with additional support from the Richard Florsheim Art Fund, Northern Trust Company, Nottingham-Spirk Design Associates, Betty and Joe Oros, Mr. and Mrs. Viktor Schreckengost, and a grant from the National Endowment for the Arts.

Lenders to the Exhibition

The Bicycle Museum of America

The Butler Institute of American Art

The Cleveland Artists Foundation

Cowan Pottery Museum, Rocky River Public Library

Everson Museum of Art

The Metropolitan Museum of Art

National Museum of American Art, Smithsonian Institution

The Rowfant Club

Virginia Museum of Fine Arts

The Western Reserve Historical Society

John P. Axelrod

Mark Bassett

Robert Bullock

Leon Dixon/National Bicycle History Archive of America

Dr. and Mrs. Michael Dreyfuss

Edward J. Karee

Donn W. Kirschenbaum

Joe and Elaine Kisvardi

Cyd Kowit

Myron N. Krotinger

Jerry and Wynne Maschino

Elizabeth Mather McMillan

Mark Michalek

Dr. and Mrs. Douglas Nowacek

Dr. and Mrs. Stephen A. Ockner

Nicole L. S. Prenevost

Private collection

Paul and Renee Schreckengost

Viktor Schreckengost

Viktor D. Schreckengost

Frank A. Simoni Sr.

Mitchell Wolfson Jr.

Foreword

This exhibition celebrates a true national treasure and Cleveland hero, Viktor Schreckengost. A contemporary of Raymond Loewy, Norman Bel Geddes, and Walter Dorwin Teague, Viktor is the last major surviving figure from the first age of industrial design. Even more remarkable, he is still professionally active today at age 94. His career has stretched for more than three-quarters of a century and has touched on almost every imaginable aspect of industrial design. Through this work, particularly children's toys such as bicycles and pedal cars, he has brought enjoyment to the lives of millions of people. Along with his industrial activities, Viktor maintained an active career in fine art, exhibiting ceramics, sculpture, and watercolors both nationally and internationally. What is more, through his activities as a teacher and the creator of the industrial design program at the Cleveland Institute of Art, he has molded the thinking and careers of countless major figures in the world of industrial design.

Viktor's most famous object is the *Jazz Bowl,* which he designed for Eleanor Roosevelt in 1930. Like the spire of the Chrysler building, it captures for many people the essence of American art deco. Other achievements include the first blunt-nosed cab-over-engine truck, the first modern American dinnerware, the most original and successful children's pedal cars ever marketed, remarkably beautiful bicycles, revolutionary new concepts for printing presses and other sorts of printing equipment, and a host of other designs for everything from lawn chairs to flashlights. During World War II, he served as head of the design laboratory of a special devices section of the United States Navy, where he carried out experiments with voice recognition, developed the first training program for radar recogni-

tion, advanced new techniques for creating topographical maps by means of aerial photography, worked on plans for the invasion of Japan, and, after the war, created better ways of fitting artificial limbs. For Clevelanders, Viktor's monumental zoo sculptures of mastodons and extinct birds are much-loved local landmarks.

We are particularly grateful to Viktor Schreckengost and his wife, Gene, who facilitated every aspect of this project and answered inquiries with unfailing patience. We owe great thanks to Henry Adams, curator of American art, who undertook this project with unbridled enthusiasm. Henry has played the role of Boswell to Viktor's Dr. Johnson, with results that are splendidly evident in this catalogue. Henry's acknowledgments record the help provided by dozens of talented members of the museum's staff. Special recognition is due to Henry Hawley, curator of Renaissance and later decorative arts and sculpture, for his insightful contributions. An exhibition committee led by honorary chair Joe McCullough and chair John Nottingham helped us spread the word about this project. Our thanks to them for their enthusiasm and assistance.

We are most appreciative of the generosity of the many lenders to this exhibition, who are listed on page ix. Finally, our thanks to Hahn Loeser & Parks LLP and the John P. Murphy Foundation, without whose support the exhibition would not have been possible. We received additional help from the Richard Florsheim Art Fund, Northern Trust Company, Nottingham-Spirk Design Associates, Betty and Joe Oros, and Mrs. and Mrs. Viktor Schreckengost. We are also grateful for the support of the National Endowment for the Arts.

Katharine Lee Reid
Director

Preface

Somewhere around the time I moved to Cleveland I came across some pictures of Viktor Schreckengost's *Jazz Bowl* in a book on 20th-century design, *The Look of the Century,* compiled by Michael Tambini. It was hard to miss because Tambini reproduced it twice—once very large, running across nearly two full pages in a splash of brilliant turquoise, and again, this time smaller, to illustrate his timeline of the century. Of course, I thought the bowl was gorgeous and on the strength of it, having somehow discovered that Schreckengost lived in Cleveland, called him up not long after I arrived, completely ignorant of anything else he might have done. Shortly afterward, he came to the museum, and we chatted in the lobby for 40 minutes or so about his career.

At the time Viktor was already well over 90, but one would not have guessed it from the quality of his recollections, which were remarkably vivid and precise. Stories, names, dates, and addresses flowed off his tongue, and in a short time I learned that he had not only designed the *Jazz Bowl* but made sculpture and designed bicycles, toys, streetlights, lawn mowers, chairs, and other things. His descriptions made highly complex technical processes of manufacture and design sound clear and simple, creating visual pictures in my mind. In addition, it was amazing to have events and people of long ago described by a witness to them: such things as a skirmish leading up to the Spanish Civil War; the New York World's Fair of 1939, in which he exhibited; or the Battle of the Bulge, where he helped install the American radar. I was also thrilled to discover that he had known American artists whom I revere, such as Charles Burchfield and Rockwell Kent, not to mention his associates in the field of industrial design, such as Josef Hoffmann, Raymond Loewy, Russell Wright, Norman Bel Geddes, and Walter Dorwin Teague. His stories made a whole epoch of modern design come to life.

It struck me that recording some of this material would be interesting, but I would surely have done nothing if one of my graduate students, Shannon Masterson, had not become interested in the project and agreed to transcribe a set of interviews with Viktor. With the innocence of youth, she thought the task would be easy and quick. Actually, transcribing interviews, if you do it accurately, is a laborious and vexing process. It took Shannon not a few hours but several months to produce a full transcript of six interviews, nearly as long as a book. That provided the foundation of this exhibition and catalogue, the first full-scale study of Viktor's work.

In the course of those interviews I visited Viktor's home, and it would have been hard to miss the massive clay vessels on the tables and the paintings on the wall and stacked in corners. Not long after the interviews had been transcribed, I proposed doing a show of Viktor's work to the exhibition committee at the museum. I had in mind a small show, tucked away in some back gallery, and had no desire to make of it an ambitious statement. To my surprise, however, the late director of the museum, Bob Bergman, suggested that Viktor's sculpture would look much better in the main exhibition gallery. What's more, he felt that Viktor's works ranked with the best ever made in Cleveland. "Isn't this as good as it gets?" he asked. Before I knew it, the show was on the schedule as a major exhibition.

Over the next few months, we moved the show forward in date, both because a few holes opened up in the schedule and because we wanted to do it while Viktor was still feeling young. As a consequence, a project that could easily have taken four or five years has been pulled together in less than two. That it was possible is largely thanks to the clarity and intelligence with which Viktor describes his work and the care with which he has kept key records.

Viktor's success in industrial design was primarily based on his great artistic and mechanical skill, but it also was pushed forward by his wonderful ability to work with people and explain his ideas. He greets a visitor with warm enthusiasm and a strong handshake. His lair is by the table in the dining room, which he keeps half-covered with unusual objects and books. The opening act of any visit is to learn about the latest item of interest there: an unusual spinning top or child's toy, a book on making faces out of fruit, a volume on coincidences or on mysterious sightings of UFOs, or an example of one of his dinnerware designs of the 1930s. Unlike many artists, he does not speak boastfully or endlessly repeat the same stories. When I have pressed him to go over stories for the purpose of this book, he invariably tells them slightly differently, so as to emphasize some new aspect. No doubt in part because of his career in industrial design, which trained him to present his work in persuasive fashion, he speaks about what he has done with precision and engaging clarity. He speaks not about himself—his talent or his genius—but about the object itself—how interesting it is, some story connected with it, or the problem of design or manufacture that it solved. He does not dwell on the past but always seems eagerly looking forward to the next adventure.

Sources

To a large extent, this book is based on two fundamental sources. The first is Viktor himself. (I also interviewed his brother Don, some old friends such as the scientist Fred Stross, and a good many students who worked with him.) In addition, I was able to consult Viktor's scrapbooks, assembled by his first wife, Nadine. They are filled with materials that normal research methods would not uncover: fliers, theater programs, ephemera, and clippings from obscure local newspapers. A major additional source has been Viktor's patent applications, which provide a record of many of his industrial designs and were particularly useful in establishing a rough chronology of his industrial work.[1]

H. A.

1. A natural question is whether Viktor's recollections are reliable, or whether he has made things up or deceptively enlarged his role in events. This complicated question is difficult to answer without tediously going into case after case, but my own firm belief is that Viktor's recollections are remarkably accurate, and, except for a few minor details, they have invariably been supported by whatever documentary evidence I have been able to unearth. Significantly, Viktor has pointed out instances in which claims about what he did are inflated or inaccurate. For example, Grace Glueck stated ("Wolfson's Warehouse: High Art to Pure Kitsch," *New York Times* [1 June 1989], Living Arts section, pp. 15, 19) that Viktor designed the first scotch tape dispenser; and the Wolfsonian Museum in Miami had two such dispensers they had catalogued as his design (*U.S. Industrial Design 51* [New York: Studio Publications, 1951], p. 104). When I asked Viktor about the matter, however, he looked bewildered and stated he could not remember them and did not think they were his work. After several weeks of sleuthing, I discovered why Viktor had looked so perplexed. The dispensers were actually designed in 1951 by Reinecke Associates in collaboration with the staff of the Minnesota Mining and Manufacturing Company.

In some cases, I must confess, I have been nervous. For example, very early in this project, when I inquired at the Smithsonian's museum of American history about Viktor's cab-over-engine truck, the curator in charge of trucks had never heard of it and could provide me with no information whatsoever. His tone was skeptical and not exactly helpful. This puzzle was solved, however, when Viktor turned up a missing page from his scrapbook, which contained the original sales literature from White Motors, describing the design. Probably 80 or 90 percent of the text in this catalogue presents material that has never before been consulted by scholars and is available in no other source.

Acknowledgments

While the list that follows may seem long, it only hints at the range and variety of assistance I received in carrying out this project. I am grateful to a number of students and associates who got it off the ground. As already mentioned, Shannon Masterson got me started on this project and worked on the initial checklist; Karinia Gobar and James Ellis helped with research; Kim Hyde was a wonderful editor and proofreader; Genevieve Hill and Michelle May read early drafts of this manuscript; and Kathleen McKeever, my right-hand man, provided much-needed assistance and counsel of all kinds.

In the curatorial arena, Diane De Grazia, chief curator, enthusiastically supported this project, as did Sylvain Bellenger, curator of 19th-century European paintings. Henry Hawley, curator of Renaissance and later decorative arts and sculpture, contributed to the selection and editing of the exhibition and carefully read an early draft of this manuscript; William Robinson, curator of modern paintings, provided encouragement and astute suggestions; Stanton Thomas and Ken Bohač reviewed the manuscript, as did Jill Jiminez, who also helped with practical matters. Lynn Cameron has been unfailingly helpful and Roberto Prcela efficiently removed every obstacle that blocked the path.

Howard T. Agriesti and Gary Kirchenbauer, assisted by Bruce Shewitz, provided sensitive but dramatic photographs that finally do justice to Viktor's work. Larry Sisson, conservator, repaired damaged pieces with a magical touch and came to my aid at a number of difficult moments. I am also grateful to Bruce Christman, chief conservator; Pat Griffin, assistant conservator of objects; Charles Eiben, preparator for prints and drawings; and Jim George and Joan Neubecker, preparators. Jeffrey Baxter has overseen the exhibition design with both creative flair and fanatic attention to detail.

The registrar's office responded with good will to the endless vexations of this unorthodox and daunting exhibition. I am grateful for the expert support of Mary Suzor, chief registrar, as well as that of many members of her staff, including assistant registrars Beth Gresham, Marlene Kiss, Sara Meng, Jennifer Qualiotto, Jeanette Saunders, and Carol Thum, packing specialist Andy Rock, and art handler Joe Ionna.

The museum's Ingalls Library staff was unfailingly helpful and did not smirk at even my strangest research questions. I am immensely grateful to Ann Abid, head librarian; Louis Adrean, assistant librarian; Christine Edmonson, interlibrary loan librarian; Sara Jane Pearman, slide librarian; Stacey Sendry, slide library asisstant; and William

Kennedy, slide cataloguer (who also kindly reviewed the manuscript).

Throughout the project I have been honored by the support and friendship of Kate Sellers, deputy director, whose enthusiasm for Viktor and his work became as great as mine. I have also been cheered by the enthusiastic and effective work of Judith Paska, senior development officer; Rob Krulak, grants manager; Jill Barry, corporate relations manager; and Fiona Green, prospect researcher.

William Prenevost, senior officer of external affairs, and Julie Limpach, administrative assistant, not only orchestrated publicity for this exhibition but laid the foundations for a documentary film that will accompany it. Joellen DeOreo developed a lecture program to accompany the exhibition. Penelope Buchanan, consultant in the education division, kindly reviewed and commented on this manuscript.

Gold medals (and purple hearts) go to Barbara J. Bradley, editor, and Katherine Solender, exhibitions manager, both of whom performed with valor beyond the call of duty in pulling this book and the exhibition into shape, often under great time pressure, not to speak of other vexations. I owe a huge debt to their expertise and skill. Thomas Barnard, graphic designer, ably supervised by Larry Channing, head of publications, produced a design for the book that pulses with energy and excitement. Heather Ulrich, exhibitions associate, competently facilitated the project.

Stephanie Stebich, assistant director, played pied piper on a memorable research trip to East Liverpool, Ohio. Finally, I am grateful to Katharine Lee Reid, director of the museum, a careful listener and inspiring leader, whose support and enthusiasm has added immensely to this project and who is a delight to work with in every way.

In conducting research for this book I drew on the help of a great number of people, including: John P. Axelrod, Boston; Mark Bassett, Cleveland; Marianne Berardi, Cleveland Heights; Daphne Cannell, mayor, Sebring, Ohio; James Corcoran, Corcoran Fine Arts Limited, Inc., Cleveland Heights; Anna M. Cottos, executive assistant to the provost, Cleveland Institute of Art; Helen Cullinan, Cleveland; Jo Cunningham, Springfield, Missouri; Giuseppe Delena, chief designer, Ford Motor Company; James F. Dicke II, CEO, Crown Equipment Corporation, New Bremen, Ohio; Paul Eickmann, provost and vice president for academic affairs, Cleveland Institute of Art; Joe Erdelac, Cleveland; Cindy Everett, Murray Company, Brentwood, Tennessee; Jay and Kathy Ferrari, Cleveland; Richard Fiorelli, Cleve-

land Institute of Art; Dee Flederjohn, Bicycle Museum of America, New Bremen, Ohio; Michael Gallagher, director, Design Center, Crown Equipment Corporation, New Bremen, Ohio; Graham Grund, Access to the Arts, Cleveland; Everson Hall, Hall China Company, East Liverpool, Ohio; Marlene Hamann-Whitmore, Memorial Art Gallery, Rochester, New York; William Hannon, CEO (retired), Murray Ohio Company, Sea Island, Georgia; J. E. Herlitz, senior vice president of product design, DaimlerChrysler Corporation, Auburn Hills, Michigan; Jerry Hirshberg, president, Nissan Design International, San Diego, California; Edward J. Karee, Sharon Center, Ohio; Joseph and Nancy Keithley, Cleveland; Joe and Elaine Kisvardi, Medina, Ohio; Ellen and Grant Kloppman, Vixseboxse Galleries, Cleveland Heights; Stephen Knapp, Fairfield Bay, Arkansas; Patricia Leathem, London; Jon A. Lindseth, Hunting Valley, Ohio; Steve Litt, *Plain Dealer;* John Mangina, Cleveland; Jerry and Wynn Maschino, Incline Village, Nevada; Joseph W. McCullough, director emeritus, Cleveland Institute of Art; Ted McMillan, Cleveland; Richard Moore, Bonfoey Gallery, Cleveland; Victoria Naumann, curator, Cowan Pottery Collection, Rocky River Public Library; John Nottingham, co-president, Nottingham-Spirk Design Associates, Cleveland; Dr. and Mrs. Stephen A. Ockner, Cleveland; Joseph Oros and Elizabeth Thatcher Oros, Santa Barbara; Joseph and Algesa O'Sickey, Kent, Ohio; Derek Ostergard, New York; Donald Peirce, High Museum of Art, Atlanta; James Platte, Hall China Company, East Liverpool, Ohio; John Rastall, Frazier, Michigan; Christine C. Rom, director, Gund Memorial Library, Cleveland Institute of Art; Melvin M. Rose, Rose Ironworks, Cleveland; Charles Sallée, design consultant, Cleveland; Don Schreckengost, East Liverpool, Ohio; Paul Schreckengost, president, Formed Fast Machinery, Cerritos, California; Frank Simoni, Commodore Tuxedo, Cleveland; John W. Spirk, co-president, Nottingham-Spirk Design Associates, Cleveland; Kevin Stayton, Brooklyn Museum; Fred Helmut Stross, Orinda, California; Annette Thompson, curator, Bicycle Museum of America, New Bremen, Ohio; Charles Venable, Dallas Museum of Art; Laszlo Vince, Cleveland Museum of Art; Albert Wasserman, Bratenahl, Ohio; Dick Williams, Murray Company, Brentwood, Tennessee; Michael Wolf, Wolf's Auction House, Cleveland; Richard Wootten, Salem, Ohio; Stephen M. Zietz, head of fine arts and special collections, Cleveland Public Library.
H. A.

CAFE

The Man Who Made the Jazz Bowl

In September 1999, I had lunch with Giuseppe Delena, a chief designer for the Ford Motor Company, who had come to give a lecture at the Cleveland Museum of Art. Delena received his design training across the street, at the Cleveland Institute of Art,[1] and he spoke at length about his former teacher, Viktor Schreckengost, who founded the design department at the school. "To this day," Delena confessed, "when I work on a design project, I can hear his voice asking me questions."[2]

Toward the end of the meal, I showed Delena photographs of one of Viktor's most striking product designs, the Sears Spaceliner bicycle, which he created more than 30 years ago, in 1965. Nothing about the bike seems extraneous, but every bar and tube of its structure is expressive and sleekly curved, so that even when motionless it conveys a desire to fly forward. For a few moments, Delena studied the photograph thoughtfully. Then he commented: "This is what we are trying to do now with car design."

The Jazz Bowl or *New Yorker,* about 1930. Diam. 29.2 cm [128]. Viktor created his first *Jazz Bowl* on the request of a New York art gallery. Guy Cowan liked the design so well that Cowan Pottery produced about 50 more. Only after he had finished the piece did Viktor learn that the woman who commissioned it was Eleanor Roosevelt.

The episode suggests the admiration, even awe, that some of the country's leading designers feel for Viktor Schreckengost's work. Yet outside the design profession his name is hardly known. The irony is that while his name is not familiar, almost everyone alive today knows his designs—they simply do not know that he created them. For Schreckengost has produced some of this century's most influential industrial designs for ceramics, trucks, printing presses, bicycles, toys, lawn furniture, flashlights, and streetlights. From teacups to bicycles, he has spent his life changing the look of things. But Viktor is an artist as well as a successful industrial designer. For 35 years he showed pottery, sculpture, and watercolors at the annual May Shows at the Cleveland Museum of Art, winning more than 50 awards. He made sculpture for the 1939 World's Fair, exhibited his works across the country, and sold ceramic sculpture to the Whitney Museum of American Art, Metropolitan Museum of Art, and other major museums.[3] *Jazz Bowl* has become a classic and is perhaps the best known example of American art deco.

Nor is that all. Not only has Viktor's influence been felt through his work, but also through the design program he created at the Institute of Art. Many consider it the first American program of instruction in modern industrial design. Generations of Viktor's students have gone on to play major roles in reshaping our products, particularly in the fields of toy and automobile design.

Regrettably, Viktor Schreckengost's very active life has never been treated as a whole. Much has been written about his work in journals, newspaper articles, and various unpublished sources, but as yet there has been no full-scale study of his career. This book sets out to fill that gap. Doing so will, we hope, help to clarify two historical phenomena, one of somewhat specialized interest, and the other almost impossibly broad. The first is the rise of a distinct Cleveland School of artists during the period between the two world wars; the second is the development of modern industrial design in this country. Viktor has played a major role in each, and the story of his life sheds light on both.

The Cleveland School

Cleveland was a natural center of heavy industry and grew rapidly during the late 19th and early 20th centuries. Indeed, John D. Rockefeller, who accumulated the single largest fortune amassed by anyone, anywhere in this period, began his career as a businessman in Cleveland. Geography helped determine the city's position as a leader in railroads and shipping, as well as in related industries such as shipbuilding. A wide variety of goods employing iron and steel were fabricated locally. By 1920, Cleveland was first in the nation in the manufacture of paints and varnishes, gray iron casting, electric batteries, twist drills, plumbing fixtures, vacuum sweepers, and printing presses and second in the manufacture of women's ready-to-wear clothing.[4] In the early years of the automobile Cleveland was home to five or six major car manufacturers and a leader in airplane construction—Charles Lindbergh's plane the *Spirit of St. Louis* was actually built in Cleveland. As industry grew, the city also took shape. In the early years of the 20th century, Mayor Tom Johnson, an outspoken visionary and controversial reformer, pushed forward an ambitious program of public building in the heart of downtown and oversaw the installation of the first electric arc streetlights and the world's first traffic lights. In 1925 the city established one of the country's first municipal airports, and in 1928 the Terminal Tower was constructed, then the tallest building in the country outside New York. This industrial growth reached its peak around 1930, when Cleveland became the third most populous metropolitan area in the United States.[5]

In such a context of industrial growth and technological innovation, it was natural that the arts became linked with industry. A number of highly successful businesses in Cleveland joined stylish design with some form of industrial process or system of mass production. Perhaps the most distinguished such establishment was the decorating firm of Rorimer and Brooks, headed by Louis Rorimer, which mass-produced deluxe furniture and decorative arts for clients across the United States and established a national reputation with its pioneering art deco look for the Statler Hotels. The firm's reputation in its chosen sphere is suggested by the fact that Herbert Hoover, then secretary of commerce, chose Rorimer to prepare the official U.S. government report on the *Exposition Internationale des Arts Décoratifs et Industriels Modernes* held in Paris in 1925.[6]

While Rorimer's was the most nationally celebrated of Cleveland-based artistic establishments, it was by no means unique. Horace E. Potter, an upscale Cleveland jewelry store, produced distinguished hand-wrought silver jewelry and other metalwork in copper, brass, and pewter. Rose Ironworks, established by Martin Rose, a former ironworker for the Hungarian royal family, hammered out some of the best art deco ironwork produced in the United States. One of their fire screens, featuring a nude woman playing a violin, has become a standard illustration in American art survey books.[7] Cowan Pottery, where Viktor worked, also fit into this tradition of translating visual ideas into the mass production of ceramics. The firm combined forward-looking artistic designs with adventurous decoration and glazes. In general, Cleveland decorative arts tended to be more boldly modern and more frankly industrial than those of most other places.

For two reasons, the Cleveland School has largely escaped the radar screens of historians of American art. First, very few of the Cleveland School's major talents produced outstanding work in oil painting, the medium that carries the most cachet among art historians and is most easily represented in museums.[8] Instead, these artists excelled in watercolor, metalwork, enameling, pottery, ceramic sculpture, and other fields often dismissed as "minor arts." Developments in these fields tended not to attract the same attention as work in painting or monumental sculpture.

In addition, the foremost Cleveland modernists often drew from different sources than the artists of other major American art centers. While most significant modern art in America was modeled on the example of Paris, a large proportion of the best work in Cleveland was inspired by German, Austrian, and Central European models. William Sommer, Henry Keller, and August Biehle all studied in Munich and kept up with modern art largely through German magazines. Martin Rose began his career in Budapest. Schreckengost and several of the other major Cleveland potters studied at the Kunstgewerbeschule in Vienna and followed the lead of the Austrians rather than the French.

Schreckengost's early work coincided with the great period of the Cleveland School, which, as a coherent phenomenon, died out shortly after World War II. American art changed and provincial centers such as Cleveland became less important, at least as artistic centers with a distinct character of their own. An exception to the general demise of the Cleveland School, Viktor continued to pursue an active career as one of the nation's leading figures in industrial design long after the 1940s.[9]

The Secret History of Industrial Design

Surely one of the most remarkable developments of the 20th century has been the transformation that has taken place in the utensils and accouterments of daily life. An amazing number of objects that we handle every day did not exist until about a century ago. Other things, while they existed, are now made of materials utterly different from those used for most of human history. Even objects that closely resemble those of earlier periods are now fabricated so differently that they have become virtually new creations. Few changes in human history have been so far-reaching and momentous as this change in "ordinary objects," yet surprisingly little has been written about how this transformation took place or who brought it about.[10]

The subject is a vast one—so vast that it can become formless. The easiest aspect of industrial design to describe is that of style—the appearance of the object. Indeed, in some design circles, notably those associated with the Museum of Modern Art, it is a stripping away of all ornament that provides the chief criterion for distinguishing "good" from "bad" design.[11] But most successful products include nonvisual factors such as some means of fabricating an object more cheaply or of improving the way it functions.

Thus, good design does not simply determine how an object looks, but also deals with a variety of equally challenging questions such as "How is it made? What does it cost? How well does it work? Is it difficult to use? Is it sexy and appealing? Does it enhance the life of its user? What are its selling points?" The visual form of product design is a truly interesting topic insofar as it leads on to more basic questions. Viktor's story illustrates issues of this sort—the "secret history" of industrial design that goes beyond surface appearance. It demonstrates some of the complex invisible factors behind successful products—particularly in the realm of physical and psychological variables that he likes to group together under the term "human factors."

Notes

1. The Cleveland Institute of Art was founded as the Cleveland School of Art, changing its name after World War II. For the sake of simplicity, we have used the wording "Institute of Art" throughout.

2. This and the following quote from Delena are from the discussion at lunch (1 September 1999).

3. Including the Museum of Fine Arts, Boston; Harvard University Art Museums, Cambridge; Cooper-Hewitt National Museum of Design, Smithsonian Institution, New York; Brooklyn Museum; Cleveland Museum of Art; Renwick Gallery of the National Museum of American Art, Smithsonian Institution, Washington; High Museum of Art, Atlanta.

4. William Ganson Rose, *Cleveland: The Making of a City* (Cleveland and New York: World Publishing Company, 1950), p. 797.

5. Mark Bassett and Victoria Naumann, *Cowan Pottery and the Cleveland School* (Atglen, Pennsylvania: Schiffer Publishing, 1997), p. 24; William Robinson, "Carl Gaertner, Painter of Industrial America," in Christine Fowler Shearer et al., *Carl Gaertner: A Story of Earth and Steel* (Cleveland: Cleveland Artists Foundation, 2000), p. 25.

6. Fittingly, Rorimer's son James went on to become director of the Metropolitan Museum of Art in New York, where he carried on his father's flair for creating a decorative ensemble. He was chiefly responsible for the creation of the Cloisters, that extraordinary medieval movie-set of a museum created through Rockefeller money during the depths of the Depression. See Bassett and Naumann, *Cowan Pottery and the Cleveland School*, p. 146–47.

7. Wayne Craven, *American Art: History and Culture* (Madison, Wisconsin: Brown and Benchmark, 1994), p. 417.

8. Charles Burchfield, for example, had a curious block when it came to working in oil. Nearly everything he did is in watercolor. For an excellent survey of Cleveland watercolorists, see William H. Robinson et al., *A Brush with Light: Watercolor Painters of Northeast Ohio* (Cleveland: Cleveland Artists Foundation, 1998).

9. For an account of the Cleveland School, see William H. Robinson and David Steinberg, *Transformations in Cleveland Art 1796–1946* (Cleveland: Cleveland Museum of Art, 1996).

10. For a survey of 20th-century industrial design, see Michael Tambini, *The Look of the Century* (London: Dowling Kindersley, 1996), and Arthur J. Pulos, *The American Design Adventure* (Cambridge, Massachusetts, and London: M.I.T. Press, 1988).

11. Arthur Drexler, curator of the design collection at the Museum of Modern Art from 1951 until 1987, boasted that the collection contains only "good design." In 1959 he explained: "The Collection as yet includes no television sets, no refrigerators, no telephones, and only a few mechanical appliances—not because such objects are intrinsically unworthy, but because too often their design is determined by commercial factors irrelevant, or even harmful, to aesthetic quality." See Arthur Drexler and Greta Daniel, *Introduction to Twentieth Century Design from the Collection of the Museum of Modern Art, New York* (Garden City, New York: Doubleday & Company, 1959), p. 4.

German Soldiers, 1915. H. 51.4 cm. [1].
Viktor made this drawing at the age of nine, when World War I was raging in Europe. It is his earliest surviving work.

According to Viktor, the word "Schreckengost" means "frightening guest" and was applied to the Vikings who raided the north coast of Europe. To the Germans, they were "Schreckengost" (with a "k"), and to the Dutch, "Schrecengost" (with a "c"). As it happens, Viktor's father's name was Schreckengost while his mother's maiden name was Schrecengost, so he is descended from frightening guests on both sides of the family.[1]

Viktor was the son of a factory worker in a factory town. His father, Warren (1877–1969), was a potter in Sebring, Ohio, which had no industry other than pottery. Many biographies of Viktor claim that he came from a long line of potters, but this is not correct.[2] The truth is darker and more interesting. Warren was the first to take up the potter's trade, though he did not begin in that profession. The son of a Lutheran minister and singing teacher, he grew up in Katanning, Pennsylvania, and began his career working for Pittsburgh Plate Glass.[3] At that time, when large sheets of glass were poured, they were allowed to float gently down, cushioned by the air, until they rested on a polished cement floor. Once on the floor, the sheet hardened completely and was then cut up into window-sized sheets. One day when Warren was at work making plate glass a horrifying accident occurred. While it was floating downward, a sheet of glass buckled, hit the floor at an irregular angle, and shattered. A sizable piece soared across the floor of the factory like a giant razor blade, about a foot above the ground, and neatly sheared off both legs of one of Warren's co-workers at the knees. After witnessing this tragedy, Warren Schreckengost collected his coat and hat and walked out of the glass factory never to return.

Viktor's father worked as a potter in Sebring, Ohio. His mother did catering for the Sebring family. This photograph commemorates their 50th wedding anniversary in 1947.

Warren then decided to become a potter and took a job working for the Ford City Pottery in Pennsylvania, where he was joined by two of his brothers, Samuel and Alan. Around 1896 the Sebring brothers, who were looking for potters, recruited all three to come to the town they had built.[4] In addition, two other potters in Viktor's extended family moved to Sebring: Billy Schrecengost, his mother's brother, and Al Brumbach, who had married his mother's sister Lucy. About the only one of Viktor's relatives who was not a potter was his uncle Ossee Schreckengost, one of the greatest baseball players of his time. Ossee played catcher for the Philadelphia A's and has won a kind of footnote to immortality, since he is mentioned in the dialogue of the Frank Sinatra movie *Take Me Out to the Ball Game*.[5]

Sebring

As the name suggests, the town of Sebring was ruled by the Sebring family.[6] The Sebrings all owned factories, situated beside the railroad tracks, that they either named for themselves or endowed with the name of an illustrious European product to give their manufactures a spurious aura of distinction and elegance.[7] These firms included the Oliver China Company, Sebring Pottery Company, French China Company, Limoges China Company, and Saxon China Company. In addition to the Sebring factories, there were two other plants that produced ceramics for specialized purposes: the Strong Manufacturing Company, which produced enamel-plated cookware, and the Gem Clay Forming Company, which produced gas mantle rings and stove radiants. In the early 20th century, Sebring produced more pottery than any other town in the United States except East Liverpool, Ohio.

Viktor (left) and his brother Paul (right), about 1930.

As a child, Viktor had known the old farmer, Noaker Pugh, who first brought the five Sebring brothers out to Sebring in a horse-drawn surrey, looking for land. They had begun scouting the Salem area and spent the night in Damascus. As they came west from Beloit they looked ahead toward a big flat area and one of the brothers said: "There's Sebring right ahead of us." Within a day, this prophecy had been fulfilled.[8] The brothers spent that night in Alliance, where they studied their maps and formed their plans. The next morning they convinced three farmers to sell their holdings for $50 an acre. By evening they had purchased 200 acres on which to create a town.[9]

Over the next year the brothers laid out the community using a grid plan, numbering the streets and naming the avenues for the States of the Union. They got the Pennsylvania Railroad to cut a spur, built a hotel, and constructed workers' housing along the railroad track. For themselves they constructed mansions along Ohio Avenue, all located near its crossing with Sixteenth Street, which became the grandest street in town. The fanciest of these structures, the O. H. Sebring residence, cost $75,000. It had 30 rooms and seven bathrooms and was designed by Jacob Myers, an architect from Pittsburgh. Viktor vividly remembers that on the Fourth of July, when he was a boy, a band came and played on the lawn of O. H.'s mansion while the Sebrings sat grandly on the porch and the rest of the town gathered around on the grass. After the band performance, O. H. served ice cream to everyone. Only one of these grand mansions still stands, that of F. A. Sebring, now owned by Viktor's nephew Paul.[10]

Although paternalistic, the creation of the town of Sebring had an idealistic, even utopian aspect. Potters of the time were notoriously undependable as workers and prone to drink. Viktor once explained this tendency, noting that the first potter, Keramos, was the bastard son of Bacchus, the god of wine, and that this lineage has continued to affect potters through the generations. Perhaps some skeptics will doubt this mythic explanation, but whatever the cause, at the turn of the century a good percentage of potters were called "floaters" because they would work for a few months, quit to go on a drinking binge, and then move on to another firm. Such an unreliable staff disrupted smooth operations.[11]

The Sebring brothers believed they could attract a steadier group of potters if each worker was able to own his own house and garden, and enjoy a good environment in which to raise a family. Consequently, the Sebring brothers arranged to sell home and garden plots to their workers on very favorable terms. This scheme also had a self-serving aspect. By selling house and land to their future workers, the Sebrings were able to raise money to finance their factories and offset much of the cost of the initial construction.

Growing up as they did in a pottery town, nearly the entire Schreckengost family became involved with ceramics, creating a virtual pottery dynasty. Pearl, the eldest child, became the head of the decorating department at the French-Saxon China Company. Her husband, Ira Eckelberry, an expert in enameling and casting, also worked for French-Saxon and assisted Viktor from time to time with his design projects.[12] Viktor became a designer for American Limoges, Salem China, and other companies. His brother Paul worked as a designer and mold-maker for the Gem Clay Forming Company. His youngest brother, Donald, worked for Salem China, taught ceramics at Alfred University in New York, and designed for various ceramic concerns in East Liverpool. Ruth worked as a decal supervisor for French-Saxon. Only one child, Lucille, did not become involved in the pottery industry.[13]

Work in the Potteries

Warren Schreckengost started at French China as a jigger man, turning out plates and other ceramic forms by hand using a lathe-like device.[14] By the time Viktor was a child, however, Warren had graduated to a more important job—stacking the bisque ware in the kiln. He was in charge of a crew that loaded up the kilns with white earthenware in stacks that stood about 30 feet high.

The stacking was all done by hand. First the pottery was carefully placed in boxes made of fire clay, called "saggers," which protected the porcelain from the direct heat of the kilns. Each piece needed to be exactly placed, or it would warp in the firing. At that point, each stacker rolled a woman's stocking into a little wad, placed it on his head, and delicately balanced the loaded saggers on top of that. With the load on their heads, the men then climbed up ladders and carefully placed each sagger on the stack, so that everything was perfectly in line. The work took patience and precision, and was physically backbreaking. Once the kiln was loaded, Warren supervised the firing. He was also responsible for the tests of special glazes and wares. At the end of his eight- or nine-hour workday, Warren returned home and tended a large garden plot on which he raised vegetables to feed his family and sell to the surrounding households.[15]

Viktor began working at the potteries as a small child, since there was always work available, even for an hour or half an hour. His first job, when he was just eight or nine years old, was to fetch cold water for the placers in the kiln from an artesian well on the hill south of town. The men would give him a few pennies for a bucket. If he worked all week, by the weekend he would have enough to buy tickets to the picture show. Children were not supposed to work until they were 16, so if word came through that the inspectors were in the pottery, Viktor and his brothers would run up a ladder and hide in the attic. From there they could look down through a skylight and see where the inspectors were within the plant. Once the inspectors were gone, they would run down and go back to work.[16]

As Viktor grew older he worked in different phases of the business until he had gone through every stage of the process from first to last, including the final finishing in the decorating shops. "During my last years in high school, I had the job of repairing wares in places where the decal had blistered. The more artistic children were given these jobs."[17] By the time he was in his teens, he had mastered the whole pottery business, without giving the matter any thought. "I didn't realize, until later in life, how easy it was for me to work in clay."[18] The one thing he did not learn was how to throw pots on a wheel, since at French China the ceramics were slip cast. They poured wet clay into the mold, let it dry for a while so that the sides hardened, and then poured out the liquid in the center. With experience, you could learn exactly how long to let the clay dry for the walls to thicken to the desired size. Viktor did not learn to throw on a wheel until he attended art school.

Viktor produced this drawing of a colonial fireplace for the French China Company when he was still in high school.

The activities taking place in the potteries provided useful lessons about the properties of materials. For example, when doing samples of the bisque or greenware, his father would stack the pieces in the kiln using a method known as dawdling. This procedure entailed placing a tiny bit of sand between each piece, to separate one from the next. The secret, his father taught him, was to place the dots of sand in exactly the same location for every piece, so the sand would form a straight column running through the whole series. If the spots of sand were out of place, the pieces would warp. Through watching and participating in such tasks, Viktor developed an intuitive grasp of principles of architecture and structure.[19]

One kiln was used to fire pieces with a color called "Mazzarine blue." They would start with white glaze over white pottery and then lay big chunks of cobalt in the kiln. When the kiln hit a certain temperature, the cobalt would effervesce, coating everything in sight with intense cobalt blue. Viktor remembers sitting inside the kiln after the fire, intoxicated with the rich blue color. "It was like being in some of those mosques in North Africa," he recalls. "Brilliant blue covered everything. I don't think you'd be allowed to do that now with cobalt—it's too dangerous."[20]

The children had plenty of drawing paper, since their father brought home the smooth tracing paper used for the transfer designs for dinnerware. It cost only ten or fifteen cents for an entire roll. Viktor's earliest surviving drawing is a sketch of German soldiers that he made during the First World War [1]. Warren also often brought home clay so that the children could make their own toys, such as soldiers and other figures. He would then take them back to the pottery and fire them. Viktor and his brothers did not have glazes, but they learned to melt paraffin, put the broken ends of crayons into it, and then paint their creations with bright colors. Making these figures led to Viktor's first venture into toy manufacture. Everyone in Sebring passionately followed the town football team, the Sebring Independents, which played in a local league against such rivals as the Canton Bulldogs, the Massillon Maroons, and the Akron Mutes. The children modeled the players in each team, giving each man the proper uniform, with a jersey that was correctly colored and numbered. Every Friday night they took their figures down to Eddie Howell's pool room and put up a display in his window of the two teams that would play the next day.[21]

Viktor's experience with design competitions also began early. When Viktor's mother and father went out at night, they assigned a drawing problem of some sort for the children. When they returned home, the children would make their presentations, from which a winner was selected. The prize was generally to go into Alliance, four miles away, and have an ice-cream sundae. All the children took the contests very seriously, although when they got older they realized that they were rigged. Although their parents always provided convincing explanations for the awards, in fact, they just passed around the prizes among the children, making sure that everyone won about equally.

In 1924, the year Viktor graduated from high school, his father had a serious accident. Warren was up about 30 feet stacking dinnerware, with several saggers on his head, when one of his assistants kicked the ladder loose by mistake. The resulting fall broke his hip and hurt his back because two of the saggers landed on top of him. For a year he was an invalid, and the injury permanently ended his work in the potteries. From that time on Viktor, as the eldest boy, became the family's principal supporter.[22]

Because of his father's fall, rather than going directly to art school, Viktor went to work for Gem Clay. The company's chief product was clay mantle rings, which glowed at the back of gas stoves, like light bulbs. By means of a carefully guarded, top-secret process, the company had developed a porous clay, so that the gas could escape. When he became an employee, Viktor learned that the trick was to mix the clay with sawdust, so that when a piece was fired the sawdust would burn away and leave little breathing holes.[23]

Although Viktor spent most of his time at Gem Clay designing patterns for mantle rings, both he and his brothers also became involved in creating mold-cast ceramic figures.[24] In addition, Viktor did freelance design work for all the other potteries in Sebring, which at that time had no professionally trained designers on staff. He also took a job trimming the windows at Bert Bayer's store in Sebring and played in a jazz band. At the end of a year, Viktor had saved up enough to enter art school, but throughout his years as a student he always found ways to earn a little money, so that there would be something to send home to his parents.

By the time he entered art school, Viktor had decided that the one thing he would never do was to become a potter. Because everybody in Sebring was a potter, it carried no distinction at all. To come up with an alternative, he walked three doors down from their home and spoke with Ed McBain, who worked as an illustrator for the Penton Publishing Company in Cleveland. No doubt aware of Viktor's skill in creating ceramic cartoon figures, McBain advised Viktor that if he wanted to make money in art he should draw cartoons. Consequently, when Viktor signed up to study at the Cleveland Institute of Art, he put down his major as cartooning.[25]

The Cleveland Institute of Art

Viktor attended the Cleveland Institute of Art from 1925 to 1929 and has been associated with it ever since. The oldest surviving art organization in the city (more than 30 years older than the Cleveland Museum of Art), the school was founded in 1883. By 1905, it had grown into a significant enterprise and that year moved into a magnificent Italian Renaissance-style building. Designed by the local firm of Hubbell and Benes, who later designed the art museum, it contained the first skylit art gallery in the city. By the time Viktor enrolled, several nationally known American painters

As a child, Viktor made his own toys, including models of the local football team.

In high school, Viktor played in Kem Webb's jazz band, performing on saxophone and clarinet. Viktor is sitting in the front row, the second from the right, in this photograph from about 1925.

had already attended the school, including Marsden Hartley, who studied there in 1892, and Charles Burchfield, who graduated in 1916.[26] When Viktor entered, the school was growing rapidly under the dynamic leadership of Henry Turner Bailey, an educator of national reputation who particularly stressed arts and crafts and the importance of industrial design.[27]

Although Viktor arrived at the school a decade after Burchfield, the split between modern and conservative that made Burchfield's student life extremely difficult was still in force. The faculty was bitterly divided between two factions: the conservatives led by Frederick Gottwald, and the modernists led by Henry Keller. Both had studied in Munich at the same time and then worked in Cleveland as illustrators, often for the same engravers. But when the Armory Show introduced America to modern art, Gottwald would not have any part of it, and Keller was all for it. The disagreement became so intense that the two were unwilling to speak to each other, or to look each other in the eye. For the students, watching them became amusing because if Gottwald saw Keller walking down one side of the double stairway at the school, he would take the other set of stairs—all the while looking sideways, in order to avoid even the slightest personal contact. Keller did the same.[28]

While attending the Cleveland Institute of Art, Viktor (front center) posed with his fraternity mates at Alpha Beta Delta, about 1926–27. The distinguished painter Clarence Carter is to his left.

Siding with the forward-looking group, Viktor chose to study with Keller and his two associates, Paul Travis and Frank Wilcox. Travis, a masterful draftsman, taught how to use a line to create a sense of mass, volume, and physical extension into the far distance. "This isn't a piece of white paper," he would say. "This is infinite space." Travis would do wonderful drawings in front of the class to illustrate his ideas. He liked to demonstrate how to draw an elephant, starting in the foreground at the trunk and working back into space until he reached the tail.[29]

Wilcox not only taught art techniques, but how to see things more intensely and grasp their meaning. One of his most unusual assignments was to fry eggs in the classroom and then make drawings of them. When the students were done, he would hold up one of the drawings and ask the class what it meant. "How far did the egg run out? How high did the yoke stand? How brown were the edges?" With a hot skillet the egg would flow out less far and have a smaller perimeter. If it was too hot the edges would burn. A fresh egg will stand up higher than a stale one. With a little practice one could look at the drawing and figure out the heat of the burner and the freshness of the egg. As Viktor recalls, "He taught us to see."[30]

Another of Wilcox's exercises was to go down to the Five and Ten on 105th Street and look at the objects in the window for 45 minutes. Back at the school, the students would make drawings of precisely what they had seen—the objects, the prices, and every other detail. After completing the drawings, they went back to the store window to make sure that everything was accurate. A good trick, Wilcox pointed out, if you have lost the image, is to close your eyes. Doing so makes the afterimage come back and you can study it. (This early training with afterimages later proved useful when Viktor worked with radar recognition during World War II).[31]

Viktor's transcripts show that he was a straight-A student and the highest ranking student in his class. He was also elected class president four years in a row. Because of his academic performance, he paid tuition for only a single year, receiving a steady string of scholarships afterward. Consequently, the entire cost

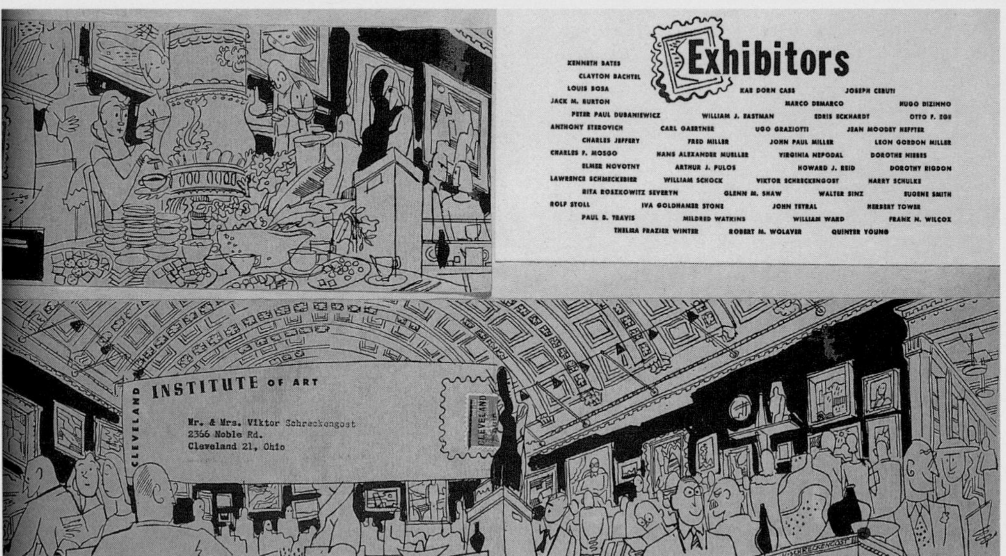

The original Beaux-Arts building of the Cleveland Institute of Art featured a skylit art gallery. Shortly before the building was torn down, Viktor memorialized the room in this invitation for the faculty show of December 1949.

of his art education was about $125. Upon graduating in 1929, Viktor received both the Departmental First Prize in design and the Mary Cushing Page Scholarship for graduate study abroad.

One of the most remarkable aspects of Viktor's activities at the school, however, does not appear on his transcript: the fact that he formed lifelong friendships with many of his teachers, including Paul Travis, Frank Wilcox, and Guy Cowan. Indeed, such long-term relationships were not limited to his teachers. While still in art school, for example, Viktor began designing window displays for Nick Simoni, who ran a laundry and tuxedo rental business. Viktor received his pay not in cash, but in laundry service and the occasional use of a tuxedo for a formal outing. After returning from Vienna, Viktor renewed the relationship, and in the 1950s designed a new logo and look for Sermoni's signs, window displays, and stationery. More than 70 years have now gone by since that relationship began, and it has been extended into the second generation. Nick Sermoni is now dead, but his son Frankie still supplies Viktor with tuxedos and has acquired several of Viktor's paintings.[32]

In the spring of Viktor's third year, the director of the school[33] called him into his office and told him that there was a job available, if he was interested, making designs for the Birge Wallpaper company in Buffalo. One of the school's graduates, Charles Burchfield, was working there and needed an assistant. Although he was not looking for a job, Viktor agreed to be interviewed. On a Monday morning he went up to Buffalo where he was met at the station by Burchfield, who asked if he had brought his painting materials. Viktor confessed that he had not and Burchfield replied: "Don't worry, I have lots of them in the car. We're going to paint today." They drove up to a park north of Buffalo, set up their easels in the woods, and painted from Monday through Thursday. From time to time they would look at each other's work, and Viktor was frankly bewildered by what Burchfield was painting. "I just can't make out what you're looking at," Viktor commented. "Can't you hear it?" Burchfield responded. Apparently he was listening to the sounds and painting them.

Over the course of their visit, Burchfield confessed that he nearly did not graduate because certain members of the faculty so strongly disapproved of his work. "Some of them said I never did learn to draw," Burchfield confided. On Friday, after four full days of painting, they finally went in to the factory. There Viktor met the boss, who offered him a job. Eager to finish school and already interested in pottery, Viktor turned it down.[34]

Viktor first took ceramics in sophomore year, when Guy Cowan began teaching a course in the subject. Cowan managed his own pottery company in Rocky River, a few miles west of Cleveland, but took off every Wednesday to teach at the school. His course stretched over two terms, from September 1928 through May 1929, with classes lasting for the entire day. There Viktor learned to throw on the wheel for the first time, since his previous experience was exclusively with molds. He also learned to make pots with coils. At one point, Cowan became involved in designing a mechanical throwing wheel and Viktor helped him on the project. During the course of this endeavor they became close friends.[35]

As with painting, a modern spirit was entering ceramics and the decorative arts. A key figure in bringing this spirit to Cleveland was Julius Mihalik, who arrived at the Institute of Art in 1922. Before coming to the

Viktor made these candleholders and bookends at the age of 16, while working for the Gem Clay Forming Company in Sebring.

United States, Mihalik had headed the Royal Hungarian School of Industrial Art in Budapest, where he befriended the abstract painter Wassily Kandinsky. He was also interested in the activities of the Wiener Werkstatte and the Bauhaus, even writing a chapter on the Wiener Werkstatte for *Art and Industry,* a volume edited by Charles R. Richards. To be sure, most of Mihalik's own work was not very radical. Nonetheless, he encouraged a number of his most gifted students, including Viktor, Russell Barnett Aitken, and Edward Winter, to study in Vienna. Thus he provided for them a direct link, even if a weak one, to the fountainheads of modern design in Europe.[36]

Viktor's eureka moment occurred in 1929, his senior year, when he saw modern Viennese ceramics for the first time in an exhibition of international ceramic art that came to the Cleveland Museum of Art. Viktor remembers going through the exhibition with Arthur Baggs, an expert in ceramic glazes, who taught at the school and whom he had met the previous year through Cowan. The Viennese pieces were so fresh that Viktor wondered how the artists could achieve such effects with molds. In fact, the sculpture was hand-formed—hence, its spontaneous effect. Schreckengost particularly admired the work of Michael Powolny, whom he learned was a teacher in Vienna. "There was a feeling of lightness, of spirit to his things," he recalled later in an interview, "like all the time he worked on them he was happy and enjoying himself. Right away I knew I had to work with him."[37] By the year's end, through the combined effect of Cowan's encouragement and the show of Viennese work, Viktor had decided to pursue a career in ceramic sculpture and travel to Vienna to study with Michael Powolny at the Kunstgewerbeschule.[38]

Mihalik, who had taught at the Kunstgewerbeschule, agreed to write to the director, Dr. Rohr, on Viktor's behalf.[39] A month or so later a letter came back from Dr. Rohr stating that they could not accept Viktor sight unseen, but they would be very much interested in interviewing him. At that point, Viktor was ready to back out, since he could not see the sense of spending money and traveling thousands of miles just to have an interview. Mihalik encouraged him to go ahead. Unfortunately, Viktor's scholarship for European study provided only $350, just enough money to get halfway across the Atlantic Ocean. By working that summer, designing radiants for stoves for Gem Clay, he was able to save more, but there was still not enough. Toward the end of the summer one of the company's vice presidents, Mr. Albright, asked if he was going to be able to get to Vienna, and Viktor told him that he was still short $1,500. Albright promptly agreed to lend him the necessary sum. With enough money to make the trip, Viktor set off for Austria in the fall of 1929.[40]

Vienna, 1930

After Viktor arrived in Vienna he went to the Kunstgewerbeschule with a translator and met with the director. After a brief exchange, Dr. Rohr called in Professor Powolny. They both looked over his work with interest and agreed he was artistically qualified to enter the school. There was one catch: it was a government school and they did not know what to charge him for tuition. Students from other countries were enrolled in the ceramic program, but Viktor was the first American. They told him to come back the next day and they would come up with a figure.

The next day, Rohr and Powolny announced that they had decided to charge 25 times the normal tuition. At that point, Viktor's heart sank.

"I'm not rich and I can't afford that," he told them. "Wait, a minute," the director replied, "how much do you think it is?" It turned out that the school was state-subsidized, and that Austrian students paid only $2.77 a year. Viktor's tuition as "guest student," even at 25 times that amount, came to only about $72.[41] His study in Vienna lasted only one year, but it profoundly affected the entire course of his career and powerfully influenced his approach to ceramic sculpture.

As a student, Viktor worked chiefly with Powolny, but also associated with the central figure of Viennese modern design, Josef Hoffmann. Hoffmann's ideas about extending the arts into daily life are perhaps best epitomized by the Wiener Werkstatte, which he founded in 1903.[42] Perhaps the most potent feature of the Werkstatte was the way it looked at every aspect of home design as related, from the architecture itself to the chairs, plates, silverware, and so forth. One obvious advantage of this approach was that it created a much more unified visual effect. To create truly cohesive designs it was necessary to develop theories and approaches that could be used for design in any media. The Werkstatte thus helped transform design from a field for specialized artisans to one for multifaceted artists, ready to attack any medium. Indeed, its tenets eventually created a new field—industrial design.

As is often the case with revolutionary movements, the early products of the Wiener Werkstatte were the most radical in approach, and today look the most modern. As the organization continued, its austerity of design became compromised. Indeed, the founding of the Wiener Keramik by Michael Powolny and Berthold Loefler in 1906 is often regarded as the event marking the end of the Werkstatte's purist phase. Art historical opinion remains divided about Powolny's small-scale sculpture. Some feel it occupies an uneasy place between knickknacks and sculpture. For others, it is precisely this informality that makes it exciting and which allowed other innovative features, such as free modeling and bright color.[43]

Powolny's class focused entirely on pottery and ceramic sculpture. About 28 students were enrolled: most were Austrian, but there were also young men from Yugoslavia, Italy, Hungary, Poland, and Russia. Viktor was the only American. For what seemed like an eternity, Viktor worked all day producing wheel-thrown vessels, using a potter's wheel that he had to turn with his feet. By the end of the day his back felt as if it was ready to break. Every afternoon around 4:30 Powolny would come in with a piece of wire and cut through the pots to examine their cross sections and see if they would support their shape. He would scrutinize the walls of the vessels for thinness and uniformity, and comment on their structure. Throughout this period Viktor was not allowed to fire anything he made. Then one day, after about six weeks, Powolny came in, smiled, turned over four or five of Viktor's pots, and marked them with the seal of the school. That meant that they could be fired and kept. From that day forward, if there was anything Viktor wanted to keep, Powolny would put that seal on it.[44]

Powolny's obsession with the structure of wheel-turned forms related to one of his sculptural approaches. He would often throw wheel forms and then cut and reassemble them to form sculpture. His students learned this technique also. After making pots, the class moved on to creating human figures with parts that were thrown on the wheel. First the students would throw a standard vessel form, and then, while the clay was still wet, make a few changes to give the shape a human quality. For example, they would cut slots to represent eyes and push out the wall of the vessel to create a nose-like shape.[45]

As their skills developed, the students in the class began working on projects for Powolny. He had a show that was going to Milan, so the class threw figures eight feet tall, in pipe-like sections that resembled sewer tile. All the figures had big dishes on their heads, filled with fruit and other things. They were shipped in pieces and reassembled on the site.[46] Powolny also had the class work on a large horse for the library in Vienna. That piece, however, was built rather than thrown.

Over the Easter break, Viktor took a long journey through Russia, visiting Moscow during the May Day celebrations and then traveling the Volga River from its source down to the Caspian Sea. After his return, he helped Powolny complete a tabernacle for the Cologne cathedral. It stood about four feet tall and was mounted on four doves covered with gold leaf. Viktor spent his Saturdays and Sundays helping Powolny burnish the gold leaf, giving it an opalescent effect with a mixture of dull and shiny spots. Around this time, Viktor's work was also included in a show of student efforts that toured Europe, South Africa, and England. The Austrians spelled his name "Viktor" in the press releases, and he decided to use that spelling also, rather than lose the publicity.[47]

Powolny was a quiet man, but very strict. The minute the door opened and he entered, everyone stood at attention until Powolny nodded. Once Viktor made the mistake of asking "Why?" when he made a criticism. Powolny immediately froze and marched out the door. The other students came over and assured

Viktor that he was in deep trouble, and a moment later he was called to the director's office and asked why he had been rude to the professor. Powolny had viewed this simple question as a challenge to his judgment and authority, particularly when it was phrased in front of a class of students. Viktor explained that he was going to leave in three or four months and would not have anyone to ask for advice very soon. After some discussion, the director called in Powolny and he and Viktor discussed the incident until they had come to an understanding. If Viktor had any questions he should not express them in the class but should come to Powolny's studio afterward. Powolny would be happy to answer questions, but not in front of the other students.[48]

On his résumé, Viktor notes that while he studied with Powolny, he also received critiques from Josef Hoffmann and Franz Cizek, who also taught at the school. Despite his distress over Viktor's abrupt question, Powolny's final assessment of Viktor's talent was generous. His report card reads:

> No. 10. Viktor Schreckengost, Guest Student, U.S.A. Behavior: Excellent. Progress: Excellent. Success: Excellent. Worked with outstanding success on pottery, ceramics, and figural sculpture. Is very talented, extremely skillful, and has a good sense of form.[49]

The 1930s

The year in Vienna marked the end of Viktor's student years. When he returned to Cleveland in 1930, equipped with modern concepts of design, he quickly established himself as the most gifted, versatile, and productive artist in the city. Within a year or so he had established a national reputation in both fine art and industrial design. Over the course of the 1930s, he produced work in a dozen separate fields, any one of which would make a respectable lifetime's output for many artists.

Viktor's accomplishments in this period were clearly aided by the fact that he was not only talented and hard working, but also charming and good looking. Women who knew him in this period declare that he was very handsome, and a brief profile about him written by the journalist Milton Fox notes that "movie stars would certainly envy his mop of blonde hair."[50] Algesa O'Sickey, who ran an art gallery in Cleveland in the late 1930s, and whose husband, Joseph O'Sickey, studied with Viktor, recalled: "He was what the Irish call 'a darlin' man.' The girls loved him and the boys loved him. Everybody loved him."[51] His one obvious fault was a fondness for fast cars. In 1930 he was injured in a car crash, and much of his work for Cowan was done with his left arm in a cast, supported by a rope from the ceiling.[52]

Viktor's career as a fine artist was boosted by an institution that no longer exists, the May Show at the Cleveland Museum of Art—an exhibition of the work of local artists and craftsmen held annually from 1919 to 1993. The show reached a peak in the 1930s, often attracting crowds of five or six thousand at the opening and as many as fifty thousand attendees by the close.

A second important venue was the Ceramic National Exhibition held regularly in Syracuse and organized by his friend Guy Cowan. There Viktor won prizes less frequently than at the May Show—in part because of the higher level of the competition, and also because he frequently served on the jury, which made him ineligible for awards. Nonetheless, the show greatly contributed to his national visibility, as the best works from it were frequently sent on tour. In 1932–33, for example, Viktor's work was shown at the *Century of Progress Exposition* in Chicago; in 1937 his work was shown at the *Paris International Exposition* and toured to museums in Scandinavia and England; and in 1939 his work was shown at the San Francisco World's Fair.

Teaching at the Institute

While Viktor was still studying at the Kunstgewerbeschule, his former teacher Guy Cowan had traveled to Vienna to meet Powolny. During the visit he invited Viktor to come work with him when he returned to the United States. He told Viktor not to accept any other job without consulting him. Viktor agreed, but when he was ready to come home, Cowan's offer was considerably less than one he received from Ohio State University, which was just starting up a ceramic design program. Once Cowan learned of the offer, he wired back with something better—for Viktor to work half the week for Cowan Pottery and the other half at the Cleveland Institute of Art. This arrangement doubled Viktor's salary, and he happily accepted.[53]

At the Institute, where he was the youngest instructor ever hired, Viktor introduced the design training he had absorbed in Vienna. Kenneth Bates, the distinguished enamelist, was teaching freshman design. Usually, the newcomer took the freshmen and the more experienced faculty member the sophomores. Bates, however, did not want to develop a new class, and Viktor's instruction was clearly at a more advanced level. Before classes started, Bates took Viktor aside and proposed that he teach the sophomore classes, which suited Viktor perfectly.[54]

Viktor had always been adept at working in different media, and his early sophomore classes explored artistic expression in such fields as ceramics, batik, and printed fabrics.

Nonetheless, he felt that Cleveland was lagging far behind the kind of design training offered in Europe at places like the Kunstgewerbeschule and the Bauhaus. So he went to the director of the school, Henry Hunt Clark, and explained that Cleveland was out of phase with what was going on in the world of design and that the situation should be rectified. Clark took a couple of weeks to think it over, and then told Viktor: "I'll give you one student. I want to see what you can do with him."[55]

The student was a boy from the Amish country named Garver Miller, who was interested in making furniture. Viktor insisted that Miller should design for mass production. The two of them started with research—a series of visits to factories. At the time, Louis Rorimer had a large business with 165 wood carvers, who were employed recarving Grand Rapids production furniture to customize it for the Statler Hotels. They visited his plant in Cleveland, as well as the Marble Chair Company and Taylor Chair Company, both in Bedford, Ohio, which made thousands of library chairs. They also went to Grand Rapids, Michigan, and visited the Herman Miller plant and other factories. Only after this exposure to practical techniques did the two sit down together and begin designing chairs.

Right after graduation, Miller moved to Washington, D.C., opened a design office, and almost immediately won the contract to refurbish the congressional offices. In a short time he had a staff of 30 people. When Clark saw how successful Miller was, he decided to open up a design department and put Viktor in charge.[56] In 1933 the Cleveland Institute of Art opened its design program.[57] For years, the department operated on a shoestring budget, but Viktor would shame people he knew in industry into donating time or materials. Soon he had 11 people working there, though often doing so for only short time slots.[58]

Cowan Pottery and the Jazz Bowl

Viktor spent the latter part of every week working for Guy Cowan, and while he worked at the pottery for only about a year, from September 1930 to December 1931, his creations are generally recognized as the firm's outstanding achievements. Founded in 1912, the company expanded rapidly during the 1920s, only to fall into financial crisis after the crash of 1929. During the period Viktor worked there, Cowan Pottery was financially shaky. In 1929, in response to those difficulties, it was reorganized. This was unsuccessful, and it went into receivership in December 1930, after Viktor had been there only a few months. Since the 1931 catalogue had just been produced and circulated, the studio remained open for another year, to liquidate its stock. Curiously, these problems seem to have had a positive effect on the work of the firm, encouraging the artists there to break out of past routines and try fresh approaches.

Viktor was only 26 when he produced the most famous piece of his career. Cowan Pottery had a hopper in the front office into which assignments were dropped. When designers ran out of projects, they reached into the basket and pulled out one of those suggestions. One day Viktor was in the office talking with Cowan, who asked him what he was working on that day. When he said he didn't know, Cowan pulled one of the requests out of the basket at random. An East Coast firm, the Brownell-Lambertson Gallery, needed a punch bowl for a woman from New York City. She wanted something with a New Yorkish theme. Cowan said, "Why don't you do that," so Viktor took the assignment.[59]

When he was done, he sent the bowl to New York with a bill for $50—the amount the woman had agreed to pay for it.[60] Shortly afterward a check for that amount came back, along with a note saying that the lady just loved the piece. In fact, she liked it so much that she wanted two more—one for her home in Hyde Park and the other for the White House. Franklin was making plans to run for president and she wanted a present to celebrate his victory, since she was sure he was going to win. Only then did Schreckengost learn that the woman who commissioned the punch bowl was Eleanor Roosevelt.[61]

Cowan Pottery went out of business soon afterward. Sadly, some of the most exciting projects were never carried out because the firm folded before they could be put into production.[62] Most of these projects were never resumed. Viktor's later work with ceramics was guided by a different set of restraints and went in a different direction. While some of his work was remarkable, he never again had a patron in the ceramic field who encouraged creative experimentation as Cowan did.

Joseph Puppets and an Excursion to Hollywood

After Cowan Pottery closed, Cowan and Viktor worked together as partners in a small design studio in Cleveland. From 1931 to 1933, Cowan split his time between projects for Ferro Enamel in Cleveland and Onandaga Pottery in Syracuse, where his father had worked. Throughout this period, he spent half the week in Cleveland and the other half in Syracuse.[63] Because of Cowan's connection with Ferro, Viktor became involved in designing enamel stoves for the Consolidated Iron-Steel Manufacturing Company of Cleveland, which wanted to update its product line by covering its cast-iron stoves with enamel panels. In addition, Viktor designed dinnerware for Onandaga Pottery.

The most remarkable of Viktor's designs for Onandaga was a service known as Econo-Rim marketed to restaurants.[64] An abortive project of this period was a scheme to produce ceramic tombstones, but Viktor backed out of the project and smashed the molds when he learned that his client simply wanted cheap imitations of stone, rather than markers emphasizing the qualities of clay that would be handsomely modern in appearance.[65] In 1933, Guy Cowan gave up his work for Ferro and moved up to Syracuse, where he worked full time as art director for Onandaga, but he continued to commission designs from Viktor, until Viktor took a position as art director for American Limoges.[66]

Along with designing dinnerware for Onandaga, Viktor also became involved in modeling figures for Helen Joseph, who ran Joseph Puppets. She had organized teams that went around the country giving puppet shows, and she also sold puppet kits, with porcelains heads and directions for sewing together the costumes. Viktor designed the packaging and advertising, modeled the puppet heads, and had thousands of them cast and fired by the pottery companies in Sebring.[67]

In the summer of 1931 Viktor decided to go with the Joseph puppet group on tour. When they got to Hollywood he lined up a job with United Studios, where he worked for two or three months, constructing huge sculptures for movie sets. First they would construct a framework of wood that they would cover with chicken wire and wrap with burlap bags dipped in plaster. Then they would do the finer modeling in plaster. Chorus girls and starlets such as Myrna Loy would drop by every afternoon to gawk, and there were constant beach parties. It was fun but the starlets were distracting, and after a few months Viktor decided that he better move on to something else or he would never amount to much.

North Africa and Spain, 1932

In 1932 his friend Fred Stross told Viktor that he planned to make a trip through Europe and North Africa, and invited Viktor to join him. Viktor has hundreds of friends, but from the sparkle in his eyes when the name comes up, it seems that his "best friend" may well be Fred. They met in Vienna on Thanksgiving Day of 1929, when they were both invited for dinner at the home of the U.S. ambassador. Trained as a research chemist, Fred is also a concert-level pianist and prize-winning photographer. He is an accomplished botanist who can rattle off the Latin names of plants. He knows shorthand and speaks eight or nine languages, including Arabic. Yet for all his accomplishments, Fred is hardly solemn. Like Viktor, he has an irrepressible sense of humor and an enthusiasm for life that is almost child-like.[68]

Fred and Viktor rendezvoused in Vienna and then headed down to Italy, where they explored each city with enthusiasm. They then took a boat to North Africa, landed in Algiers, and traveled across Algeria into Morocco, where they visited such cities as Fez, Casablanca, Marrakech, and Tangier. From Tangier they crossed over into Spain at Gibraltar, where they spent about a month, before returning to Vienna.

In Spain they witnessed one of the ominous preludes to the Spanish Civil War: an abortive military revolt led by the right-wing General José Sanjurjo, a military associate of Franco, on 10 August 1932. On that day, Viktor and Fred were on a train to Seville, where Sanjurjo briefly took control, until government forces arrived to suppress the rebellion. Even today, accounts of the Sanjurjada are confusing, and for Viktor and Fred, arriving in the middle of the action, it was clearly a perplexing experience. As they approached the city, they saw troops of cavalry galloping in the distance and smoke rising from burning buildings. Inside the city they dodged both insurrectionists and troops of soldiers, while struggling to find food and a place to stay. The international rise of fascism was still a few years off, but Viktor and Fred had been given an early wake-up call.[69]

At the end of the trip, Fred decided to accompany Viktor back to the United States and pursue his postgraduate education in Cleveland. At the time it was not easy for an Austrian to get a visa, but fortunately Fred had been born in Egypt (and spent his childhood in Alexandria). When he applied for a visa as an Egyptian, he got one without difficulty. Don Schreckengost picked the two up in New York, and the three drove to Cleveland, where they moved into a house on Hessler Street, in the University Circle area. At the time, Viktor was teaching at the Cleveland Institute of Art, Don was studying there, and Fred was getting a master's degree in chemistry from Western Reserve University. They all kept strange hours. Don worked at night and came in late, but he remembers that sometimes he would wake up at three in the morning because Fred was playing Gershwin's *Rhapsody in Blue* on a grand piano on the top floor. The group broke up when Don took a teaching position at Alfred University and Fred headed west to get his doctoral degree in chemistry from Berkeley.[70]

On his return from Europe, Viktor began focusing intensely on industrial design. In 1932 he presented a modern line of dinnerware to the executives at American Limoges, which was in a slump due to the Depression and the competition from foreign imports. They rejected it, but invited him to try again, and in 1933 he came back with two strikingly modern patterns, which they accepted and put into production the following year. Both proved to be big sellers, and on the strength of them, Viktor was moved from a consulting role and appointed chief designer for the firm. For the remainder of the 1930s, Viktor turned out dinnerware patterns on roughly an annual basis and also designed several hundred different decorative treatments.

The Worst-Looking Chicken Coop

At the same time that he was introducing a new look to American dinnerware, Viktor became involved in designing trucks. This came about in a curiously indirect fashion. Viktor's friend, the painter Paul Travis, was teaching an art class for professional women at the Church of the Covenant on Euclid Avenue and found that the women grew tired of making only paintings. He asked if Viktor would come over and help. So Viktor did, teaching them to make Christmas cards, lampshades, batiks, or whatever else caught their fancy. He had been focusing on such diverse media in his classes at the Cleveland Institute of Art, so it was not difficult to present them to another group.[71]

One Saturday morning, while the class was still running, there was a knock at the door of Viktor's studio, and when he opened it there stood one of his students, Mrs. Spiller. She had come to introduce her husband to Viktor and to show him some of the designs that Viktor was working on. "Mr. Schreckengost, I want you to meet Huz," she said.[72] At the time, Viktor was designing a double-decker steam-powered bus for a New York company that wanted to eliminate gasoline and cut down on pollution.[73] Ray Spiller first studied the drawings with enthusiasm and then revealed that he was the chief engineer for the White Motor Company in Cleveland. He asked how long it would take Viktor to finish his work on the bus. "About six weeks," Viktor replied. "Call me the minute you're through," Spiller told him. "We have an idea I'd like to tell you about." Once his steam bus was finished, Viktor gave Spiller a call and arranged to meet with him down at White Motors.[74]

At that time, the length of a truck was limited by law to 42 feet. Consequently, anything that could be taken off the nose could be added to the back. Spiller had come up with the concept of putting the engine right under the cab, which would add cargo space to the back. But the process of making things fit together in a reasonable way had stymied him. He had constructed a mock-up of plywood, but it was an ungainly thing. When he first showed it to Viktor and asked him what he thought, Viktor laughed and told him that it was "the worst-looking chicken-coop I ever saw." "Well, fix it!" Spiller replied.[75] Viktor's final design took five feet off the front and thus added five feet to the hauling load. With the extra space, you could pay for the whole rig in a single year.

Europe, 1937

On 6 September 1935, Viktor married Nadine Averill, a former student at the Cleveland Institute of Art, who became his "critic, secretary, keeper of files and scrap books, and general greaser of domestic and artistic wheels."[76] (She also supplied the titles for many of his ceramic sculptures.) The couple settled in an apartment on Noble Road in East Cleveland, "done entirely in modern

Viktor was hired as a full-time designer by American Limoges in 1933. He first fabricated his dinnerware designs in plaster, and his precise measurements took into account the shrinkage of the clay during the casting process.

style" and "decorated with a dazzling array of Mr. Schreckengost's art pieces." The place was so striking that it was featured in an article in a Cleveland newspaper in 1948. "But it isn't big enough when one room has to serve as a studio," Nadine sighed, when interviewed.[77]

In 1937, Viktor returned to Europe with Nadine, visiting Germany, Austria, Sweden, and Norway, as well as the *Paris International Exposition*, where some of his ceramics were on display. Hitler had come to power, and fascism was on the rise. Even to a casual visitor it was clear that war was on the way. On the airfields in Germany, he saw lines of fighter planes, although according to the Treaty of Versailles, Germany was supposed to have no armaments. In Berlin they were pouring concrete 20 feet thick to make a "subway." He was in Berlin in 1937 when Mussolini came to meet Hitler and saw the two ride together in a motorcade down the main street. As they passed, Viktor was roughed up by the crowd because he was not holding out his arm in a fascist salute.

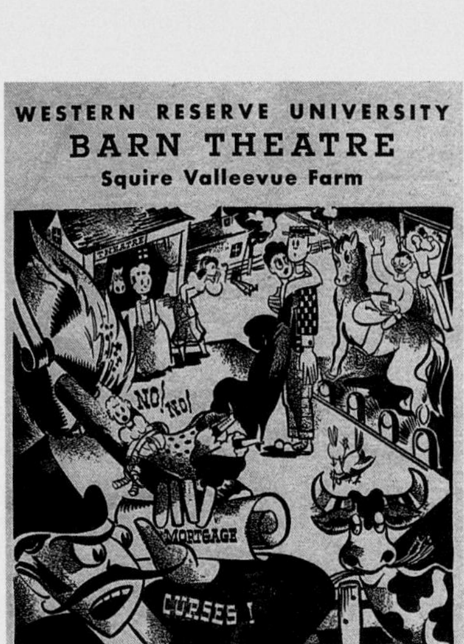

Along with sets and costumes, Viktor designed programs and posters for the theater program of Western Reserve University. This ad is from the summer of 1941.

As with the 1932 journey to Spain and North Africa, the trip seems to mark a slight shift in Viktor's activities. While some of his former interests continued, such as his activity designing dinnerware for American Limoges, the greater part of his energy seems to have gone into a different set of interests, such as ceramic sculpture, stage and costume design, and the design of bicycles and pedal cars for Murray Ohio.

Stage Design

Concurrently with his work in ceramics and industrial design, Viktor produced dozens of set and costume designs for theater productions in Cleveland. Viktor's first ventures in stage design came when he was still in art school. Early in his studies at the Cleveland Institute of Art, Barclay Leathem, head of the theater program at Western Reserve University, came to the school to speak about his work. At the end of the presentation he asked if any of the students wanted to get involved in stage design. Viktor raised his hand, and as a consequence produced three or four stage sets before he left to study in Vienna. He had hardly arrived at the Kunstgewerbeschule when he heard someone exclaim "That's Viktor!" and found that the speaker was Leathem's wife, Ruth. She informed him that Barclay had come to Vienna to study stage design with the famous theatrical impresario Max Reinhardt. The coincidence of being together in Vienna cemented Viktor's friendship with the Leathems, and on their return to Cleveland they often worked together on theatrical projects.[78] This activity reached a peak in the late 1930s. From 1938 to 1943, when he left Cleveland to join the U.S. Navy, Viktor designed sets and costumes for five or six productions every year.

A curious outgrowth of this work with stage design was the invitation to produce costumes for the Akron Rubber Ball—an annual extravaganza lavishly supported by the major rubber companies of Akron. The gala was intended to attract national attention to the Rubber City's newest products, and Viktor's costumes were entirely created from synthetic rubber fabrics and materials.

Bicycles

Improbably, this work on costumes and theatrical projects led Viktor to bicycle design. In 1937 the Dunham Tavern, the oldest building still standing on its original site in Cleveland, needed to be repaired and refurbished. There was a red barn behind it, and Barclay Leathem came up with the idea of staging plays in the barn during the summer and early fall to raise money. He selected an

Viktor began the process of bicycle design with full-scale drawings in pastel. Sadly, most of his drawings of this type have been lost.

old-fashioned melodrama titled *Murder in the Red Barn, or Maria Marten,* which had been first introduced to the stage at the Marlebone Theatre in London on 6 April 1840. Though hardly subtle, the play provided lively entertainment, with much active involvement from the audience, which was encouraged to hiss the villain and applaud the hero. Performances ran 14–18 September 1938 and did indeed raise enough money to refurbish the tavern, as Leathem hoped. As usual, Viktor designed the sets, which was a technical challenge, since the settings shifted abruptly from Mister Marten's cottage, to a wood, the Polestead village green, a drawing room in London, a prison cell, and a street.[79]

Early in the design process, when Viktor had made some sketches, he went over to Leathem's apartment to discuss them. They were joined by Leathem's friend and upstairs neighbor, Ralph O'Brien, a vice president at the Murray Company, a metal-stamping firm. O'Brien's wife made some mint juleps, and after looking at the drawings they sat down to have a drink. Before long an entire bottle of whiskey had disappeared and they were feeling a little woozy. At that point, the conversation turned to bicycles.[80]

Up to that time, the Murray Company had been getting its bicycle designs from a well-known graphic artist, Count Alexis De Sakhnoffsky, who had a national reputation since he did monthly drawings of automobiles for *Esquire* magazine. De Sakhnoffsky had made sketches for Murray's Steelcraft line of bicycles, but since he was not interested in engineering, the company found that his designs were not always practical, and that it was often difficult to figure out how to translate his drawings into a physical object, with working pedals, brakes, gears, and other mechanical appurtenances. Murray was looking for someone new. Had Viktor ever designed a bicycle? He confessed that he hadn't. Would he like to? "Of course." [81]

They arranged to meet at the Murray Company the next Monday. When Monday came, since they had all been tipsy, Viktor didn't know whether to keep the appointment or skip it. He was thinking that maybe he would skip it when he got a call from Ralph asking where he was. With that encouragement, he went down to the company as promised, and met with the president, C. W. Hannon. By the time the meeting was over, Viktor had been commissioned to create a bicycle design that would be unveiled at the 1939 World's Fair.

Viktor was not sure what to charge, since he had never designed a bicycle before, so he agreed to do it for whatever they had paid the count. For months he worked on the design, modeling all the parts in clay except for the tubing, which he had made in a machine shop. When he was done Murray paid him a measly $1,500. Nonetheless, the commission marked the beginning of a relationship with Murray that lasted for the next 35 years.[82] Before Viktor had completed his first bicycle, he had begun to design cabinets, fans, pedal cars, and chairs. His relationship with Murray also brought additional projects, such as the design of bicycle lights for Delta Electric and consulting work for Sears, Roebuck, one of Murray's largest customers. In addition, shortly before the war Viktor made his first venture into what would become one of his major interests, the design of printing presses. His first such project was to redesign a one-cylinder offset press for Chandler Price.[83]

The O'Neill Memorial of 1949 was Viktor's first venture into monumental sculpture.

Ceramic Sculpture

While producing these industrial designs, Viktor remained active as a fine artist. During the early 1930s, he had concentrated chiefly on pottery and ceramic decoration, but in the late 1930s he focused on ceramic sculpture. The year 1937 marked a turning point, for then Viktor received first prize for ceramic sculpture in the May Show for the first time with a group of three works. From 1937 onward, he was the principal prize winner in this field. As his work became known he began to receive commissions, including several memorials and the trophy for a women's air race. In 1939 he was asked to produce sculpture for the United States Building at the New York World's Fair.

In fact, 1939 was a peak year for Viktor, during which he not only produced sculpture for the New York World's Fair and exhibited his Mercury bicycle there, but also staged a show of his industrial designs in Cleveland at the Institute of Art, and displayed his ceramics at the May Show in Cleveland, the Ceramics National in Syracuse, and the San Francisco World's Fair. Shortly before the New York World's Fair he received a call from Walter Dorwin Teague, declaring that a space had opened up and was available if Viktor wanted to show any more of his ceramics at the fair. By that time, Viktor had nothing left to show. All his significant work was already on the road.

World War II

When World War II broke out, Viktor was 37. He was too old to be drafted, and he also had a deferment because of his involvement in defense work for Murray and other Cleveland manufacturing companies. Nonetheless, he was eager to do his part. In 1943, Murray Ohio received the first Army-Navy Excellence Award in Cleveland, and the company asked Viktor if he would organize the event in which the award was to be given out. Viktor took an old warehouse on East 152nd Street, painted it light khaki inside, and installed lighting, a stage, and seats for 2,000 employees. Then on 9 April 1943, Captain A. S. Wotherspoon from the Naval Ordinance Plant at Center Line, Michigan, presented the award to the president of Murray, C. W. Hannon. In addition, every one of the Murray employees got a certificate, each of which Viktor arranged to be framed.[84]

Wotherspoon was profuse in his compliments over the way the ceremony had been organized and, when he learned who was responsible, encouraged Viktor to put his name in for navy work. "The navy could certainly use a man like you," he commented. With Wotherspoon's encouragement, Viktor went down to take a physical and be interviewed. When the examining board had finished their questions they told him that they were way behind in processing applications, but that he could expect to hear from them in three or four months. Five days later he got a phone call saying that an assignment had been found for him and that he should report for duty immediately.[85]

Making Sense of Radar

After basic training in Quonset, Rhode Island—a process he claims to have enjoyed—Viktor was summoned to Washington to meet Captain (later Admiral) Luis de Florez, one of the most brilliant and unorthodox figures in the U.S. Navy.[86] The American-born scion of an aristocratic Spanish family, de Florez was a short, energetic man, with a pompadour and carefully waxed mustache. After graduating from M.I.T. with a degree in engineering, he made a fortune in industry constructing and managing oil refineries, and developing a technique for cracking gasoline from kerosene. He was also an enthusiastic amateur flier and skilled marksman, with a talent for shooting upside down, with his head between his legs.

When World War I broke out, de Florez enlisted in the navy and promptly devised 39 inventions for the cockpit of navy airplanes, including all the instruments except the tachometer and the oil gauge, as well as the first seat belt and shoulder harness. When World War II erupted, he returned to the service and pioneered the use of "virtual reality" to simulate flight and combat situations. When this practice produced dramatic improvements in combat, while drastically cutting training costs, de Florez was placed in charge of a special devices section to find novel ways to solve military problems.[87]

De Florez wanted Viktor's help on a top-secret project. The technology of radar had just been developed—the very name "radar" was still a secret—but the challenge of interpreting the strange blips and beeps that showed up on the radar screen had not yet been mastered.[88] No method had been developed for interpreting the strange scatter-patterns that showed up on the scope, or for establishing whether they portrayed a squadron of enemy bombers or a gaggle of geese. De Florez had come up with the notion that the scattering had to do with shape, and that no one would be more sensitive to that than a sculptor. When he came upon Viktor's application, he immediately pulled it out of the pile.

Within two weeks Viktor had taken charge of the Landfall Studio, where he worked on two interrelated projects: developing an effective program of radar recognition and producing accurate terrain models to guide bombing missions. Once he had successfully solved these problems, Viktor was placed in charge of making models for the invasion of southern Honshu, to end the war with Japan. Since the project was top secret, parts of the model were manufactured in different parts of the country and then transported to a secret base in New Jersey, whose perimeter was surrounded by barbed wire and watched night and day by 32 hulky U.S. Marines.[89]

Viktor's work on map-making was interrupted by even more pressing matters during the Battle of the Bulge. The American radar was not functioning properly, so Viktor was hurriedly flown to France, bringing

In the months just after Pearl Harbor, Viktor designed posters to support the war effort and worked on plans to protect Cleveland from an aerial attack.

In the navy's section of special devices, Viktor worked on radar recognition and a new process of making topographical maps from aerial photography. He also developed maps for the invasion of Japan.

his radar recognition system with him. His help was needed to get the troops to read the radar returns properly and re-site malfunctioning radar installations so that they would work.[90] After a harrowing flight to Europe through blinding snow, he was sent out to the front. While the enemy was close, his one near-death experience came when he found himself staring down the barrel of an American tank, which was not sure of his identification.[91] He quickly discovered that the Americans were half-blind because of the way they had placed their radar. The problem, of course, was that an exposed position was often vulnerable to enemy fire and a thoroughly camouflaged one, hidden behind a screen of trees, was completely useless. The trick was to clear away the trees and other obstacles just enough to get a full image, but still leave the site relatively protected.

Commander of Naval Research

Viktor stayed in France only four or five weeks since he was needed back in the United States to help plan the invasion of Japan, which was scheduled to take place in early August. Viktor and his team had everything ready, but early that month atomic bombs were dropped on Hiroshima and Nagasaki, and the invasion was canceled. Within two days of the Japanese surrender, Viktor recalls, all his highly sensitive projects were canceled and then started up again with new code numbers. Thus, they could be hidden from America's so-called allies, such as Russia.[92]

After fighting ended, Viktor was assigned to New York and became the commanding officer of the Naval Research Center on 9th Street, where he had everyone from doctors to scientists from NASA in his unit. Consequently, he got to see the latest technology that was being developed and explore how to use it most effectively. One of the more amusing projects entailed determining the best way to transmit orders through static. After recording voices with all kinds of accents and intonations, Viktor's team found that the dialect that could be most readily understood through any kind of sound interference was that of West Virginia. Once they discovered that a particular pitch carried clearly through almost anything, they found ways to tune the equipment to that pitch, so you did not need to come from West Virginia to be understood.[93]

The aftermath of war entails clean-up: collecting bodies and putting the wounded back together as well as possible. Viktor got involved in both these tasks. He designed steel body containers that were stackable and easily labeled. He also became involved in fitting amputees with artificial limbs, since the navy discovered that slight differences of measurement made a great difference in how people could walk. Viktor and his team put lights on the joints of normal people to see how they moved and then tried to duplicate the effect with people of the same size who had lost a limb. They carefully measured and charted the movements of people of every weight and size.[94]

One of Viktor's last projects was to install a major exhibition on naval training and naval science at the New York Hall of Science that included extraordinary action photographs and films of the navy at war taken by Edward Steichen. Viktor used various tricks to make the material seem lifelike. One of the displays, for example, was a mock-up of the runway on an aircraft carrier. A dummy of a full-sized man stood in the foreground, and scaled-down figures created the effect of perspective. At the end of the line of men was a tiny model airplane. Thus, in a small space, the display created a convincing illusion that you were standing on an actual runway with all those men. Another display featured a model of an atom 22 feet across, constructed out of stainless steel rings. Visitors could walk under it and get a sense of how the layers of spinning electrons went together.

But the most exciting and popular spectacle of the show was not in the script. They had arranged to bring in a fighter plane from the Brooklyn Navy Yard, a plane so large that to get it in the building they had to take its wings off and lift it by crane through a large window on the second floor. Unfortunately, when it was halfway through the window, the labor union handling the move went on strike. They had to stop work from Friday afternoon until Monday morning until they got the difficulties settled. The plane looked quite startling, half-in, half-out of the building, and some of the navy's top brass, including Admiral Nimitz and Admiral Halsey, came by to goggle.[95]

Viktor entered the U.S. Navy as a lieutenant. He left it as a four-striper, with the secretary of the navy's commendation, and a blue ribbon he could add to his uniform.[96]

The citation reads as follows:

> The Secretary of the Navy, Washington
>
> The Secretary of the Navy takes pleasure in commending Lieutenant Viktor Schreckengost United States Naval Reserve
>
> For outstanding performance of duty as head of the design labora-

In October 1944, Viktor went out on the minesweeper *USS Kestrell* to test the range and accuracy of radar.

Viktor often brought painting materials with him on research flights. This watercolor, *And out to Sea*, was on view in the 30th May Show in 1948.

Viktor not only designed dinnerware, but promoted his patterns at the trade shows. Here he poses with his Tempo design of 1949.

tory of the special devices division of the bureau of aeronautics from November 1943 to May 1945. Carrying out his essential work with skill and initiative, Lieutenant Schreckengost expertly developed new and improved techniques to construct and utilize three-dimensional terrain models for use in briefing pilots and air crewmen and, in addition, rendered invaluable assistance in the operation of radar planing devices for the location and evasion of enemy radar installations in bombing and invasion tactics. By his leadership and ingenuity Lieutenant Schreckengost inspired a high quality of research, design and workmanship in the production of models for specific operations against Japan and thereby contributed materially to the effectiveness of the special devices program and the successful prosecution of the war.

His superb professional ability and conscientious devotion to an important task were in keeping with the highest traditions of United States Naval Service.

A copy of this citation has been made part of Lieutenant Schreckengost's official record and he is hereby authorized to wear the commendation ribbon.

Signed.

James Forrestal
Secretary of the Navy.[97]

On his departure, Viktor was offered the opportunity to attend the Naval War College and possibly become a rear admiral. However, he was eager to return to his career in art and design, and he declined.

Viktor stayed in the Naval Reserves after the war, which gave him an opportunity to meet interesting people and go to interesting places. De Florez seemed to know everyone. For example, Viktor met the inventor Igor Sikorsky, who showed him a drawing of a 300-passenger helicopter with 16 propellers across its top. The machine was never fabricated, but it was an exciting concept. Viktor also went to the Goddard Space Flight Center in Maryland and spent two weeks examining the files on UFOs. The files were filled with descriptions of radio signals from outer space that were being broadcast toward Earth at strange but regular intervals, whose cause and origin were as yet unexplained.

The Postwar Period

Viktor was just 40 when he left the navy in 1946. According to those who knew him at the time, he was still strikingly handsome. Helen Cullinan, the former art critic for the *Plain Dealer,* remembers attending a party at the home of Barclay Leathem shortly after the war, and being stunned by the sight of Viktor standing by the piano in his navy uniform. She also recalls that Viktor was "wonderful with children."[98] Once when he came over to a party at her home, her baby, Thomas, was in a cranky mood and wanted to be held. Viktor spent the entire evening strolling around the living room carrying the boy, who fell asleep on his shoulder, while he chatted cheerfully with other guests. Barclay Leathem's daughter Patricia also remembers Viktor from this period.

> Vik (and Nadine) were my Christmas people—they were both so tall and beautiful and filled with laughter and joy as they arrived Christmas Eve bearing gifts, perfectly wrapped-jewels in themselves.
>
> I remember one year when Vik was in uniform. He drew out and explained the structure of the atom. He was creating the visual

"teaching package" of atomic energy to inform the armed forces of the "new technology" which was so soon to change the world. Always the Navy and Vik were linked. He designed the interior of the nuclear submarines so that all the surfaces—flooring, walls—were contrasting textures offering tactile as well as visual stimulation in order to reduce the tedium of the limited environment offered to the submariners.[99]

During the war Viktor found it difficult to work in clay and turned to watercolor, an easily portable medium. After the war he began to exhibit his watercolors and participate in national watercolor exhibitions. He also returned to work in clay. In 1947, the year after his return, he won first prize at the May Show in both pottery and ceramic sculpture, and he introduced a series of slab forms that treated vessel forms not as pottery but as sculpture. He continued to work actively in clay until the late 1960s, when he abandoned such work on his doctor's orders, because of trouble with his back.

In addition, Viktor once again immersed himself in industrial design. The year after his return he worked with the engineers at Murray to develop a method of fabricating bicycle frames. Over the next decade, through a combination of such cost-saving methods and racy visual design, Murray became the world leader in the bicycle and pedal car field. He returned to dinnerware design for Salem China and produced a string of successful shapes and patterns, culminating in his Free Form design of 1955. In addition, shortly after his arrival in Cleveland, he got a call from Ray Spiller, his friend from White Motors, who had just become the chief engineer at Harris-Seybold, a manufacturer of printing presses and equipment. From the late 1940s into the 1960s, Viktor designed presses for that company which dramatically changed the whole nature of printing.

Around 1950, Viktor designed the Murray showroom in New York. He also redesigned the Murray logo.

Viktor first sculpted his pedal cars in clay, then moved on to working models (photograph about 1940).

Viktor's designs often took into account the different preferences of boys and girls. Boys generally liked police cars and fire engines, girls preferred vending trucks and station wagons. Boys liked bright red, girls preferred blue and white. Such color coding broke down when Viktor introduced magenta bicycles in the mid 1950s. It turned out that boys and girls like them equally.

Notes

Much of this text is based on a series of interviews with Viktor Schreckengost. These discussions were transcribed and are on file at the museum. Other information comes from the artist's scrapbook and is so indicated in the notes.

1. Interview #1, p. 5.

2. For example, this misinformation is provided in Karen McCready (with an introduction by Garth Clark), *Art Deco and Modernist Ceramics* (London: Thames and Hudson, 1995), p. 173. The mistake appeared in print as early as 1931. See "Youthful Cleveland Designer Inherited His Taste for Art," *Cleveland News* (2 November 1931); and "Youngest Art Teacher," an article from an unidentified newspaper, probably from Cleveland (no month or day indicated, 1931) (Schreckengost scrapbook).

3. Interview #1, p. 5.

4. Warren went to work with the French China Company (owned by O. H. Sebring); Samuel went to work at the Sebring Pottery (managed by Frank A. Sebring); and Alan went to work at American Limoges (owned by Frank A. Sebring).

5. Viktor was born on 26 June 1906 in the family home at 266 West Indiana Street, the third child and eldest son. He had two brothers and three sisters: Pearl Schreckengost Eckelberry, 27 March 1899–1 March 1976; Ruth Schreckengost Key, 16 March 1901–20 February 1986; Paul Schreckengost, 1 January 1908–7 October 1983; Don Schreckengost, born 23 April 1910; Lucille Schreckengost Jackson, 2 April 1913–28 January 1986. My thanks to Gene Schreckengost for providing the life dates (memo, April 2000).

6. The Sebring dynasty was started by George E. Sebring (1834–1915), who began in the grocery business. He soon found that farmers needed crockery to hold eggs, butter, and other items that he sold. The demand for these crocks became such that he decided to cut out the middleman and go into the business of manufacturing china. Before long, he expanded into dinnerware as well as crocks, and pottery became more profitable for him than groceries and produce. In the next generation, the Sebring fortune was managed by five of George's sons: Oliver Howard, known as "O. H." (1857–1929), George Eugene (1859–1927), Ellsworth Henry (1861–1937), Frank Albert (1865–1937) and Frederic E. (1868–1925). For a time the various members of the Sebring family operated potteries in East Liverpool and East Palestine, Ohio, but they could not keep up with the orders they received, so they became interested in constructing new factories. Being close to the main railroad line was important so that they could bring clay and glazes to their factories and ship the finished wares to urban markets. In April 1898 the brothers set out together on a scouting expedition to locate an appropriate site.

Three of the Sebring brothers died too early to play an active role in creating the town of Sebring: Joseph (1872–1890), William Henry (1870–1904), and Charles (1872–1877). In addition, there were two sisters, Eva (1865–1956) and Emma (1872–1957), who both settled in Sebring but did not play an active role in business affairs.

7. Interview #3, p. 2. Craig S. Bara, *Images of America: Sebring, Ohio* (Charleston, South Carolina: Arcadia Publishing, 1999), p. 9. For information about Sebring, I am also indebted to Daphne Connell, mayor of Sebring, and Frank Barrett, Sebring.

8. Interview #8, p. 1.

9. In 1899 they filed articles of incorporation, with a clause forbidding the sale of intoxicating beverages. On 9 May 1898 the *Alliance Review* announced that the new community just to the east would be named Sebring.

10. Bara, *Images of America,* p. 79.

11. Joy Stoer, "The Ceramic Industry of Sebring, Ohio," master's thesis (Ohio State University, 1948), p. 32.

12. Interview #3, p. 5.

13. One of Viktor's childhood friends from Sebring, Charles Murphy, also went into ceramics, becoming the chief designer for Redwing Pottery.

14. See note 4.

15. Interview #3, pp. 3–4.

16. Ibid., p. 3.

17. Schreckengost, in Jane Dwyer Garton, *Pedal Cars: Chasing the Kidillac* (Atglen, Pennsylvania: Schiffer Publishing, 1999), p. 28.

18. Ibid.

19. Interview #1, p. 7.

20. Ibid., pp. 7–8.

21. Interview #3, pp. 2–3.

22. Interview with Don Schreckengost (29 July 1999). The other children also helped as much as they could. Don, for example, although he wasn't yet in college, was earning money from working in the potteries and singing in a musical group, as well as from playing semi-pro baseball on weekends. He passed on most of this income to his parents.

23. Interview #4, p. 1.

24. The work of Don and Paul is described in detail in "Comic Page Figures Made in Clay," *Youngstown Telegraph* (1931).

25. Interview #8, p. 3.

26. Interview #1, p. 8.

27. Nancy Coe Wixom, *Cleveland Institute of Art: The First Hundred Years, 1882–1982* (Cleveland: Cleveland Institute of Art, 1983), pp. 13, 15, 21.

28. Interview #1, p. 8. In 1911, William Sommer and a group of his friends organized the Kokoon Club to promote modern and postimpressionist styles. In 1913 these artists were thrilled when some of the key paintings of the Armory Show were exhibited at the Cleveland Museum of Art. Reacting against the Kokoon Club was the Cleveland Society of Artists, an academic group supported by Frederick C. Gottwald and Walter Sinz.

29. Interview #1, pp. 8–9.

30. Ibid., p. 9.

31. Ibid., p. 10.

32. Viktor designed Sermoni's sign, which featured a man with a tuxedo who was reflected in a mirror, so that you could see back and front at one time.

33. Henry Turner Bailey was the director of the Cleveland Institute of Art from 1919 to 1930.

34. Interview #2, p. 9; letter from Viktor Schreckengost to Alyn Rosser (14 July 1997).

35. Interview #8, p. 3.

36. Interview #1, pp. 10–11, and Interview #8, p. 3.

37. Sckreckengost, in Marlene S. Hamann, "The Ceramic Sculptures of Viktor Schreckengost," master's thesis (Syracuse University, 1993), p. 7. *The International Exhibition of Ceramic Art* toured the United States under the auspices of the American Federation of Arts from October 1928 to September 1929. The show, on view in Cleveland, 21 February–21 March, included the work of several artists from Vienna, including Michael Powolny and two of his students, Vally Wieselthier and Suzi Singer (Shinner). Schreckengost has stated that he was even more impressed with their work in the show than by Powolny's. Powolny exhibited two hand-built animal figures, a bull and a colt, both glazed in brilliant Persian blue. He also exhibited a breakfast service he had designed that was executed by the Wiener Porzellanfabvrik Ausgarten. See *International Exhibition of Ceramic Art* (New York: American Federation of Arts, 1928).

38. Interview #8, p. 3.

39. Ibid.

40. Ibid., p. 4. Albright was later delighted that he had loaned Viktor this sum, since Viktor repaid it when he returned from Europe. Shortly after the stock market crash of 1929, Citizens Bank in Sebring folded, and Albright lost most of his life savings. He would have lost this sum as well had he not loaned it to Viktor.

41. Interview #4, p. 5.

42. Hoffmann was joined in this venture by another artist, Koloman Moser, and the businessman Friz Warndorft, who provided financial support.

43. For the Wiener Werkstatte, see Jane Kallir, *Viennese Design and the Wiener Werkstatte* (New York: G. Braziller, 1986). For Powolny, see Elizabeth Frotter, *Michael Powolny* (Vienna and Cologne: Bohlau Verlag, 1990).

44. Interview #4, p. 8.

45. Ibid., pp. 8–9. Viktor produced his *Chinese Head* [69] in Vienna.

46. Ibid., p. 10.

47. Ibid., p. 8.

48. Ibid., p. 6.

49. Copy in the possession of Viktor Schreckengost.

50. "Impressions, Viktor Schreckengost," sketch by Schreckengost, words by [Milton] Fox, *Cleveland News* (c. February 1932). In 1938 Ray Bruner described Viktor as "long, lanky, and blonde"; see Ray Bruner, "Art: Schreckengost Models a City of Tomorrow," *Cleveland News* (21 May 1939).

51. Interview with Algesa O'Sickey (28 May 2000).

52. Fox, *Cleveland News* article (c. February 1932).

53. Interview #1, p. 1, and Interview #8, p. 5. When Viktor returned to Cleveland in the fall of 1930, he worked Monday, Tuesday, and Wednesday teaching the basic design course for sophomores, and Thursday, Friday, and Saturday making designs for Guy Cowan. Viktor's friend Paul Bogatay ended up taking the job at Ohio State, and remained there for his entire professional career.

54. Interview #8, p. 13.

55. Ibid.

56. Ibid.

57. Carnegie-Mellon University in Pittsburgh and the Pratt Institute in New York also opened design programs around this time. As will be discussed, however, Viktor's program was apparently unique in the degree to which it provided students with direct exposure to the challenges of designing for industry.

58. Interview #8, p. 14.

59. Ibid., p. 5.

60. Ibid., p. 6.

61. Ibid., pp. 6–7. The Roosevelt punch bowls cannot now be located, but articles of the 1930s indicate that Eleanor Roosevelt provided the commission. The claim is made, for example, in "Youthful Cleveland Designer Inherited His Taste for Art," which states: "Recently governor Franklin D. Roosevelt's wife wanted a pottery bowl in modern design. They considered Peter Arno, the cartoonist, as the designer. But a New York concern induced them to commission this young Cleveland artist. He designed a bowl, *The New Yorker,* with a pattern of skyscrapers and musical notes. The concern came back with an order for 50 more." This statement is repeated, with near identical wording, in "Art Alliance Dinner for Cleveland Artist," *Youngstown Vindicator* (4 December 1932).

62. Interview #1, pp. 13–14.

63. Interview #8, p. 7. After all the pottery had been sold off, Cowan donated many of his leftover materials to the Institute of Art. At the time people were not fully aware of how dangerous some of the glazes were. Uranium was used to create a bright red-orange glaze, and Cowan gave five bags of his leftover uranium to the school—several hundred pounds of radioactive material. It lay around the studios for years but, miraculously, does not seem to have caused any ill effects.

64. "I designed almost all of the new restaurant ware for him," Viktor recalls, "with short rims and things that were a little more practical. That made it look as though there was a lot of food on the plate." Interview #6, p. 1.

65. "Youthful Cleveland Designer Inherited His Taste for Art"; William Daley, "In Conversation: Viktor Schreckengost/William Daley," *American Craft* 57 (June/July 1997), p. 47.

66. Interview #1, p. 14.

67. In the early 1910s, Helen Haiman Joseph produced marionette shows for adults at the Cleveland Play House. She also wrote the first English history of marionettes and spent three years in Europe visiting puppet theaters. In 1931 she published a children's book titled *Little Mr. Clown* and produced a marionette of Mr. Clown to be sold with it. When it proved a great success, she created additional puppets and became actively involved in toy manufacture. See Edwin T. Randall, "Santa Claus is Loading Up with 'Made in America' Toys," *Plain Dealer* (1 December 1935). Viktor owns one of the puppets heads he designed, and an advertisement for Joseph Puppets is in the Schreckengost scrapbook.

68. Interviews with Gene and Viktor Schreckengost (undated); telephone interview with Fred Stross (20 April 2000).

69. See Hugh Thomas, *The Spanish Civil War* (New York: Harper & Brothers, 1961), p. 78; and Stanley G. Payne, *The Franco Regime, 1936–1975* (London: University of Wisconsin Press, 1987), p. 62.

70. Interview with Don Schreckengost (29 July 1999).

71. Interview #8, p. 9.

72. Interview #1, p. 16.

73. This design was never put into production.

74. Interview #8, p. 9; Interview #1, p. 15.

75. Ibid., p. 10.

76. Cornelia Curtiss, "Many Roles of an Artist's Wife," *Cleveland News* (29 March 1948) (Schreckengost scrapbook).

77. Ibid.

78. Interview #7, p. 20. For Leathem's obituary, see Alma Kaufman, "Barclay S. Leathem, 80, famed leader in theatrical education," *Plain Dealer* (3 February 1981).

79. Interview #7, p. 17; Interview #8, p. 11. The program for the play is in the Schreckengost scrapbook. The red barn was torn down shortly afterward.

80. Interview #7, p. 17.

81. From 1936 through 1938 Murray produced a Mercury bicycle designed by De Sakhnoffsky. While De Sakhnoffsky's drawings seem to have been vague, the bike did contain a number of innovative design and mechanical features, probably for the most part introduced by the engineers at Murray. They included the first streamlined pedal cranks (with no dogleg to clear the chain guard), the first built-in side kickstand and anti-shatter rear reflector, and hubcaps. See http://home.earthlink.net/~oldbicycle/indexoaklandA.htm, p. 12.

82. Interview #7, p. 18.

83. Interview #8, pp. 20–22.

84. Ibid., p. 17. On 10 April 1943 the *Plain Dealer* carried a photograph of Captain Wotherspoon presenting the award to C. W. Hannon (Schreckengost scrapbook). In addition, Murray published a booklet at the time of the award, *The Story of Conversion of the Murray Ohio Manufacturing Co. from Peace to War Production* (c. 1943).

85. Interview #2, p. 1; Interview #8, p. 18.

86. Interview #2, p. 1.

87. Robert Lewis Taylor, "Profiles: Captain among the Synthetics" (part one), *New Yorker* (11 November 1944), pp. 34–38, 40, 43.

88. Interview #8, p. 18. Radar stands for radio detection and ranging.

89. Interview #2, p. 2; Interview #8, p. 19.

90. Interview #2, p. 3.

91. Ibid., p. 3.

92. Ibid., pp. 4–5.

93. Interview #2, pp. 7–8.

94. Interview #2, p. 4.

95. Ibid., pp. 5–6.

96. Viktor entered the navy as a lieutenant, was promoted to lieutenant commander during the war, left active duty as a commander, and became a captain during his 20 years in the reserves after the war.

97. Copy in the possession of Viktor Schreckengost.

98. Interview with Helen Cullinan (8 October 1999).

99. E-mail from Patricia Leathem, London (30 November 1999).

The Work

Viktor's work in art and design often entailed solving problems unique to a particular medium, and it is necessary to understand these challenges to grasp fully the originality of his work. Consequently, it is useful to consider each medium he explored in turn, beginning with his artistic work and proceeding to his work in industrial design.

Drawing and Watercolor

At the heart of Viktor's success as an artist, in both fine art and industrial design, is his ability as a draftsman and watercolorist. He began drawing very early, as is evident from a watercolor he made at the age of nine, showing German officers of the First World War [1]. He perfected his skills as a student at the Cleveland Institute of Art. The program there was rigorous, and from his teachers Viktor developed proficiency in making various types of drawings, which are so distinct that they amount to virtually separate fields, for example, cartooning, figure and landscape drawing, memory drawing, anatomical and medical rendering, mechanical drawing, perspective rendering, and costume design. Viktor's work as a sculptor contributed to the confidence with which he drew, for he was able to grasp relationships of form and space and give them substance. Very often, he added tonality to these renderings through the use of watercolor. He seldom painted in oil, despite a few efforts, such as *Blue Revel* of 1931 [2] and *Moroccan Lutes* of 1934 [3], which reveal real talent in that medium.

Viktor's facility as a draftsman was nicely demonstrated in 1939, when he and Nadine went on a beach vacation to Cape May, New Jersey, with Barclay Leathem, William Ramsay, and their families. Through a fluke of weather, they were hit by a northeaster, and it rained all nine days of the trip, stranding them indoors. Indeed, thanks to a leaky roof, the party spent the first night sleeping in their cars. To amuse the children, and because "you can't play poker all the time," Viktor produced several dozen humorous sketches, many of them on yellow-ruled grammar school paper, which were so impressive that his fellow vacationers urged him to make them the subject of an exhibition. Modestly, Viktor held back from doing so, but a few weeks

Blue Revel, 1931. H. 127 cm. [2]. Visits to the Globe Theatre, where a group of faculty members from the Cleveland Institute of Art had rented a box, inspired this painting. It was included in the 1931 May Show at the Cleveland Museum of Art, along with Viktor's *Cocktails and Cigarettes* punch bowl.

BLUE REVEL

Moroccan Lutes, 1934. H. 85.5 cm. [3].
Viktor acquired the lutes pictured in this design during a trip to North Africa in 1932. The cubist style of the painting pays tribute to Picasso, whose work was admired by Viktor's companion on the North African trip, the chemist and photographer Fred Stross.

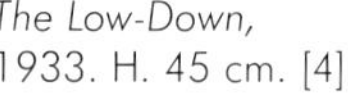

The Low-Down, 1933. H. 45 cm. [4].

Harlem Hoofers, 1933. H. 44.5 cm. [5].

Christmas (Salvation Army), 1933. H. 44.5 cm. [6].
Viktor exhibited these three watercolors in an exhibition of caricatures by local artists on view at the Cleveland Museum of Art in January 1933.

later, apparently without his knowledge, five were reproduced in the *Cleveland Press,* and they provide remarkable evidence of his proficiency and technical skill. Casually dashed off, for the most part without models, they nonetheless contain convincing renderings of fish, locomotives, buildings, and people, including very recognizable caricatures of his fellow vacationers as well as himself and Nadine.[1]

Despite this display of artistry, drawing and watercolor remained a sideline for Viktor through the 1930s. While these skills provided the basis for his designs in other media, it was not until World War II that he seriously explored watercolor as a medium in its own right. Indeed, he often took watercolors with him when he went on research flights to map the Earth's terrain with radarscopes and stereometric photography. These missions made him grasp the experience of space in new ways. As he later recalled:

> My eyes were opened to another dimension of space, where you seemed completely detached from immediate surroundings. What on the earth's surface, appeared to be very large forms, became, at high altitude, merely part of a pattern. Yet, as light cut across at certain times of day, you could tell where these forms were.[2]

He also noted that flying created astonishing differences in the perception of color, whether because of some side effect of the altitude or because it created an actual change in tone and hue. Color no longer seemed to belong to specific forms, but suffused the field of vision as a whole in an almost mystical fashion. As Viktor commented:

> All I know is that real color no longer seemed to exist on the earth. It was in the sky itself, and consequently, it was difficult to find a painting surface big enough to catch the impression.[3]

With his painter's eyes, he was able to see beauty even in the terrifying flight to Europe, to participate in the Battle of the Bulge.

> I remember once when we were flying over Scotland between two storms. One storm was overhead; one far below us. We broke out into the space between the two. Overhead it was still very black and brown, but beyond the sky was a brilliant lime green—a strange new color that all fliers experience, yet none can accurately describe. Immediately under us was a heavily

All Quiet, 1946. H. 54.3 cm. [7]. Viktor was horrified by the ruins of French villages he encountered in France in 1945, when he took part in the Battle of the Bulge. He produced watercolors such as this one to bring home to Americans the terrible devastation of war.

> rolling white mass, while below that the lower storm was pushing up what appeared to be huge black ice cream cones.
>
> I tried endlessly to capture these new forms, but I have never exhibited the results. They would require too much explanation.[4]

At this time he also recorded the devastation of war in such watercolors as *All Quiet* of 1946 [7]. As he told the reporter Dorothy Grafly:

> It left such an impression that I had to put it down. I found, however, that one of the most difficult things in the world is to paint rubble and destruction. Even the illusion of chaos must be carefully planned.[5]

To his distress, when he exhibited these works he found that the public was largely indifferent.

> People were not interested. When they reacted at all it was with a shrug that seemed to imply: all that is over now, so let's forget about it.[6]

As with his political sculpture in clay, however, Viktor was unwilling to let the public response dictate the art he produced.

> We artists should do more, not less of that sort of thing, and we should do it now to show the sheer hopelessness of war.[7]

When he returned to Cleveland, he continued to work seriously in watercolor, shifting his subject matter to evocative renderings of old mansions [8], in a style somewhat reminiscent of the work of other Cleveland School artists such as Charles Burchfield and Clarence Carter, and still-life compositions [10]. He also began regularly showing watercolors at the May Show as well as exhibiting in national watercolor exhibitions. In January 1948

House of Memories, 1946. H. 53.5 cm. [8].
Like other watercolorists of the Cleveland School, Viktor was fascinated by Victorian mansions, with their evocation of nostalgia and decay.

he held his first one-person show of watercolors at the Town and Country Gallery in Cleveland. During this period, his work in watercolor was regularly singled out for favorable mention in the press, and from 1946 to 1958, the last year in which prizes were given, he won awards in watercolor or freehand drawing at the May Show every year. Indeed, art critics and jurors were not the only ones impressed by Viktor's watercolors of this period. In 1948 a young girl, Jean Chandler, used up her entire savings to acquire one of his watercolors from the May Show.[8]

O. H.'s Place, 1947. H. 55.9 cm. [9].
This watercolor records the ruins of Oliver H. Sebring's mansion in Viktor's hometown of Sebring, Ohio. During the Depression, the family lost its fortune and this mansion became a rooming-house. It was destroyed by fire in 1947.

During this period, Viktor produced so many watercolors that it is difficult to chart their many shifts of style and subject matter. Generally speaking, over the course of the 1950s, his watercolors grew increasingly stylized, with angular lines like those in the work of Lyonel Feininger, which function like lines of lead in stained glass to surround bright sparkles of color. His subject matter often related to trips or current projects. During the early 1950s, for example, when he was doing sculpture for buildings at the zoo, he made a large number of animal studies [64–67]; in 1977, after a trip to Egypt with Fred Stross, he painted several watercolors of Egyptian subjects; and in 1980, after a simi-

Dried Fruit, 1946. H. 53.5 cm. [10]. This still life was arranged in one of Viktor's slab form ceramic vessels.

Fall Festival, 1962. H. 53.5 cm. [13]. By the 1960s, Viktor had begun fragmenting shapes in a decorative fashion that brings to mind both cubist painting and stained-glass windows.

Studio Window, 1947. H. 53.5 cm. [11]. Concurrently with more realistic watercolors, Viktor produced renderings such as this one that emphasize abstract qualities of design.

Floral, 1973. H. 97.5 cm. [14]. Viktor's confident mastery of the wet textures and brilliant colors possible in watercolor are evident in this work.

First Snow, Last Flowers, 1974. H. 53.5 cm. [12]. While best known for his clean, geometric renderings, Viktor also produced fluid, nearly abstract paintings. He created the unusual textures in this watercolor by sprinkling salt on the wet pigment.

Derelict, 1947.
H. 54.5 cm. [15].

Tornado's Wake, 1956. H. 54 cm. [16].

Late Show, 1964. H. 54 cm. [17]. On research flights during World War II, Viktor became fascinated by how the world looks from the air. He returned to such subject matter in this watercolor.

lar trip with Fred to Guatemala, he turned to Mayan themes. Perhaps his most striking late watercolors focus on the New York skyline [18, 20], often featuring landmarks of the art deco period such as the Chrysler Building, and on musical instruments [21].

The success of these watercolors led to a number of commercial projects. For example, after winning a prize in a show of American watercolor in New York, Viktor was invited to make Christmas cards for the American Artist's Group. He produced such cards annually from about 1947 to 1996—a period of nearly 50 years. In 1979 he created a series of watercolors of Cleveland landmarks, including the West Side Market and Terminal Tower for a Cleveland calendar, and his watercolors were frequently featured on the programs of concerts, civic events, and charitable affairs in the northeast Ohio area.

Light on the River, 1975. H. 53.5 cm. [18].
The blue mood of this romantic city view evokes the feeling of jazz.

Pattern of the Sea, 1985. H. 74 cm. [19].
This watercolor of fish shows Viktor's gift for decorative pattern.

New York Buildings, Blue Background, 1997. H. 98.5 cm. [20].
Viktor's late watercolors often dramatically abstract forms in a fashion that brings to mind the wiring of a computer.

Big City Jazz, 1987. H. 99 cm. [21].
Many of Viktor's watercolors explore the shapes of musical instruments. Not surprisingly, he was particularly fond of rendering the instrument he played—the saxophone.

VIKTOR
SCHRECKENGOST

Stage Sets

Viktor's skill with watercolor allowed him to do distinguished work in stage and costume design, although sadly most of his work of this sort is now lost. Just enough survives to demonstrate that his work in stage design was often ingenious, on a par with the best work of its type produced anywhere in America in the period. It does not seem to have bothered Viktor that much of this work reached only a tiny audience, since the Eldred Theater at Western Reserve University, for which he produced most of his sets, seated only 200.

Viktor seems to have enjoyed the practical constraints of stage design, such as the need to create grand effects with a small budget and work quickly. From 1938 to 1943 he produced four or five stage sets a year. Loosely speaking, his sets can be divided into three types: those that created a period effect with painted backdrops; those that explored sculptural volumes; and those that used light to create changes, with a minimal use of scenery.

Painted backdrops were a cheap way of creating rapid scene changes. Viktor often used this technique for Victorian melodramas such as Augustin Daly's *Under the Gaslight* (1867), which featured 11 different scenes, including a bridge from which the heroine was thrown and a railroad track onto which the hero was bound. Backdrops were also an effective way to evoke a period flavor, which again made them well suited for plays with a Victorian setting. In October 1940, Viktor produced striking backdrops and costumes for a farce by Thornton Wilder, *The Merchant of Yonkers* (1938), in which he spoofed the theatrical conventions and manners of New York around 1880. "What lends more color and humor to this fandango than anything else," noted Glenn Pullen of the *Plain Dealer*, are "Viktor Schreckengost's imaginative settings and amusing costumes. His sets vividly catch the mood of mad mockery, while the quaint zebra-striped suits and billowing gowns of the 1880s also help sustain much of the tomfoolery."[9]

For more serious productions, Viktor created more sculptural stagesets, often using shrewd tricks to construct them inexpensively. For a production of T. S. Eliot's *Murder in the Cathedral* (1935), for example, he created lofty columns out of standard cardboard tubes, with the addition of a few plywood arches. To create a sense of spaciousness he followed the rules of perspective and put a diminutive, strikingly backlit stained-glass window in the background, at the end of a long line of columns and arches. Theater critic William McDermott appreciatively noted that the effect was "a cathedral-like setting which is all reverence, and eerie, candlelit beauty—shadow, towering, and evocative."[10]

Still more original were Viktor's sets for August Strindberg's *Spook Sonata* (1907) and William Saroyan's *Jim Dandy* (1941)—the world premiere of the play. Both are strange and unusual plays. Drama critic Jack Warfel noted that attempting to detail "the tingling heights and depressing depths" of Strindberg's play in story form would be "like trying to nail jelly to a wall," and he reported that the audience responded with "inspiration and bafflement. Mostly bafflement."[11] But whatever the meaning of it all, Warfel noted that the spirit of the play was evocatively captured in Schreckengost's stage settings, which created "an illusion of vastness, and enhance the eerie mysticism."[12] A clever gimmick of Viktor's scheme was the movable panel in the front, which gradually opened up to change the setting from the outside of a building to the inside of a room. This interior was vast and ambiguous in scale, with strange green columns and arches that receded into an infinite distance. The unfolding of the set perfectly paralleled the unfolding of the dramatic action and matched its increasingly eerie mood.

Jim Dandy [22, 23] also presented an unusual challenge. In his preface, Saroyan boasted that the play "contains no characters, no imitations of people, and no plot," and that "the realm in which this play...takes place is the realm of the constant and continuing heart of living things—a most enormous realm—which includes the whole miracle of the writer himself, and reader, and him who beholds the play."[13] Creating a set from such directions was clearly difficult, but Viktor took his hint from the remark that the stage should extend from here to eternity, that it was neither inside nor outside, and that it resembled a public library. His design showed trees growing in the library, and five-foot books extending from the front of the stage into the distance to a vanishing point. In the center of the stage was a revolving door through which the characters entered and exited, with a glass ball on top that sparkled every time the door turned. Other objects, including a cash register and a red child's wagon that Viktor had designed for Murray, were scattered across the stage in surrealist fashion. Critics agreed that this setting was "extraordinarily right and effective," and one confessed, "I

Stage Set Rendering for "Jim Dandy," 1941. H. 35 cm. [22].

The set for the world premiere of William Saroyan's play *Jim Dandy* was daring, with clouds and trees in a library and shadows falling across the sky. Viktor included one of his own little red wagons on the right-hand side as a surrealist object.

Character Design for "Jim Dandy," 1941. H. 33 cm. [23].

This costume drawing for *Jim Dandy* shows Viktor's skill and assurance in rendering the human figure.

found myself fascinated by a child's wagon that stood front stage throughout the play, bathed in bilious pinspot."[14]

Finally, Viktor designed sets for two summer productions at Cain Park, an outdoor theater with a large, open stage that made it necessary to create scene changes largely with light. Both productions were organized by a remarkable Italian actress, Marta Abba. Abba had started her career performing in Rome in the theater troupe of the modernist playwright Luigi Pirandello, who dedicated the play *Trovarsi* (1943) to her. The Cain Park productions marked her return to the stage after an absence of nearly four years following her marriage to the Cleveland businessman Severance Millikin.

Abba's first production was a Victorian comedy by Victorien Sardou, *Divorçons! Comédie en Trios Acts* (1880), in which she played a bored wife who wanted a divorce. (The subject was unfortunately prophetic: Abba and Millikin divorced a few years later.)[15] The numerous scene changes presented a challenge for an outdoor theater. Viktor's solution was to arrange a series of rooms on a circular stage that turned. Between scenes the lights were directed out toward the audience, and with a turn of the stage a magical transformation would take place. Local critics concurred that the effect was marvelous. William McDermott declared that Schreckengost had "managed the remarkable feat of contriving a background that brought the intimacy of a French drawing room to the open spaces of Cain Park. Count the evening a distinguished success."[16] His judgment was echoed by Albert E. Prudence, who declared that "the stage designs by Viktor Schreckengost are perfect."[17]

Similar in concept was Viktor's staging of Pirandello's play *Right You Are! If You Think So*

(1923). The key character was a mother-in-law, the role performed by Abba, whose behavior appeared sane to half the characters in the play, and insane to the other half. The challenge of the performance was to make both interpretations equally plausible. Viktor's stage design was essentially a simplification of the one he had developed for *Divorçons*. Rather than using a revolving stage, he arranged a series of rooms in a line and used lighting to move from one to another. Critics concurred that the staging was a triumph.

"I wasn't interested in pinning down a superficial doorway, or in period styling," Viktor later recalled. "Instead I wanted to study the position of a door in relation to the action on the stage. Finally, I worked into big outdoor theatrical productions and learned that the movement of the actor within space limitations must be given the support of costume design as well as of an adequate stage set; and that figure movement in and out of light gives another dimension."[18]

One of Viktor's last little triumphs in stage design occurred during the war, when he devised inventive ways to use materials at hand to create interesting visual effects. When stationed at Quonset Point Naval Station in Rhode Island, he created a picturesque grouping for the glee club by used metal lockers four feet high and eight feet long as platforms for the men to stand on. While the chorus was practicing, Viktor went to the back of the room to study how it looked. "That's a beautiful presentation," a man standing there said to him. "Who did it?" "I did," Viktor replied. "My name's Henry Fonda," the man stated, coming over to shake his hand. "I think it's wonderful."[19]

Viktor's last venture in theatrical design occurred just after the war, when he designed the setting for a television production of Charles Dickens's *A Christmas Carol* (1843), which he worked on with Barclay Leathem. Taken on their own terms, Viktor's schemes were a success, but they did create some unintended social disruption. To produce an effect of London fog and mystery, Viktor used dry ice. During breaks in the filming it was stored in a refrigerator at the television station. Unfortunately, the refrigerator was also being used to keep the food for the *General Electric Kitchen Show* cold. When the chef arrived for the filming, the food she planned to prepare had frozen rock solid—the eggs were so hard they bounced off the floor like squash balls. Her filming had to be postponed.[20]

In an interview just after the war, Viktor discussed designing for television, pointing out some of the unique qualities of the medium.

> Television is a definite challenge. First of all, it is necessary to find some way to keep production costs down. Sometimes there is a simple solution. I discovered, for instance, that by elevating the cameras I could use the floor for a background. In the movies you shoot in scale for a 20-foot screen. Any such scale is useless for television where the size of the screen limits your action to greatly reduced space.[21]

While Viktor's stage sets never received the kind of national attention they deserved, the experience certainly contributed to his skill in the field of industrial design. When he designed household appliances, he made use of his discoveries from stage design of how light can transform the nature of form. As he stated in an interview of 1949:

> When I tackled a refrigerator, I first developed a working knowledge of the reflection of light from surfaces. Light, I found, can so distort surfaces that it changes the appearance of the object itself, adding an illusion either of stability or speed. If a cabinet looks too high for the dimensions of its base, you can lower its appearance by using highlights [so] a basically heavy, squat form can be given the illusion of vertical lightness without added ornamentation.[22]

Technical tricks aside, perhaps the most impressive thing about Viktor's theatrical work was his sensitivity to the inner mood of a play, even when it pushed toward emotions that were bizarre or unusual. To use Eliot's terms, his stage sets provide the perfect "objective correlative" to the text, capturing the emotional essence of the drama in the language of visible things. His most ambitious and finest stage sets were associated with plays that were strange, uneasy, and surreal in mood, such as Strindberg's *Spook Sonata* or Saroyan's *Jim Dandy*. In person, Viktor is so relentlessly cheerful and upbeat that it is a little surprising to find that he was so sensitive to distraught and anxious moods, and so skillful in capturing them.

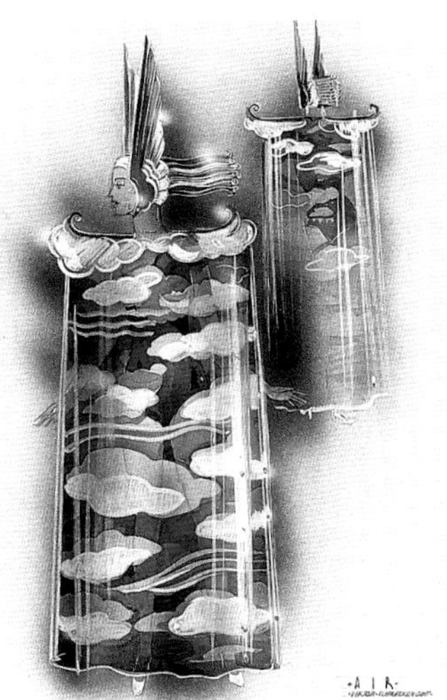

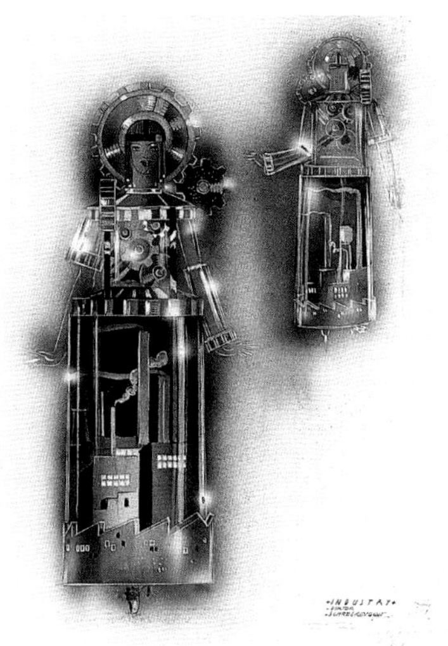

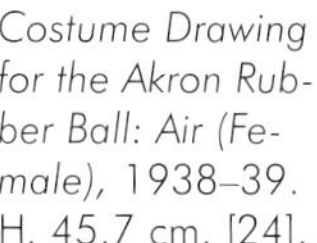

Costume Drawing for the Akron Rubber Ball: Air (Female), 1938–39. H. 45.7 cm. [24].

Costume Drawing for the Akron Rubber Ball: Industry, 1938–39. H. 45.7 cm. [26].

Costume Drawing for the Akron Rubber Ball: Fire (Female), 1938–39. H. 45.7 cm. [28].

In 1939, Viktor designed costumes made entirely of rubber fabrics for the ball sponsored by the rubber companies of Akron.

The Akron Rubber Ball

A curious offshoot of this work in stage design occurred in 1939, when Viktor was commissioned to design costumes for that year's Akron Rubber Ball [24–29]. The invitation required guests to come in "rubber costume"—a term that included both pure rubber and products or cloth that had been processed by the rubber companies. The organizers, however, set guidelines to make the event "an impressive and beautiful costume affair, discouraging such freak costumes as the gigantic hot water bottles, tires, and water showers which marked last year's ball."[23] Three nationally known painters—John Sloan, Rockwell Kent, and Charles Burchfield—served as judges of the costume competition.

Viktor was hired to design costumes for the king and queen of the ball and their court, nine men and nine women whose garments were to represent the four basic elements of rubber—earth, fire, air, and water—as well as other factors contributing to its fabrication, such as transportation, power, chemistry, and industry. These courtly robes were to be worn by vice presidents of each of the rubber companies and representatives of the city's three largest department stores.

For inventiveness, extravagance, and sheer oddity, Viktor's costumes have surely seldom been surpassed. They were fabricated from about 15 different rubber fabrics and products, some of which had never been shown in public before, including cord fabric, rubber tubing, rubber sheeting, clear plastics, suede-finish sheeting, sponge and plastic rubber materials, Corosheen, Pliofilm, Koroseal (familiar in raincoats and umbrellas among numerous other uses), and Controlastic (used in corsets and other webbings). The unusual qualities of these fabrics were exploited to the full, for they were used in a complete spectrum of colors and layered to create interesting shimmering effects that would change according to the play of light. Many of the women's gowns, for example, used colored appliqué drapes over basic white transparent fabrics and vice versa, which provided depth and introduced interesting variations in color and light values.[24] A newspaper article of the time provides a detailed description of the construction of several costumes, which makes it easier to imagine the overall effect.[25]

Hand-Formed Ceramics

Along with drawing and watercolor, the first medium Viktor mastered was ceramics, and ceramics have played a central role in his artistic output throughout his career. Indeed, Viktor was perhaps the most versatile artist of the 20th century in the medium of clay. He produced noteworthy sculpture, pottery, commercial dinnerware, and monumental architectural reliefs. While carrying out these projects, he explored virtually every technique known to the medium, for example, cast forms, hand-thrown and hand-built vessel forms, freely shaped carved slab forms (an approach he introduced to American ceramics shortly after World War II), hand-painted plates and vessels (often with delicate modeling and shading, like that found in paintings) [30, 31], and sculpture that was cast, built, carved, or constructed by assembling units from hand-thrown vessel forms. In many instances, Schreckengost's work of the 1930s and 1940s, which ranges from colorful and funky to monochromatic, austere, and tastefully abstract, startlingly prefigures the work of such contemporary masters in clay as Robert Arneson or Peter Voulkos. Clay also provided Viktor with a bridge into other areas of art and design. For example, until the recent introduction of computer graphics, automobile and product design was largely modeled in clay. Viktor's virtuosity in clay also led naturally into the design of bicycles, pedal toys, lawn mowers, and other products.

When Viktor first encountered Viennese ceramics in 1929, he was delighted by the fact that they were unique hand-modeled pieces rather than cast. By working directly in clay it was possible to achieve a spontaneity not possible through more indirect means. Such freely modeled pieces formed a major focus of Viktor's work from 1930, when he returned from Vienna, up to about 1970. During the early 1930s, he used the May Show and other exhibitions to build up a reputation as a master quickly. In 1931 he received first prize for ceramics, with his *Cocktails and Cigarettes* punch bowl [134], and in the same year he sent his work around the country in a fashion unprecedented for a Cleveland artist. For the rest of the 1930s, Viktor was the darling of the Cleveland art critics, and over the course of his career he won more prizes at the May Show than any other artist, in any medium.[26]

This success in winning attention and prizes was waged against fierce competition, for during this period a number of other Cleveland artists, most of them former employees of Cowan Pottery, also produced highly original work in clay. Like Viktor, these artists combined Viennese and American techniques and subjects to create a synthesis. Their work is often considered the first concerted "movement" of American sculpture in clay. During the early 1930s, Viktor shared the spotlight with two other young men, Russell Barnett Aitken and Whitney Atchley. One Cleveland journalist even wrote of them as "The Three Horsemen" who "galloped into the May show ... with such clattering hoofs that the thunder is making pleasant reverberations all through the country."[27]

A rival to Viktor in talent, but not in discipline, Aitken never quite decided whether to excel as an artist or as an adventurer, sportsman, and raconteur. The son of a wealthy Canadian electrical engineer, he spent much of his childhood wandering through the woods, either shooting at animals or making sketches of them. Like Viktor, Aitken attended the Cleveland Institute of Art, although he never graduated. Also like Viktor, he went on to study in Vienna, although Aitken was too adventurous to settle down to a formal program of schooling. Rather than throwing pots under the stern eye of Powolny, he spent much of his time in athletic pursuits. He skied across Austria, canoed in Germany, rode with Hungarian cowboys, and was initiated into the Corps Hilaritas, a Viennese dueling society, where he became expert in fencing and saber fighting. On his return to Cleveland, Aitken began producing vigorous, freely formed, humorous clay sculpture, colored with garish tin glazes in the Viennese manner.[28]

From 1930 to 1940, both Viktor and Aitken won a first prize at the May Show nearly every year, with Viktor generally receiving the prize in pottery, and Aitken the prize in ceramic sculpture. Toward the end of the decade, however, Aitken moved to New York, where his interests shifted from ceramics to journalism. Only after Aitken left Cleveland did Viktor shift away from decorated plates and begin showing ceramic sculpture at the May Show. Less colorful as a personality, and less original as an artist, was Whitney Atchley. His forte was decorated plates and vessels whose harmonious balance of figure and ground drew on his early training as a printmaker. Like Aitken, Atchley left Cleveland in the late 1930s and dropped out of the ceramic field. He spent his later years teaching, first in Dallas and then in San Francisco.

After 1940 both Aitken and Atchley stopped exhibiting at the May Show, and Viktor's principal competition in ceramic sculpture came from two women, Thelma Frazier Winter and Edris Eckhardt, both of whom won a string of prizes throughout the 1940s. Winter was attracted to subjects from theater, opera, and classical mythology, which she treated in a slightly sentimental fashion. Her greatest honor came in 1939 when she became the first woman to win a first prize in ceramic sculpture at the Ceramic National Exhibition in Syracuse.

The Seasons Vase, 1931–33. H. 27.3 cm. [30].
The design of this vase resembles Viennese posters.

Floral Vase, 1931, H. 29.5 cm. [31].
Viktor often mixed his glazes with varnish and turpentine to control their flow. This practice allowed him to create effects similar to oil painting.

Eckhardt also favored romantic subjects, but her figures often possess El Greco-like elongations that give them a somewhat anguished character. The wretched Pierrot in *Painted Mask* of 1946, for example, allegedly resembled Eckhardt's husband, who suffered from tuberculosis at a time when the disease was not curable.[29]

Decorated Plates

From 1930 up to about 1937 Viktor focused on plates and vessels with hand-painted decorations. Always shrewd in his marketing skills, he was undoubtedly aware that such objects dramatized a skill in painting that few potters possess. Perhaps the tour de force of these pieces was his Leda plate of 1931–32 [32], a masterwork of American art deco on par with the sculpture of Paul Manship. Its design was created through the sgraffito technique—that is, by scratching through a covering of

Leda and the Swan, 1931–32. Diam. 41.8 cm. [32]. For this plate Viktor used sgraffito, a challenging technique. To create the design he scratched through a surface covering of black engobe to the white ceramic underneath.

black engobe (clay mixed with glaze) to the white clay vessel underneath. While Viktor's design looks effortless, in fact, the technique presented formidable difficulties since, like drypoint in printmaking, it does not allow the artist to make any changes or corrections.[30]

After exploring sgraffito, Viktor moved on to painted wares that are more pictorial in effect. Some of these early works are on hand-thrown forms, but he also worked on blanks from Cowan Pottery and (after 1932) American Limoges, treating these surfaces much as a painter does a canvas. These plates and plaques cross a great range of subject matter, which is most often presented with a touch of humor, such as Pegasus [33], baseball players [34, 35], polo [36], Neptune [38], cocktails [40], Janus [41], warriors [42], still life [43], Lady Godiva, Nero fiddling while Rome burns, zebras, and giraffes. Their style draws variously from American cartoons, Viennese posters, the French "ocean liner style," and the cubist compositions of Braque and Picasso. While they use

Pegasus Plate, 1931. Diam. 42.5 cm. [33]. Flying horses were a popular art deco motif because they evoked power, speed, and flight. Viktor created the pictorial design with curves that dramatize the roundness of the plate.

Baseball Plate: Pitching, about 1930s. Diam. 27.9 cm. [34].

Baseball Plate: Batting, about 1930s. Diam. 27.7 cm. [35].

Polo Plate (one in a series of ten), about 1937. Diam 24.3 cm. [36].

The Hunt, 1931. Bowl, Diam. 41.9 cm; plates, Diam. 29.2 cm. [37]. This service portraying a fox hunt has the same punch bowl shape as the *Jazz Bowl*. The fox is hidden inside the bottom of the bowl.

Neptune Plaque, 1936. Diam. 38.8 cm. [38].

Danse Moderne, 1931. Diam. 28.5 cm. [39]. Those who could not afford a *Jazz Bowl* from Cowan Pottery could purchase this jazzy wall plaque, which was similar in style.

Cocktails Plate, 1931. Diam. 29.2 cm. [40].

Janus Plaque, 1936. Diam. 39 cm. [41].

Warrior Heads Plaque (No. 5), 1932. Diam. 45.7 cm. [42].

simple materials, many of these plates are technically ingenious, using various devices to get the tonal richness of a painting, as well as interesting color effects. To make the colors flow properly, Viktor mixed the glazes with a variety of mediums, including water, turpentine, and glue. (The turpentine allowed him to get more gradation in the colors.) Sometimes he did several firings, one for the basic design and another to add some of the brighter colors that do not fire at such heat, such as reds and blues. He sometimes used overglaze painting on top of the fired piece, particularly for metallic lusters such as copper, gold, and platinum, which created an iridescent look.

In 1937, Viktor showed ceramic sculpture at the May Show for the first time, exhibiting three pieces, each markedly different from the others in subject and technique. One was a bull carved from a solid lump of clay; another was a head modeled from a vessel-like hollow form; the final piece was an African-American subject, baptism, that used clay additively to build up the different forms. From this time onward Viktor showed painted vessels less often, concentrating instead on ceramic sculpture.

Still-Life Plaque, 1931–32. Diam. 41.3 cm. [43].

Alces Americanus Shirasi, 1948. H. 44.1 cm. [44]. To emphasize how ridiculous it is, Viktor gave this figure of a pompous moose its full Latin name.

Animals

Most of Viktor's sculpture from 1937 until 1943 can be divided into the same subject groupings as his first May Show sculpture entry: animals, heads, and African-American subjects. Most of the animal sculptures were first modeled as solid forms and then carefully cut in half or in sections, hollowed out, and then reassembled. In many cases, Viktor made interesting simplifications, which one often does not notice unless they are pointed out. For example, his impressive *Brahman* [45] has legs that end at the ankles, in the interest of both structural strength and visual simplicity. As with his figural sculpture, that of his animals is often humorous, and he generally provided the pieces with playful titles. A pompous moose he titled by its full Latin name, *Alces Americanus Shirasi* [44]. A lamb jumping over a lion he provided with the punning title *Spring* [52].

Loosely speaking, Viktor employed two artistic approaches when rendering animals. On the one hand, he was interested in linear silhouette and used the outline almost like a line drawing. Several of his early sculptures, including a rendition of two giraffes and a camel [47], exploit this principle.

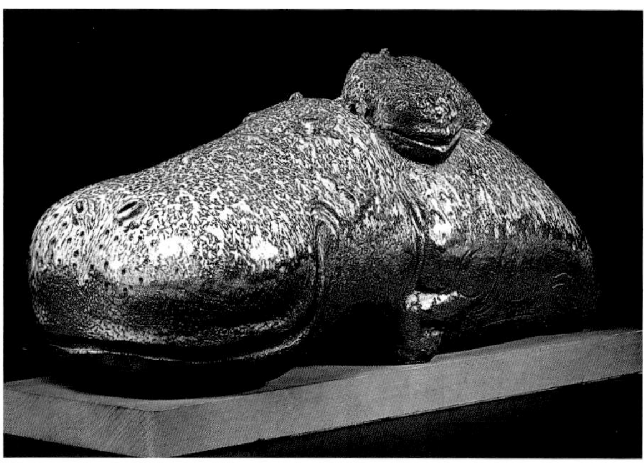

Brahman, 1951. H. 54.5 cm. [45]. The bold carving of this bull brings to mind a drawing by Picasso. To strengthen the piece and create a more massive effect, Viktor cut off its legs at the ankles.

Beauty Nap, 1948. H. 23.6 cm. [46]. Viktor made this hippo with its baby at the same time he produced his massive slab form vessels. It shows a similar interest in working with massive chunks of clay.

Naama, 1939. H. 44.2 cm. [47]. Viktor rode camels when he visited North Africa in 1932 and became fascinated by their ungainly shape. This sculpture emphasizes the unusual outline of a camel in a fashion similar to a line drawing.

Mountain Sheep with Sea Green Glaze, c. 1922. H. 26 cm. [48].
This early sculpture, made when Viktor was a student at the Institute of Art, shows his gift for simplification. It takes a moment to realize that the sheep have horns but no ears. Designed to be cast, the piece employs shapes that will fall easily out of a mold.

Charger, 1929. H. 46 cm. [53].
In Vienna, where he studied at the Kunstegewerbeschule, Viktor mastered a variety of ways of making sculpture in clay. *Charger* pays tribute to Austrian baroque sculpture of the 17th century.

Fish, 1948. H. 26.7 cm. [50].

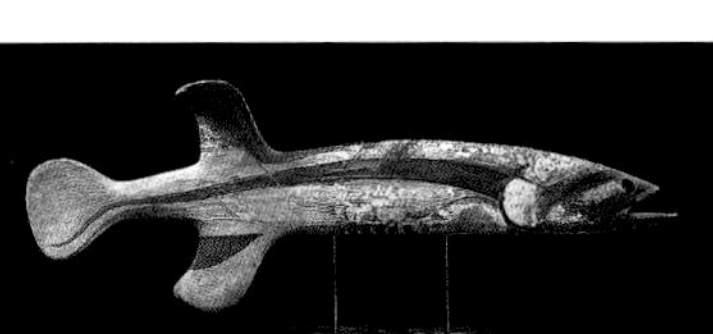

Kublai, 1950. H. 39.5 cm. [51].
While every feature of front and back is clearly indicated, we never forget the massive slab of clay from which this elephant is carved.

Balashan, 1942. H. 52.5 cm. [54].

Spring, 1941. H. 38.1 cm. [52].
A frisky lamb jumps over a lion in this punning portrayal of spring.

These works were also technically tricky because their forms were so attenuated that they required physical support while being fired, to prevent them from drooping. He used various devices to solve this problem, sometimes burying the figures in sand, which provided support, and sometimes making clay buttresses to hold them up.

On the other hand, he was interested in using clay to create seemingly formless blobs, which we must study closely to "find" the creature. A remarkable instance of this is his *Beauty Nap* [46], executed just after the war, in which a baby hippopotamus rests upon its mother's back. While we can see them as hippopotami, we never forget that they are made of lumps of clay. Perhaps even more fascinating is an elephant, *Pachyderm* [57], which is almost unrecognizable from some viewpoints. Move around it and it shifts from a shapeless lump of clay to a recognizable creature. Through this visual trick, the viewer goes through an experience not unlike that of the sculptor himself, creating something recognizable and distinctive from a shapeless lump of clay.

Still a third device, though Viktor used it more rarely, was creating a kind of dazzle effect through

Bull, 1948. H. 30.7 cm. [55].

Leap Frog, 1950. H. 50 cm. [56]. The irregular flowing glazes add greatly to the impact of these pieces.

Pachyderm, 1951. H. 61 cm. [57]. As we move around this object, an elephant appears from a shapeless blob of clay.

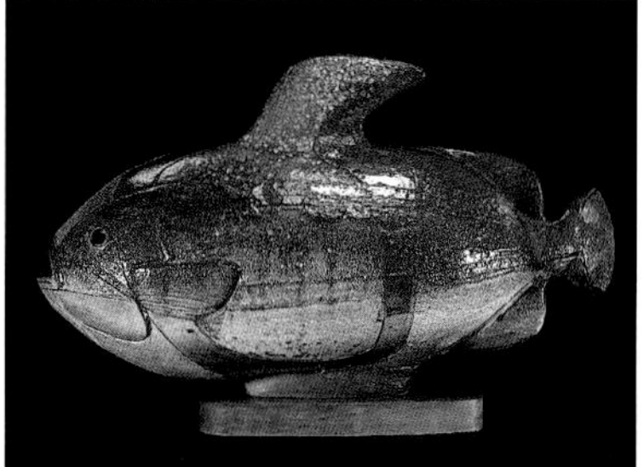

Samoa, 1950. H. 46 cm. [58]. This fish was on view in an exhibition of work by contemporary sculptors at the Metropolitan Museum of Art in 1950. It was the only ceramic included in the show.

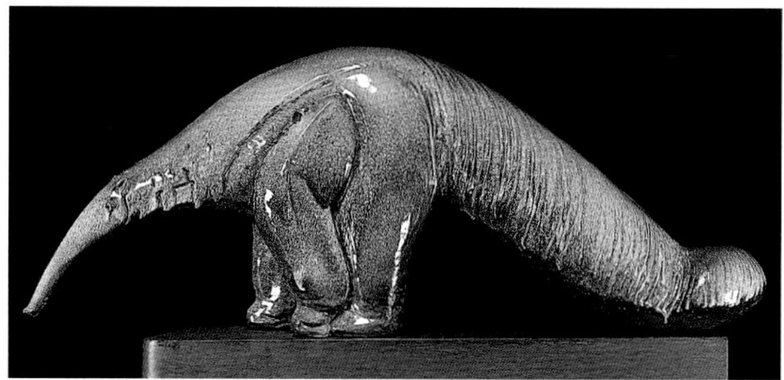

Anteater, 1950. H. 29 cm. [59]. In 1950 the Cleveland zoo acquired an anteater, which provided the inspiration for this sculpture.

Bumptious and Toto, 1951. H. 31.6 cm. [60]. Many of Viktor's animal sculptures focus on the bond between mother and child.

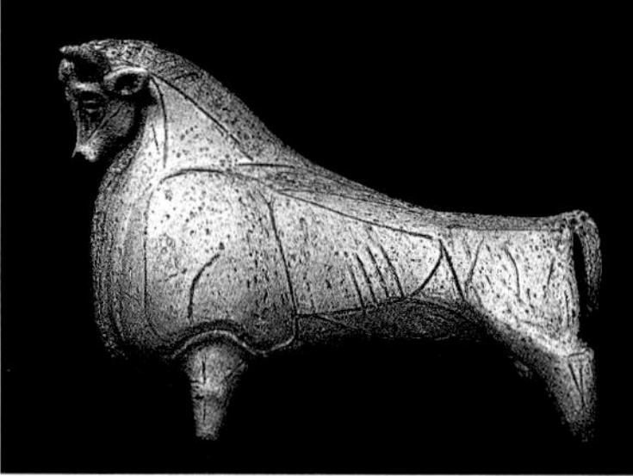

Bovine, 1955. H. 32.4 cm. [61].

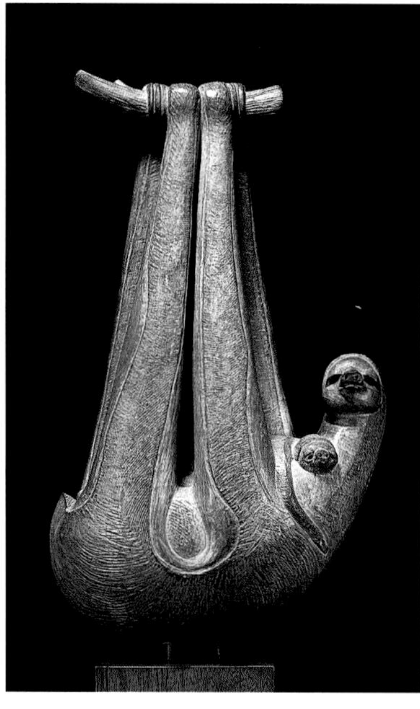

Three-Toed Sloth, 1957. H. 79.5 cm. [62]. Even though this sloth rests firmly on its base, it appears to be hanging from an invisible tree.

decorative pattern, as in his renderings of giraffes and zebras. Such use of decorative pattern brings to mind the work of Carl Walters, which Viktor could have seen throughout the 1930s at the Ceramic National in Syracuse. Originally trained as a painter, Walters began producing whimsical animals in clay, which he decorated with swirling designs reminiscent of folk art. Viktor's use of patterns has affinities with that of Walters but indicates closer study of actual natural forms. In addition, rather than glazing the whole surface, Viktor enjoyed creating an interplay between the glazes and the clay. To create his zebra stripes, for example, he did not use pigment or colored glazes, but incised through charcoal black engobes to the white clay underneath.[31]

Tiger, 1951.
H. 26.2 cm. [63].
Viktor often focused on movements that bring out the unique features of an animal. Tigers, for example, are designed to leap.

Bull #4, 1953.
H. 16 cm. [64].

Camel, 1953.
H. 18 cm. [65].

Buffalo Sketch, 1953. H. 18 cm. [66].

Bovine #9, 1953.
H. 16 cm. [67].

Hand-Thrown Head Form, 1929. H. 23.7 cm. [68]. Sometimes nicknamed "Mr. Cup Head," this piece forms a humorous head out of cup and vessel forms.

Chinese Head, 1930. H. 34.3 cm. [69]. Viktor's teacher in Vienna, Michael Powolny, often created clay heads out of cut and modified vessel forms. Viktor followed that technique here, making the features appear strange so that we remember how they were created. The square shapes on hat and base refer to cubist painting, and give the piece a modern effect.

Keramos, 1939. H. 48.9 cm. [70]. Keramos, the patron deity of sculpture, was the son of Bacchus, the god of wine, and Ariadne, who became a constellation. Thus, he is crowned with stars and has hair of purple grapes. Appropriately, his head is vase-like and he holds a jar in his hand.

Ceramic Heads

In 1937 and 1938, Viktor produced several mask-like heads in clay, which form a loosely related series. In them he started with a vase-like shape and then modified it slightly to create a human head, pushing out the wall to create a nose and pushing through it to create hollow eyes. The technique was one Powolny sometimes used, and Viktor employed it in Vienna for pieces such as his *Chinese Head* [69]. The method grew out of the notion that ceramic sculpture should explore the unique qualities of clay as a medium, and that, as the Viennese sculptor Vally Wieselthier once wrote: "The real technique for pottery is always the pot."[32] In accordance with this idea, Viktor never fully humanized his clay heads of this type. They always retain a quality that is somewhat strange and exotic, even a little frightening. Although beautiful, they exist in a realm that is only half human.

In 1937, Viktor produced his first piece of this type, a mask of *Niobe* lamenting her lost children, with a tear running down her cheek. The piece bore a slight resemblance to his wife, Nadine, and was photographed beside her in an article for the *Cleveland News*.[33] In 1938 he followed with four exotic and beautiful heads, *The Seasons* [71–74], each in different colors of clay, with writhing hair ornaments of plants belonging to the seasons appropriate to each. Then, in 1939 he produced *The Elements* [109–11] for the New York World's Fair, as well as *Keramos* [70] surrounded by his attributes. The figure of Keramos holds a simple Greek vase in his hand, and his head is garlanded with stars and deep purple grapes—references to his mother, Ariadne, who became a constellation, and his father, Bacchus, the Greek god of wine.[34]

As a variation of this theme, in 1937 Viktor also produced a piece called *Potter's Holiday,* in which he combined fragments of pots that had broken apart in the kiln into an assemblage. Today we might well consider it the most interesting piece of the whole lot, but that quality of being random and accidental was ahead of its time. When Viktor exhibited it the reaction was cool. Disappointed by its poor reception, he eventually discarded it.[35]

The Seasons: Winter, 1938. H. 44 cm. [71].

The Seasons: Spring, 1938. H. 43.1 cm. [72].

The Seasons: Summer, 1938. H. 45.3 cm. [73].

The Seasons: Fall, 1938. H. 45.3 cm. [74]. Viktor's four seasons are deliberately strange—half jars and half people.

African-American Subjects

Probably about a third of Viktor's ceramic sculpture of the 1930s is devoted to African-American themes, and one may well ask why he chose to devote so much effort to imagery of this type. Such subject matter was as sensitive in the 1930s as it is today. Indeed, for contemporary audiences, Viktor's ceramics of this type present a definite challenge and evoke mixed responses. Some see them as celebratory, others as stereotyped and demeaning. Both responses suggest the sensitive nature of any representation of black skin or African-American figures, for it brings to mind a long history of slavery, discrimination, and social injustice, as well as the vital role of African Americans in giving a distinct character to American culture, particularly in music, with such idioms as ragtime, soul, doo-wop, and the blues.

Today scholarly writing about images of black-skinned people tends to follow a series of somewhat hypocritical rules. Generally speaking, prettified images are extolled, even when they were not generously intended; less pretty ones are reviled. On the one hand, a large literature exists that praises the renderings of African Americans by the 19th-century genre painter William Sidney Mount, even though it is well documented that Mount thought them inferior and supported slavery. On the other hand, the harsher images of artists such as Thomas Hart Benton are often criticized, although it is equally clear that Benton was distressed by the unfair treatment of black-skinned people and hoped that his paintings would awaken Americans to do something about it.

Severe criticism tends to fall on those who exaggerate those traits characteristic of African people—very black skin, thick lips, and an arrangement of features that looks different from Nordic peoples—particularly if it is done in a humorous fashion, or with a strong sense of caricature. In such criticism, however, a double standard is generally applied, for when the artist is African American, or even Hispanic, this kind of caricature is viewed as positive. Thus, for example, while Benton's renderings of blacks have often been vilified as racist and demeaning, the considerably more exaggerated caricatures of the African-American painter Archibald Motley, or the Mexican cartoonist Miguel Cavarrubias, have never been attacked. The racial double standard of such evaluations is evident. Moreover, if applied across the board, this objection to strongly African characteristics becomes ridiculous, for surely an important function of art of any ethnic subject is to bring out its distinguishing qualities and discover the particular beauty of these qualities.

In Viktor's case, the first thing to be said is that he was not a racist, and, in fact, he was the principal mentor of the first black students at the Cleveland Institute of Art. Yet it would be false to pretend that his pieces do not make use of caricature. The question then becomes, what was the purpose of this caricature, and what message was it sending? To answer these questions, we must consider the social and artistic context in which Viktor worked.

During this period, the number of African Americans in Cleveland was growing dramatically as they emigrated from the South, lured by factory work and other forms of employment. Cleveland's African-American population more than doubled every decade between 1910 and 1930, reaching a total of about 72,000 by 1930. Most of the newcomers concentrated in a single district, "The Roaring Third," located between the downtown business center and the art museum.[36]

In general, this period was one of rising social tension and increasing racial discrimination. But it also gave birth to positive developments, such as the creation of the Playhouse Settlement, later renamed Karamu House, which promoted African-American participation in all aspects of city life, particularly the arts. In the 1930s, the Playhouse Settlement initiated the careers of a number of successful black artists, including Elmer Brown, Hughie Lee-Smith, Charles Sallée, and William E. Smith. In addition, during this period, Cleveland was home to a number of Caucasian artists who were profoundly interested in African and African-American themes.

The central figure of this group was Paul Travis, a farm boy from Wellsville, Ohio, who graduated from the Cleveland Institute of Art in 1917 and took up a teaching position there shortly after. In 1927, when Travis won an award for foreign travel, he made the unconventional choice of shunning his expected destination, Europe, for a year in Africa. For seven lively months, Travis wandered in the interior of the continent, through savannas and jungles, making sketches and having unusual adventures. Once, for example, he was thrown from his train berth when the locomotive hit a giraffe. On another occasion, he fell into a deep pit filled with poisoned stakes made by pygmies to trap antelope. ("I had heavy boots on, so the stakes didn't hurt me. But believe me, I was scared.")[37] With funds from

Harlem Hoofers, 1930. H. 33 cm. [75].

Harlem Melodies, 1930. H. 31.8 cm. [76].
Viktor made these ceramic sculptures while he was in Vienna. The Viennese were fascinated by jazz and African-American dancers and musicians, finding such subject matter exciting, exotic, and uniquely American.

Karamu House, Travis also acquired a notable collection of African art, much of it purchased directly from tribal chiefs, which was divided up among Karamu House, the Cleveland Museum of Art, and the Cleveland Museum of Natural History.

On his return from Africa, Travis found that "everything seemed to be clarified."[38] He staged shows of his African work in 1929 and 1931, and for the rest of his life he concentrated largely on painting African subjects.[39] He also passed on his enthusiasm to others, including the two most talented young artists in Cleveland at the time, Viktor Schreckengost and Clarence Carter.

Because Travis went to Africa and exhibited his paintings of Africa before Viktor went to Vienna, it seems likely that at least at a subliminal level his example played some role in turning Viktor toward African-American themes. Viktor's work, however, was generally somewhat different in spirit. With the exception of a few bronze busts, he never focused on Africa itself, but rather on people and music.

Viktor began making clay figures of African Americans when he was a student in Vienna, and his work of this type was greatly admired by Josef Hoffmann, who would watch with evident delight while Viktor was working on them. At the time, black-skinned people were very rare in Austria, and Viktor recalls that the doorman of the Grauben Cafe in Vienna was so unusual that a crowd would gather outside to watch him open and close the door.[40] American jazz, however, was beginning to attract attention, and the black nightclub performer Josephine Baker was the rage of Paris. Indeed, Viktor's first statuettes, *Harlem Hoofers* [75] and *Harlem Melodies* [76], focused on dancers and musicians.[41] Painted with exaggerated colors, they are very similar in feeling to the caricatures of Cavarrubias.

From the European perspective, pieces of this sort clearly seemed exotic and singularly American. Moreover, this was an area of expression that offered unexplored possibilities. The fact that African Americans were often considered inferior or low class, or that their clothing and attitudes could be seen as vulgar, was very much part of the message of these pieces, with their exaggerated features, blackness, flamboyant posturing, and garish costumes. There can be no question that these qualities were intended to be seen as somewhat humorous, but overall, they seized upon a negative stereotype and reversed it into something positive, much as 18th-century Americans took the hick stereotype of "Yankee Doodle" and made it a badge of pride.

Apparently Viktor made no more ceramic figures of African-American subjects until 1936, when he exhibited *The Baptism* (private collection) at the May Show. It portrays a black preacher in a white robe, holding a Bible in his right hand and placing his left hand on a little boy's head as he reads a blessing. At this time Viktor began to produce African-American subjects in great numbers. Essentially, his pieces of this type divide into three themes: classical mythology, music and religious celebration, and motherhood.

The Abduction, about 1940. H. 34.6 cm. [77]. This piece depicts Europa and the Bull, a theme often treated by sculptors of the period. Having heard that Europa was born in Africa, Viktor showed her as African, making her resemble the famous dance hall performer Josephine Baker, whom he had seen in Paris.

The first group of sculptures shows familiar themes from classical art and mythology, but populates them with black-skinned figures. The myth of Europa and the Bull [77], for example, was frequently treated by Paul Manship, as well as other nationally known art deco sculptors of the period. Viktor's rendering of this theme follows the usual conventions but with one twist. Somewhere he had read that Europa was originally from Africa, and he showed her as a black beauty. Indeed, in Viktor's rendering, Europa bears a striking resemblance to Josephine Baker. In another instance, Viktor was inspired by a famous antique Roman sculpture that shows the river Nile as an old man, surrounded by tributaries in the form of little cupids. Viktor had the thought that if the Nile is in Africa, then perhaps the figure should be represented as African. Consequently, he showed the river as a bearded African man, surrounded by little black children.

Humor generally points in more than one direction, and the subversive, dangerous wit of these pieces has a double aspect. In one sense, Viktor's intention was ennobling. At a time when black Americans were carefully segregated from whites, it must have been a shock to walk into a hallowed art museum and find black figures who were not only allowed to come in and join the festivities, but were looking down at everyone from their place high up on pedestals. In addition, Viktor's use of black figures served as a device for bringing life back to subjects that had been treated so often they had almost ceased to be of interest. By populating these classical scenes with black Americans, similar to the people one passed in the street, rather than idealized white gods, he made them provocative and interesting. In their rendering, these pieces often play up, even caricature, African features. Yet their fundamental message is that people, and even the gods, of all times and races are pretty much the same, and that the African Americans of today are not all that different in their emotions and desires from the revered deities of classical times.

The second group celebrates the excitement of music, or of religious faith, or of the two combined. As noted, Viktor's first African-American statuettes, made in Vienna, showed singers and vaudeville performers, but when he returned to this theme in the 1930s he generally gave his representations of dance and music an additional religious aspect, which stressed the themes of fortitude and faith. *Glory, Glory* (National Museum of American Art, Smithsonian Institution, Washington), for example, presents a group of female black gospel singers, arms raised in ecstasy, while *Shadrach, Mesach, and Abed Nego* [78] shows the three ministers of King Nebuchadnezzar, who refused to worship his golden idol and were thrown into the fiery furnace. In both instances, Viktor's designs have close parallels in the African-American popular music of the time. *Glory, Glory,* for example, is very close in feeling to the 1927 Bessie Smith recording, "Preaching the Blues," which contains the lines: "Now one old sister by the name of Sister Green, Jumps up and down the shimmy [like] you ain't never seen."[42] Similarly, *Shadrach, Mesach, and Abed Nego* brings to mind Louis Armstrong's jazz recording of the popular song, "Shadrach," of 1938, which had been adopted from a Negro spiritual of the same name.[43]

In fact, Viktor's interest in African-American religion dates back to his childhood, when he and his brothers would sneak in to listen to the black preachers and gospel singers at the outdoor tabernacle just south of Sebring. "That's where I first heard a real Negro spiritual," Viktor recalls. Appropriately, in the 1930s, when Viktor showed these sculptures, alongside work by Paul Travis, at a Baptist church in Cleveland, the opening was celebrated with a performance by a black gospel choir.[44] Interestingly, in the 1930s, this aspect of Viktor's work was recognized as one of his most important artistic contributions. His clay statue *Shadrach, Mesach, and Abed Nego,* for example, was purchased by the Metropolitan Museum of Art in New York, an honor for an artist in his 30s.[45]

Shadrach, Meshach, and Abed Nego, 1938. H. 71.7 cm overall. [78].
When they refused to worship a golden idol, these ministers of Nebuchadnezzar were thrown into the fiery furnace. Much to everyone's amazement, they emerged from the flames unharmed: their faith in God had saved them. Viktor depicted the figures as African Americans, perhaps in reference to "Shadrach," Louis Armstrong's jazz recording of 1938.

As with the classical subjects, the emotional power of these designs depends on the fact that we read them simultaneously in two ways. On the one hand, the figures are not idealized, but are ordinary, even homely figures, who suffer from poverty, discrimination, and injustice because of their black skin and African features. On the other, they are also figures who are infused with the ecstasy of music and suffused with the glory of religious faith. Standing on a museum pedestal, they are no longer social inferiors, as they might be in real life, but figures we can admire, even envy.

The final theme Viktor explored was the most provocative of all, that of the beauty and fecundity of black figures. *Mother Earth* of 1939 [79] portrays a nude black woman covered with small babies of various colors designed to represent the various nationalities of the world. As is often the case with Viktor's work, the meaning of this choice vibrates at different levels. Earth, the soil we stand on, is black or brown in color, so what could be more natural than to represent Mother Earth as a black woman? In addition, as we now know, the human race originated in Africa, so a black-skinned ancestor was the mother of us all. Perhaps the riskiest aspect of Viktor's piece, at a time when interracial liaisons were taboo and even illegal, is that it portrays a black woman as provocatively sensual and fertile. Indeed, a persistent theme of Viktor's sculpture is that of deliciously cute small children, generally with black skin, surrounding or crawling over larger figures. Since Viktor had no children of his own, this persistent theme seems to express some form of longing.

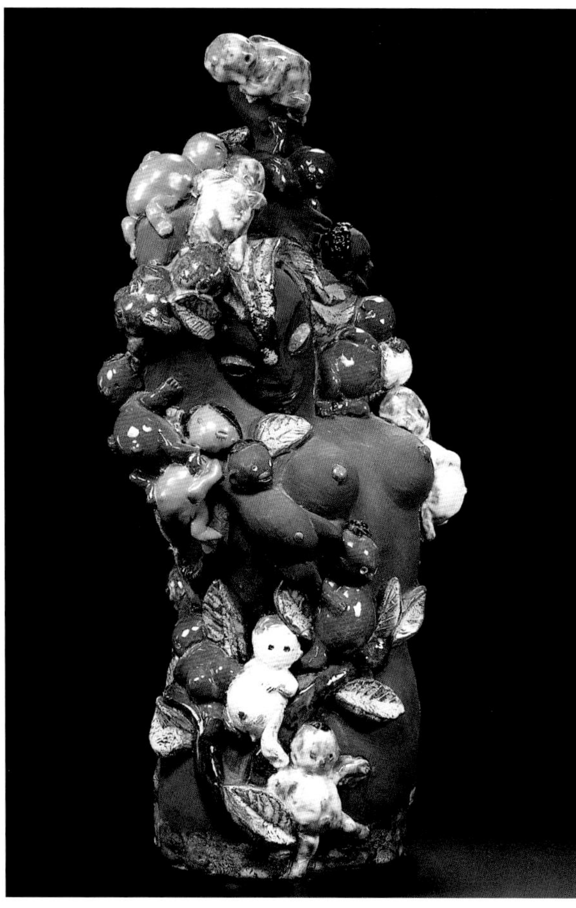

Mother Earth,
1939. H. 42.3 cm.
[79].
Because the human race originated in Africa, Viktor showed Mother Earth as an African woman, covered with babies of all races and colors.

Clearly, African-American culture was an important guiding force for Viktor that not only influenced his renderings of African-American themes, but colored all his work. His rendering of black figures seems to express a desire to absorb and capture things he admired in a culture utterly different from the one in which he had been raised. Viktor's background, even his family name of Schreckengost, has a fearsomely Nordic character, and the factory-town world where he spent his childhood was one of almost humorless discipline, religion, and constant hard work. Perhaps the world of African Americans, and the values expressed in their music, provided a liberating element, opening up a world of casual fun, exuberance, and sensuality. While the dichotomy should not be made too simple, African-American culture brought a passionate, sensuous, Dionysian element to Viktor's work, which played off against the stern, disciplined, Apollonian principles of his Nordic, working-class heritage. One of the almost constant elements in Viktor's work, whether fine art or industrial design, is its sense of fun, and its sensuous, curvaceous forms. At some level, if only a subliminal one, this quality was surely based on his fascination and love of African-American music and the culture that created it. Overall, Viktor's sculpture of black subjects shows a remarkable fearlessness in crossing the usual boundaries of culture, race, even artistic good taste, to make a fundamental connection with people and things.

Apocalypse '42

Viktor marked the end of the 1930s with two remarkable pieces of political sculpture, which vigorously protest the rise of fascism. The first, *The Dictator* of 1939 [80], shows Nero strumming a lyre while the British lion sleeps at his feet and the diminutive forms of Hitler, Mussolini, Stalin, and Hirohito climb up his throne. Each figure holds his appropriate attribute: swastika, fasces, hammer and sickle, and flag with rising sun.

When he made the piece, Viktor had recently returned from Europe, where he had witnessed the rise of fascism firsthand. The statuette represented his attempt to issue a warning of things to come. When it was exhibited the piece stirred up considerable controversy, in part because the director of the Cleveland Museum of Art, William Milliken, had just received a cultural award from Mussolini. Milliken complained that the piece would offend the Italian-American community, insisting that such a subject had nothing to do with art.[46]

The Dictator, 1939. H. 33 cm. [80]. During visits to Europe in the 1930s, Viktor was disturbed by the rise of fascism. Here contemporary dictators Hitler, Mussolini, Stalin, and Hirohito crawl up the throne of the Roman emperor Nero, while the British lion sleeps at his feet.

Filibuster, 1949. H. 49.5 cm. [81]. The piece recalls the work of radical cartoonists of the period such as William Gropper.

Even more remarkable was Viktor's subsequent political sculpture, *Apocalypse '42* [82], in which the figure of Death, dressed in a German uniform, rides a horse accompanied by smaller figures representing Mussolini, Hirohito, and Hitler. "In the Four Horsemen of the Apocalypse," Viktor wrote, "I saw a strange resemblance to the four beasts that have been let loose on the world today. Certain liberties have been taken in my interpretation, for instance I felt one horse was enough for the whole gang.... Perhaps it is humorous, but I really believe that it tells a true story."[47] Viktor applied red glaze to the globe of the earth the horse straddles, and by a lucky accident it streaked in the kiln, giving it the appearance of a flow of blood and underscoring the ominous nature of the four horsemen.

The delicate task of handling an unpleasant subject with humor has never been better finessed. Once again the piece caused offense in some quarters. Indeed, with its garish colors and vulgar imagery, the piece still looks a bit rude, but also amazingly contemporary. Viktor's approach was

Apocalypse '42, 1942. H. 40.6 cm. [82].
The figure of Death, dressed in a German uniform, rides a horse in the company of Hitler, Hirohito, and Mussolini.

roughly 20 years ahead of its time, for the style of *Apocalypse '42* could be a work of Funk art, the school of irreverent ceramic sculpture introduced in the 1960s. From our vantage point today, more than half a century later, *Apocalypse '42* stands out not only as technically remarkable, but as one of the most passionate and artistically important ceramic sculptures of the period.

Slab Forms

James Stubblebine and Martin Eidelberg, in an article on Viktor's ceramic sculpture, end their analysis of his work with *Apocalypse '42* and conclude their essay with the claim that the Cleveland School of ceramic sculpture ended abruptly with the outbreak of the Second World War.[48] Actually, while the war did mark a turning point, ceramic sculpture in Cleveland did not end then, but simply changed in character. Much of Viktor's postwar work is even finer than that of the 1930s. In general, he moved away from the humorous subject matter and garish tin glazes of his early work toward a more monumental approach, which made greater use of the natural properties of clay. As Viktor noted:

> When I began my experiments, all ceramic sculpture in this country was completely glazed. I wanted greater variety; so I poured water over the original clay piece to spot where the highlights would hit after firing and glazing. In this way, I found that underlying forms gain in importance when subjected to high glaze, since the glaze accents them. This has a distinct advantage, as it means you can obliterate incidental detail. When I felt that detail was important I tried self-glazing bodies, actually mixing the glaze right into the clay in order to produce a hard semi-gloss surface without the obliteration. In turn, this led to variations in textural qualities of clay, and meant that forms could be simplified by suggesting detail through change in texture. Now my work is based primarily on form and texture, and I use colored clays, except when I wipe the glaze into the clay, or put lamination of a different sort of clay over.[49]

Viktor's most unusual and controversial pieces of 1947 were a line of pottery vessels that, rather than being thrown on the wheel, were carved from slabs. An article in *Craft Horizons* described the technique in detail.

Sappan, 1947.
H. 57.2 cm. [83].

Shell, 1949.
H. 12.9 cm. [84].

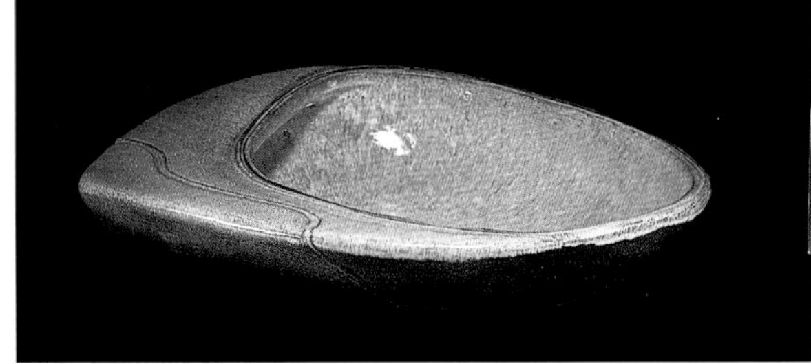

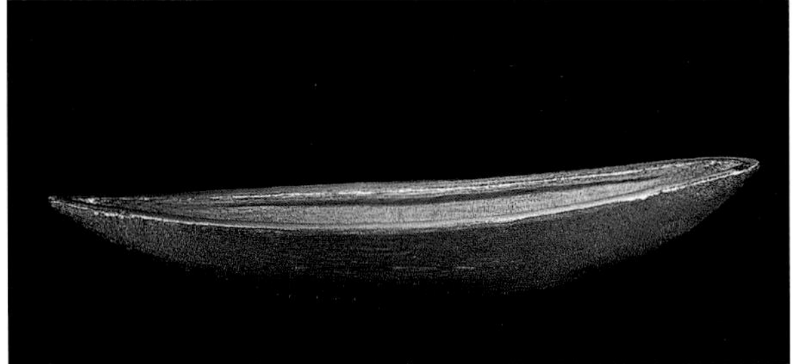

Canoa, 1951.
H. 13.5 cm. [85].
The technique of hollowing a clay slab used here is similar to the method used to create a dugout canoe.

Cellular, about
1950. H. 41.4 cm.
[86].

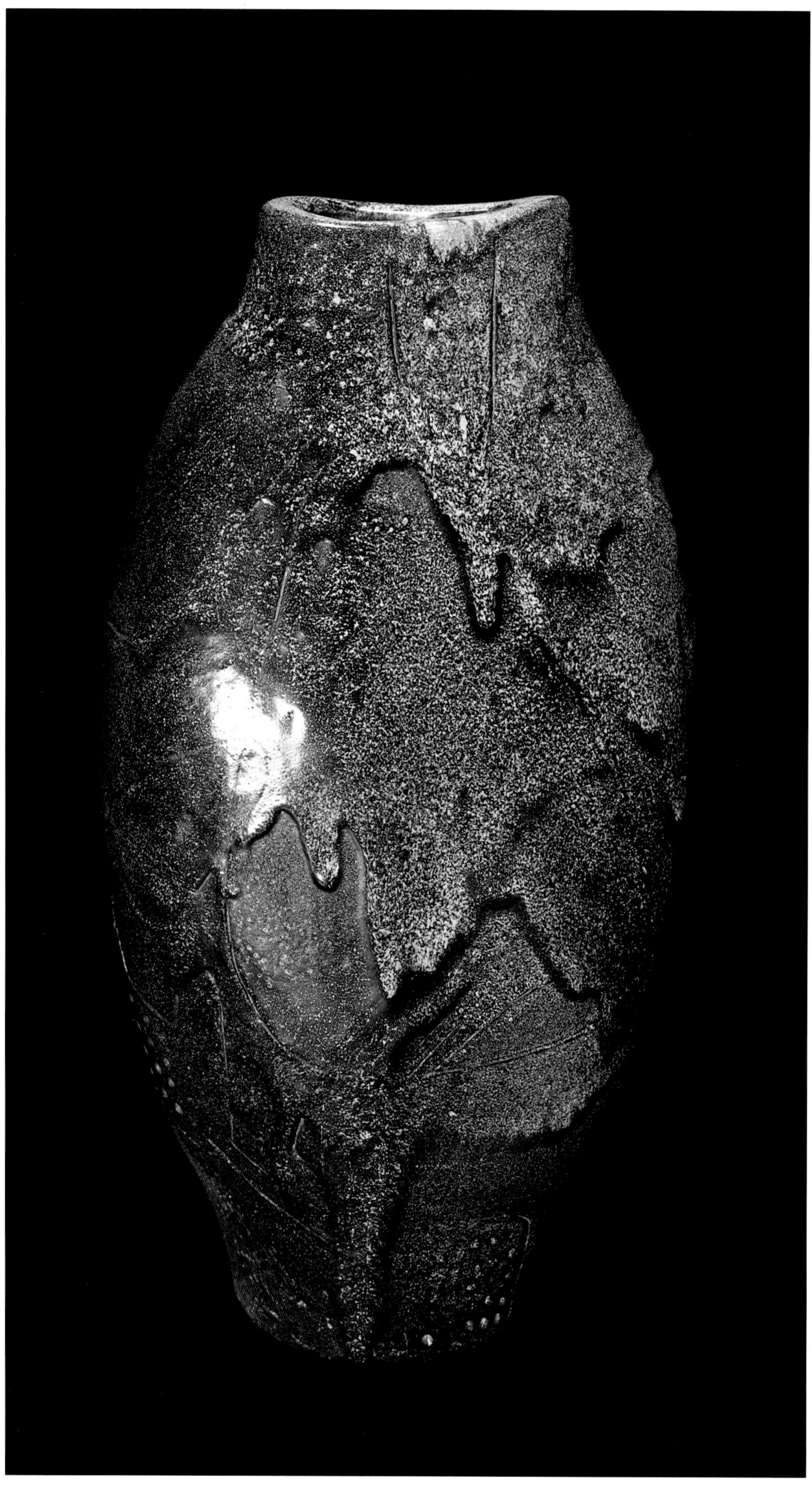

Butternut Vase,
1947. H. 45.7 cm.
[87].

The idea is a simple one. It consists of adapting to objects of use the techniques of the sculptor, formerly reserved for statues or bas-reliefs. Perhaps we should say the technique of the stone carver for Mr. Schreckengost does not add clay to his forms but cuts clay away from the solid block until he achieves his desired end. Thus pottery acquires sculptural quality. It is freed from the limitations of the rounded form imposed upon it by the traditional wheel.... With the clay block ready and of the right overall shape, the outside of the object is carved upside down so that the moisture is retained in what will ultimately be the inside of the bowl. When the outside is sufficiently dry to retain its shape it is turned right side up and the inside scooped out.... In one case, which Mr. Schreckengost calls his "Lagenaria" (gourd in Latin), a further experiment of carving first the lower half then the upper and then fusing them together was tried. This piece Mr. Schreckengost claims proves his credo that pottery need not be functional but should be sculpturally fine enough to justify its existence by beauty of form alone.

This is a somewhat challenging statement on which we'd like to hear from our readers.[50]

Beyond its virtues as a technique, Viktor's method represented a new conception of ceramics that took it out of the realm of utility or craft and treated it as a pure art form. Schreckengost himself stated: "I was stymied by mechanical methods and tried to imagine pottery not as a handicraft, but as a fine art. I wanted to get away from the normal medium that dictated utilitarian shapes, and looked for a method where form, rather than utility was of primary interest."[51] Much as Viktor's satirical sculpture anticipates the work of Robert Arneson, his use of slabs of clay, and his emphasis on art rather than utility, anticipates the other major direction of contemporary work in clay, the non-utilitarian slab forms of Peter Voulkos.

Oblongata, 1950. H. 40.6 cm. [88]. Shortly after leaving the navy, Viktor startled the ceramic world with slab forms—vessels that were not thrown on a wheel but carved from slabs of clay.

"I tried to imagine pottery not as a handicraft, but as a fine art," Viktor recalled. "I looked for a method where form, rather than utility was of primary interest."

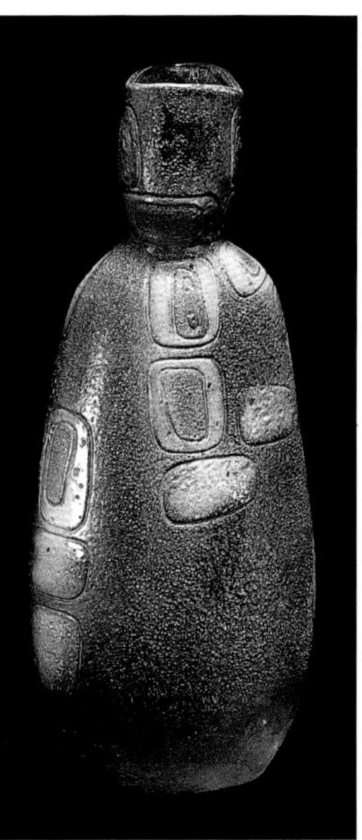

Crater, about 1950. H. 72 cm. [89].

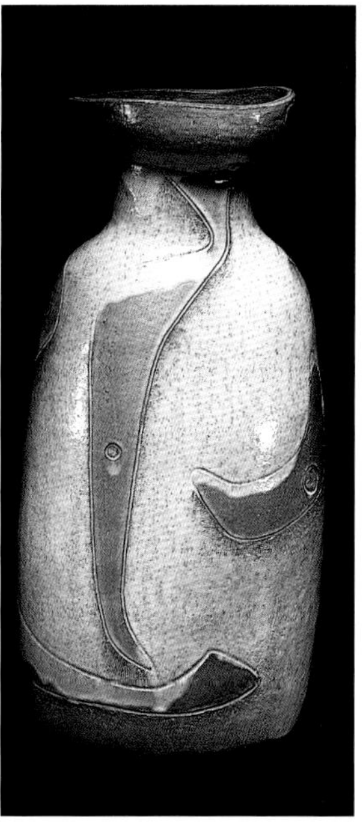

Fusion, about 1950. H. 69.5 cm. [90].

Cast and Monumental Sculpture

In addition to his work with freely formed ceramic sculpture, Viktor designed cast sculpture throughout his career. He produced three such works while working with Guy Cowan. Since Cowan's principal modeler, Waylande Gregory, resented intrusions into his domain, all three pieces approached sculpture in a somewhat unusual fashion.

The *Crusader Decanter* of 1931 [92] is a humorous piece. After Prohibition went into effect, an informal group of Cleveland artists and writers began calling themselves "The Crusaders"—their crusade being to end Prohibition. They met in one another's homes to campaign for their cause, and in 1931 they asked Viktor to design a decanter in which to hide their liquor. His design doubled as a liquor container and a desk-top sculpture. The warrior is two-faced, to express the two-faced nature of Prohibition. On one side the crusader's shield is emblazoned with three X's, symbolizing whiskey, and on the other it carries three stars, for Three-Star Hennessey Malt Liquor. The sword is a corkscrew. Because of the sensitive nature of the piece, it did not carry a Cowan mark.

Madonna of 1931 [93] took a traditional subject and translated it into simplified modern forms that resemble the sculpture of Brancusi. Viktor executed the figure at the Cleveland Institute of Art and made his own molds there, but he then cast and fired the piece at Cowan Pottery, using Cowan's special ivory glaze. Viktor exhibited the piece in New York and elsewhere, and it was reproduced in the *International Studio* but it was never produced in large numbers.[52]

Finally, Viktor created a little statuette of a colt. It was closely modeled on an earlier piece by Michael Powolny, which Viktor had seen in 1929 in the show of Viennese ceramics that came to Cleveland. Viktor's *Colt in Egyptian Blue* [94], however, lifts its head in a livelier fashion, and while Powolny's piece was glazed in dull earthen tones, Viktor employed an electric blue. In this choice of color Viktor's work thus refers back to the source that surely inspired Powolny as well, the blue horses of Franz Marc, the great German Expressionist painter of the Blue Rider group. William Milliken saw Viktor's blue colt shortly before the 1931 May Show, and liked it so well that he com-

Crusader Decanter, 1931. H. 38.1 cm. [92]. This sculpture, made at the height of Prohibition, doubles as a place to hide liquor.

Madonna, 1931. H. 24.6 cm. [93]. The radical simplification of shapes here brings to mind the work of the modern Romanian sculptor Constantin Brancusi.

Colt in Egyptian Blue, 1931. H. 20.2 cm. [94]. This figurine pays homage to the work of Viktor's Viennese teacher Michael Powolny as well as to the canvases of the German Expressionist Franz Marc, who painted animals in bold primary colors.

missioned 15 examples in Egyptian blue to give out as wedding presents. By that time, Cowan Pottery had already closed, so Viktor fired them at the Institute of Art. Doing so entailed negotiating with the formidable Mrs. Dyer, who was in charge of the ceramics studio there. Milliken agreed to pay $25 each, a generous sum for the time, but Mrs. Dyer charged Viktor $12.50 each for the use of the school's kiln, significantly cutting into his profit. The piece is not marked Cowan, but carries Viktor's die-impressed signature at the base.

Jeddu, 1931. H. 62.2 cm. [95]. The dramatic profile of this figure recalls the bust of the Egyptian queen Nefertiti in the Berlin Museum. It was inspired by photographs that Viktor's friend Paul Travis brought back with him from Africa.

Academic Sculpture

Along with these works in clay, in the 1930s Viktor also produced a group of highly realistic heads in clay, based on photographs that Paul Travis brought back from Africa. The first of these, *Jeddu* [95], was inspired by a photograph taken by George Sprecht in about 1924, *Nobasodrou, Femme Manbbettu*.[53] Interestingly, Malvina Hoffman, a gifted academic sculptor of this period who had studied with Rodin, was also inspired by this same photograph, and used it as the basis for her bronze, *Mangbettu Woman* of 1930, now in the Field Museum, Chicago.

Hoffman's piece is more realistic. Viktor, however, expressively simplified the design. The moment he saw Sprecht's photograph he clearly recognized its uncanny similarity to the famous bust of the Egyptian queen Nefertiti in Berlin. Consequently, he cut off the figure at the neck, to bring out the resemblance to the Egyptian bust, and rendered his forms with a bold simplicity reminiscent of Egyptian sculpture. Viktor was clearly proud of this piece. He exhibited it widely and for years it was the dramatic focus of his living room.[54]

Viktor's other African head was a more modest bronze, *Mangbettu Child* of 1933 [96]. It was surely based on a photograph of Paul Travis in Africa with a Mangbettu child sitting on his lap.[55] Once again, Viktor was clearly struck by the beauty of the profile as well as by the marvelous way in which the line of the head was continued by a beautifully fashioned coil of hair. While realistic, his rendering shows a wonderful simplicity of form, which endows it with a modern character. These two pieces, and still a third African head, *Congo* (location unknown), are exceptional in Viktor's oeuvre because of their essentially academic approach to sculpture. All three were intended to be translated into bronze, although for reasons of expense only one of them was actually cast.

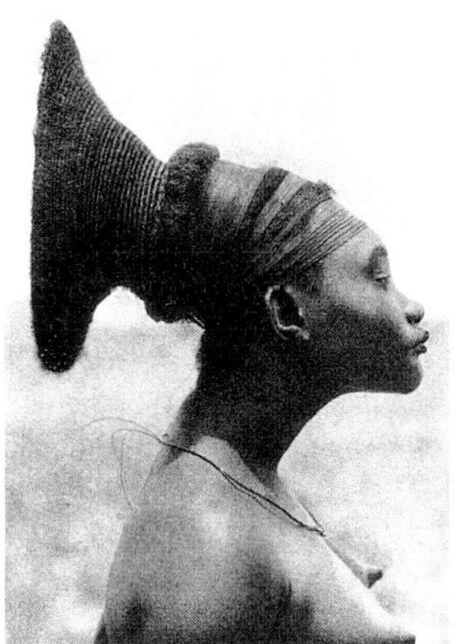

This photograph was taken by George Sprecht around 1924.

Malvina Hoffman's *Mangbettu Woman* is in the collection of the Field Museum in Chicago.

Mangbettu Child, 1933. H. 47.3 cm. [96].

Paul Travis holding a Mangbettu child on his lap during his trip to Africa in 1927. This picture by an anonymous photographer was most likely the inspiration for the portrait on the left.

Viktor also produced cast sculptures that were more consciously modern in approach, although they were intended as ceramics rather than bronze. Bracketing this group of academic heads in date are two efforts—one a single work, the other a group—that show Viktor's interest in more modern sculptural developments.[56] In both cases, he seems to adopt the mode of other artists, although with an inventiveness that makes the stylistic jump feel interesting. *Madonna* [93] represents an attempt to adopt the highly simplified forms of Constantin Brancusi to popular taste. *Circus Group* of 1935 [97–101] reflects the influence of folk art and the sculpture of Eli Nadelman.

Memorials, Trophies, and Public Sculpture

Viktor's first piece of public sculpture was a small memorial he created in 1938 in memory of F. A. Sebring. Modeled first in plaster, and then cast in bronze, it stood just 30 inches high and 16 wide and was placed at the employees entrance of the

The Circus Group #1: Henri the Great, 1935. H. 22.8 cm. [97].

The Circus Group #1: Jum and Jumbo, 1935. H. 25.8 cm. [99].

The Circus Group #1: Little Nel, 1935. H. 14.4 cm. [98].

The Circus Group #1: Madame Kitty, 1935. H. 21.8 cm. [100].

The Circus Group #1: The Great Cellinis, 1935. H. 39.5 cm. [101].

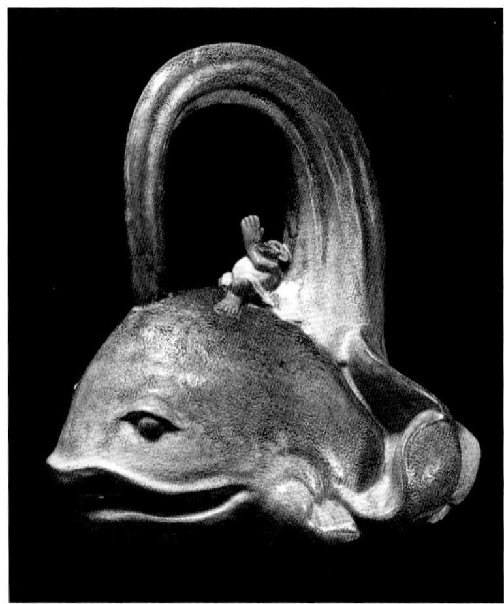

Jonah, 1937. H. 29.1 cm. [102]. Most of Viktor's early ceramic sculpture was humorous, with bright glazes like those he had seen in Vienna.

Rhythm of the Soil, 1947. H. 28 cm. [105]. This figure makes an interesting contrast with Viktor's earlier sculptures of African-American themes. In this piece, he avoided bright glazes and emphasized the natural qualities of clay. He also used a more abstract and cubist type of design.

Ichabod Crane, 1948. H. 30.6 cm. [106]. Forms become rubbery and expressive in this humorous rendering of Washington Irving's tale of a schoolmaster scared out of town by a headless horseman.

Samson and Delilah, 1940. H. 25.4 cm. [103]. Viktor's sense of humor extended even to his treatment of biblical themes.

Judas, 1949. H. 41 cm. [104]. In this piece, the almost expressionless head takes on an emotional quality because of the dripping of the glaze.

Peter the Fisherman, 1954. H. 76 cm. [107].

Limoges plant in Sebring. Viktor's simple and strikingly beautiful design featured simply Sebring's name and a nearly abstract pyramid, the shape of a potter's cone. The symbolism of the piece was explained by Jack Lindsey, sales representative of Limoges, at the dedication: "All of you know what a potter's cone means to the master potter. It is an exact record of the degree of heat to which the ware has been subject. Placed beside a piece of ware to accompany it through the kilns, the potter's cone tells the story in its minutest detail. What could more clearly represent the life of F. A. Sebring than a potter's cone, standing straight and firm after passing through all the years of stress and fire?"[57]

In 1939, Viktor took on his first major commission for figurative sculpture, when he was commissioned to create the Culver Air Trophy by K. K. Culver, the head of the Dart Aircraft Corporation in Columbus, Ohio [108]. The award was intended for a woman's air race over a 50-mile straight course, an event being added to the Miami All-American Air Maneuvers in Florida. Viktor's design, completed in February 1939, featured a graceful horizontal figure, representing the feminine spirit of flight, suspended from an angled, tapering shaft, which contributed to the sense of uplift and forward movement. Contestants needed to win the race three times in order to keep the trophy, but they did get the small model of an airplane the figure held aloft in her hands, which was intended to be changed annually.

Art critic Grace V. Kelly praised the piece as "an impressive example of what a sculptor may do with aerodynamic forms."[58] An important aspect of the effect was the use of shimmering metal surfaces. While the piece was cast in bronze, it was plated with silver, except for the airplane at the top, which was plated in gold. As Kelly noted: "Subtle highlights play over its surface and become an integral part of the design. Its effect should be wonderful to behold in the brilliant sunshine of Florida."[59]

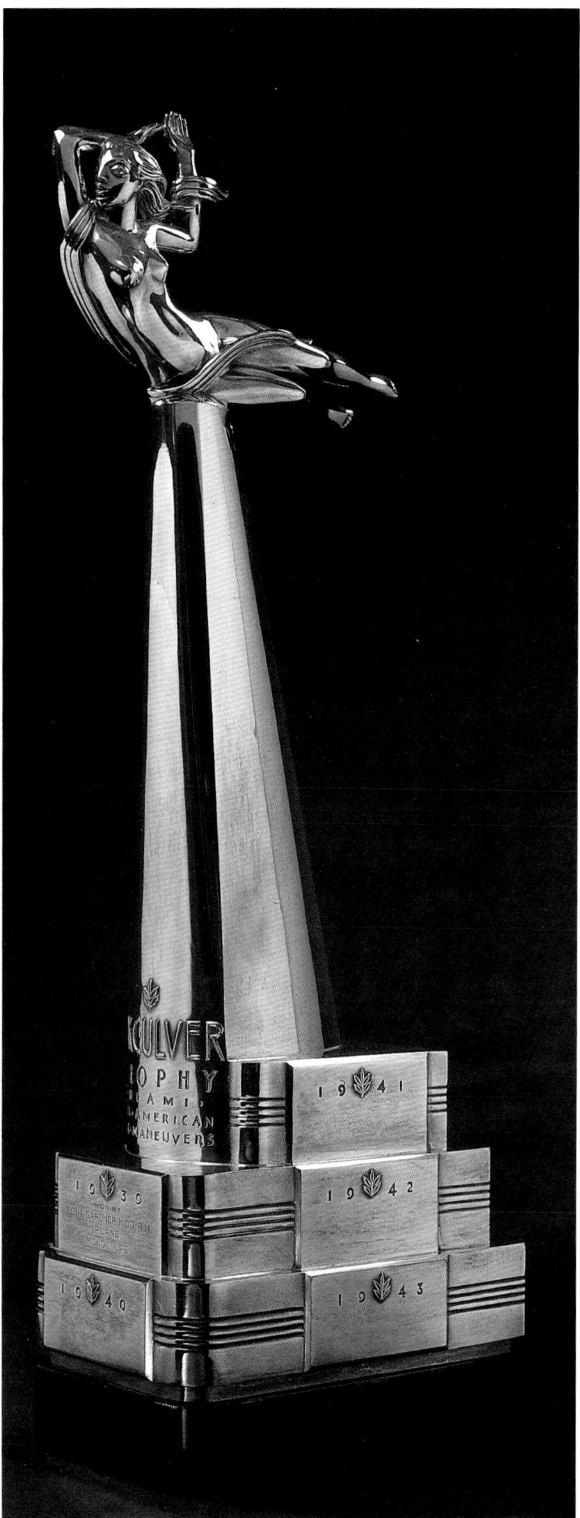

Women's Flying Trophy, 1939. H. 101.6 cm. [108]. A figure representing the feminine spirit of flight dominates this trophy, created in 1939 to honor the winner of the Miami 50-mile air race for women.

The Four Elements: Water, 1939. H. 50.5 cm. [109].

The Four Elements: Air, 1939. H. 50.5 cm. [110].

Ceramic Head for the 1939 World's Fair (The Four Elements: Fire), 1939. H. 51 cm. [111]. Viktor made four heads personifying the elements for the American Pavilion of the 1939 New York World's Fair. They were displayed on white pedestals ten feet high and beams of light streamed through their eyes.

The 1939 World's Fair

In the head *Niobe* of 1937, Viktor returned to a technique he had employed while studying in Vienna, that of modifying a vase-form to create a face. In 1938 he used the same technique for striking heads of *The Seasons* [71–74] mentioned earlier as well as the witty sculpture *Keramos* [70]. These works attracted the attention of the sculptor Waylande Gregory, who was serving as an advisor for the 1939 New York World's Fair. In October 1938, Gregory invited Viktor to make a proposal for four similar ceramic heads to be displayed in the United States Building at the fair. Viktor promptly sent off four airbrushed watercolors, showing female heads emblematic of air, earth, fire, and water that he was interested in making.[60]

Because of administrative confusion, however, Viktor's designs were not accepted until March 1939, when Walter Dorwin Teague, who had just been placed in charge of the decor, wrote to Viktor asking him to carry out the proposal as quickly as possible. By that time, less than six weeks remained to accomplish the task. To get varied color effects, Viktor used different clays for each head.[61] Rather than doing the usual bisque firing, he applied glazes to the unfired clay and then fired both clay and glaze in a single step. While unconventional, the results were extremely interesting, since the glazes flowed and soaked into the clay in an interesting way. The pieces arrived at the fair just days before the opening and were dramatically installed in the foyer to the state dining room. There they attracted the attention of the journalist Royal Cortissoz, who devoted an entire illustrated article to them in the *New York Tribune*.[62]

The O'Neill Memorial

Viktor's first work of public sculpture in the round was his O'Neill memorial in Cleveland in 1949, created to honor Hugh M. O'Neill, a Cleveland horseman and dealer in fine horses, who played a major role in establishing the Cleveland mounted police. The sculpture was placed near the Troop A stables of the mounted police at East 38th Street.

VIKTOR

The Hugh M. O'Neill Police Memorial Monument, 1949. H. 68.5 cm. [112]. Hugh O'Neill played a major role in establishing the Cleveland mounted police. This plaster version is a model for a bronze honoring O'Neill that stands near the Troop A stables.

For the project, Viktor designed a heroic horse's head in plaster [112] that was cast in bronze by the Gorham Foundry. Unfortunately, the casting was not ready in time, so the colored plaster was used for the ceremony. No one knew the difference, and the next Saturday Viktor took over the real one and set it in place. The bronze statue was cleaned a few years ago and finally got its own dedication.[63]

In 1955, Viktor designed a metal wall sculpture for the Cleveland airport: a series of geometric shapes symbolizing earth, air, water, and the signs of the zodiac.[64] In 1957 he modeled two wall reliefs for the headquarters of Marathon Oil in Findlay, Ohio: oil derricks and airplanes symbolizing the source of power and its uses.[65] Both projects were fabricated by Rose Ironworks, then run by the founder's son Melvin Rose, who had been one of Viktor's design students at the Institute of Art.

Architectural Sculpture

In the 1950s Viktor produced three major ventures in architectural sculpture thanks to his friendship with the most forward-thinking Cleveland architect of the period, J. Byers Hays. In a general way, the stylistic development of Viktor's architectural ceramics parallels that of his smaller sculptures. In both cases, he moved from bright colors produced with tin glazes to greater use of the natural clay, and in both cases the later works are more simplified in their massing and concentration of form.

Shortly before the war, Viktor and his wife began to plan a radically modern dream house on a piece of property they had purchased just outside of Cleveland.[66] For help executing the design, Viktor called on the services of Byers Hays. Hays had started his career working in a classicizing manner, but by the 1930s had become the city's major advocate of modern architecture. Before long the scheme began to take a more lively shape, with a curving front and a cantilevered back porch. In the end the house was never built, for just after the war Viktor purchased the house where he has lived ever since on Stillman Road in Cleveland Heights. But the game of designing a house led to a warm friendship with Hays, which in turn led to Viktor's zoo commissions.

In 1948, Hays was commissioned to produce a master plan for the Cleveland zoo. Shortly after it was completed, he was asked to begin filling in the blueprint by designing structures for the birds and the pachyderms. Hays's scheme for the bird house required a tower 60 feet high for ventilation. He and Viktor came up with the notion of facing it with large, brightly colored sculptures of birds that would create what Hays described as "a contemporary totem pole" and clearly proclaim the building's purpose.[67]

Working with his nephew, Don Eckelberry, the distinguished ornithologist and author of four Audubon guides, Viktor came up with a program that pictured the history of birds from their first appearance, 140 million years ago, up to the present day. He started at the bottom with the first known bird, the *Archaeopteryx,* a fierce-looking carnivorous creature, with a crocodile face, wicked serrated teeth, and sharp claws. Next came the four-foot-long *Hesperornis* of 100 million years ago, the first amphibious bird, with huge webbed feet [113]. Then came the *Diatryma* of 60 million years ago, a giant bird with hair-like feathers and a head two feet long [114]. The fourth panel showed the

Hesperornis, 1950. H. 47.2 cm. [113]. This creature, the best known bird of the Cretaceous period, was clearly a good swimmer.

Diatryma, 1950. H. 48.7 cm. [114]. Fossils of this giant bird have been found in North America and Europe. Its small wings and powerful legs suggest it ran rather than flew.

Dodo, 1950. H. 44.5 cm. [115]. Native to Mauritius, an island in the Indian Ocean, this bird had blue-gray plumage and stout yellow legs. It could not fly and was easy prey for human predators.

American Bald Eagle, 1950. H. 45.2 cm. [116]. Not really bald, this eagle has a distinctive white-feathered head.

In 1950, Viktor completed five large sculptures for the bird building of the Cleveland zoo portraying the development of birds from the first known prehistoric bird, the *Archaeopteryx,* to the bald eagle. These cast plaster plaques are Viktor's presentation models for four of the five panels. The full-size panels are five by eight feet and glazed in brilliant colors.

dodo (*Raphus cucullatus*) [115], a flightless pigeon weighing about 50 pounds that became extinct about 250 years ago. At the time, experts did not know whether it had webbed feet or not, so Viktor hid the feet. Finally, at the top soared the bald eagle (*Haliaeetus leucocephalus*) [116], which at the time was seriously endangered.

In addition, Viktor produced 24 smaller plaques, representing recently extinct American birds: the Eskimo curlew, the heath hen, the great auk, the Carolina parakeet, the passenger pigeon, and the Labrador duck. ("I remember when they used to sell roasted passenger pigeons on a stick for 15 cents along the coast," Viktor recalls).[68] Once he had sketched out his designs, his nephew Don as well as researchers at the Audubon Society and the American Museum of Natural History in New York carefully checked over the drawings feather by feather to make sure that they were thoroughly accurate.[69]

Viktor wanted tiles that would not just hang on the face of the tower but would have eight-inch extensions on the back so that they would become part of the bearing wall itself. There was not a kiln in Cleveland large enough to fire pieces of this type, but one day as he was driving through the

Holland Tunnel in New York, he noticed that it was lined with white tile that still looked perfect, with no cracks. After asking around he found that it was made by Federal Seaboard in Perth Amboy, New Jersey, so he arranged to visit the two Danish brothers who ran the place. They informed him that they could handle as much as 80 tons of terracotta in a single firing. Viktor did not want any distortion or warpage, so he asked if he could use the center of their kiln. "You can have any part you want," they replied.[70]

Each of the large plaques was five by eight feet and weighed about a ton. (The smaller plaques were about two feet square.) That was too large to fit in his usual studio, so Viktor modeled the first test piece, the *Archaeopteryx,* at the Fillous & Ruppel Co. in Cleveland.[71] The other birds he produced in a studio at Perth Amboy from one-quarter scale models. Since the birds were too large to fire as a single piece, the full-scale models were cut into sections, a mold made of each section, and terracotta pressed into each mold for the finished sculpture.[72] Since the upper panels were considerably farther away from the viewer than lower ones, Viktor increased the depth of the relief as he moved upward, to make sure that the detail of the upper panels was still visible. Thus, the *Archaeopteryx,* the bird lowest on the tower, has a relief of only 14 inches, while the eagle at the top is 28 inches deep.[73]

After the tiles were cast, they were glazed with as many as 22 different colors, using a variety of techniques. Sometimes glazes were superimposed on one another to create special effects. Some of the glazes were sprayed on; others were hand-brushed to produce shaded effects, particularly to suggest the variegation of feathers. When the glazing was complete, the finished sections were subjected to five-day heat treatments in kilns reaching 2,200° F and then allowed to cool for a week before they were removed. Since the vermilion and orange glazes could not withstand such a high temperature, those sections were glazed after the first firing, and then fired again at 1,640° F. These low-fired colors have held up well to the weather, since the surface on which they rest was smooth and fully hardened.[74]

The completed panels were then crated in straw and trucked to Cleveland, where they were mounted in the chimney of the birdhouse. On 19 October 1950, the structure was dedicated with much fanfare, including speeches by the mayor of Cleveland and Dr. Alexander Wetmore, secretary of the Smithsonian Institution. The project got some national attention as well. After Viktor won a medal for the project, his work was written up in *Newsweek.*[75]

Viktor had been nervous when he took on the commission, since he signed a contract that the terracotta would last 25 years. If it deteriorated in that time he would replace it at his own expense. Today the sandstone around the panels has flaked and decomposed, but the tiles remain in perfect shape. A nice side benefit of the project was that it brought Viktor out for frequent visits to the zoo and led to a flood of sketches and sculptures of animals. The marvelous *Anteater* Viktor modeled in 1950 [59] is surely a rendition of the anteater the zoo purchased that year.

The Early Settler at Lakewood High School

Shortly afterward, in 1954, Hays built the extension to Lakewood High School, and again he asked Viktor to produce a piece of sculpture that would give the building dramatic interest. To expand the building, they had cleared an old apple orchard that historians were almost sure had been planted by Johnny Appleseed when he came from Pennsylvania up through the Ohio Valley. It seemed natural to make Johnny Appleseed the subject of the piece, and Viktor made presentation drawings of the grizzled planter skipping through the woods planting seeds. Unfortunately, the authorities thought Johnny looked like a vagrant and were not sure that he provided a good role model for children. So Viktor made a few changes and then titled his design *The Early Settler*. What had formerly been an apple tree became the Tree of Knowledge, and in the background he placed the rising sun of the Ohio State seal. In the sky are bright red cardinals, the state bird.[76]

To make sure the design would read clearly, Viktor greatly exaggerated the size of the hands and facial features. In addition, he turned the head so that it would respond to the natural changes of the light. "The wall is curved," Viktor noted, "with the sun breaking in over the left side of it, so I modeled it so his face changes in the morning as the sun moves across it."[77]

Constructing the piece at full scale presented a technical challenge. Although the figure is kneeling, he measures 17½ feet from feet to head, while the setting on which he stands is 34 feet across. Up to his waist, Viktor modeled the figure in relief. Above his waist, Viktor made him fully three-dimensional so that he would project outward from the wall by about three feet. To accomplish this forward lean, the upper torso was mounted on an I-beam and the tiles were hung from it with bronze hooks. Since Viktor was only able to fire terracotta sections that weighed between six and eight hundred pounds apiece, it took careful calculation to design the individual pieces. In addition, the whole construction was made slightly flexible, so that as the curved wall heated up or cooled over the course of the day and night the sculpture could swell and shrink. With this project a full-size plaster model would have been too large to ship, so Viktor modeled the relief at one-tenth size, and then went to Perth Amboy with the model to make the enlargements and castings. Once again, Viktor glazed the piece with colorful glazes of blue, yellow, red, and earth tones.

Mammoths and Mastodons

Meanwhile, Hays was still busy with the zoo. After completing the aviary, he moved on in 1956 to the pachyderm building. Again he asked Viktor to provide a visual identity for the structure. Once again, Viktor chose to depict the extinct ancestors of the creatures housed inside, in this case modeling full-scale mammoths and mastodons on the outside wall. He designed this relief so that the animals rise up directly from the ground. People passing by can stand beside them to get a sense of scale. It is a natural place for children to have their photographs taken, and today, more than 40 years after the piece was installed, it remains the most photographed place in the zoo.

This project was even larger than the first, requiring 32 tons of clay. The mammoth is 25 feet wide and 13½ feet high, while the mastodon is also 25 feet wide but only 12 feet high. Both had an eight-inch relief surface extending back into the bearing wall. So that they would fit the kilns, the animals were divided into sections weighing about six hundred pounds apiece—50 for the mammoth and 37 for the mastodon. Again, each piece was cast from a mold so that it could be duplicated if it warped or buckled during the firing. In this case, rather than using glazes, Viktor used four different kinds of clay, which produced four different color tones after firing.[78]

After making a small clay model, Viktor modeled the full-scale sculpture at Federal Seaboard. To support it he constructed a framework two by twelve feet, covered it with plywood, and then put big cleats in to hold the clay. Unfortunately, the wall against which this plywood framework was leaning began to buckle from the weight, opening up a large crack of daylight between the wall and roof. Viktor and a team of helpers propped it up with telephone poles and then used steel rods with tighteners to pull the wall back into line until it was reinforced. Everything else about the project went smoothly, and it was fully installed at the zoo in time for the dedication on 13 May 1956.[79]

In 1954, Viktor's *Early Settler* won first prize for an architectural ceramic at the 18th Ceramic National in Syracuse, and shortly afterward he won the American Institute of Architects Fine Arts Medal.[80] Sadly, the pachyderm building proved Viktor's last venture in architectural sculpture. Further ventures were tentatively planned but never carried out. As Viktor recalls: "The next one was to be the cat building and then the reptile house. It would have been nice to have the whole zoo finished in the same concept. I don't know what happened, whether they ran out of money or what. A whole new management came in, and we never did any more buildings at the zoo."[81]

Radar Recognition and Topographical Maps

The most unusual application of Viktor's sculptural skills came during World War II, when he used his understanding of sculptural form to develop the navy's first program of radar recognition and to invent techniques for producing highly accurate topographical maps based on stereometric aerial photography. As Admiral de Florez told Viktor: "When I saw 'sculptor' on your specifications, I wanted you to come work with us."[82]

Radar shows up on a screen in a scatter pattern. To figure out how such images were formed, Viktor first produced models of various kinds of aircraft. He then moved little lights around these models, to see how the light would reflect off the shapes. He found that if you know the angles of the beams of light you could work back from the scatter pattern to a precise definition of the original shape. Radar works in essentially the same fashion, so after working with beams of light, Viktor was able to come up with a system of radar recognition that would predict the image radar will produce if it hit a plane of a particular type.

Viktor also carried out practical experiments to determine the range of radar. In October 1944 he went out on the North Atlantic, on board the minesweeper *USS Kestrell* to test the distance at which one could detect the periscope of a submarine.[83] He discovered that a mast 32 feet high with radar on it would read up to 150 miles. After that point the reading disappeared because of the curvature of the earth. Viktor and his team also worked on helping fliers use radar to stay on course. If there was a specific area of coastline being targeted for a bombing mission, for example, he and his team could use topographical maps to develop a precise picture of what the radar return would look like. Thus, a bombing crew could match the image coming in with the prediction. When the two precisely corresponded that meant the flight was on target and the crew could start dropping bombs.[84]

Further, Viktor developed and perfected a technique for producing highly accurate terrain models based on aerial photography. To create such models, extensions were placed on some of the navy planes with cameras mounted four feet out on the ends of the wings, so that when they photographed together they produced a stereometric pair.[85] Once the film was developed, they then projected the two images, superimposing one upon the other until they matched. After this match was made, a technician could build up the shapes of the landscape with white modeling clay, simply piling up the clay until it met the edge of the image. Compared to conventional methods, the technique was both quick and accurate because it created a perfect replica of a shape from the photographic image, without requiring exact measurements.[86]

Viktor and his assistants then went one step further. Using the clay as a mold, they vacuum-formed plastic shapes, put emulsion on them, and printed all tactically useful information back onto them—such as roads, buildings, and the location of military targets. In planning an approach they could rephotograph the model from any direction, giving fliers an exact picture of what to expect.[87] While they used the new technologies of radar and aerial photography, all these techniques were fundamentally an extension of sculpture.

In 1956 Viktor produced a monumental wall relief, *Mammoths and Mastodons*, for the pachyderm building of the Cleveland zoo.

Industrial Design

Viktor Schreckengost started his career as an industrial designer in 1930, when the profession was just starting in the United States. While there were precedents dating back to the 19th century in the work of such figures as Christopher Dresser in England and Peter Behrens in Germany, through the 1920s most products, particularly in the United States, were created not by trained designers but by artisans or engineers within an industry. As late as 1931, a survey carried out by the magazine *Product Engineering* established that only 7 percent of its readers felt that the exterior design of a product was a crucial factor in its sales. This attitude changed fundamentally, however, during the 1930s, as streamlining captured the imagination of the public and as manufacturers looked to industrial design in a desperate effort to revive flagging sales.[88]

The term "industrial designer" was apparently first used by Norman Bel Geddes in 1927, and the importance of design for mass production was dramatically illustrated that same year when Henry Ford, who had resisted the seductions of styling, finally succumbed to competition from General Motors and abruptly halted production of the Ford Model T. The cost of closing down the factory and retooling to produce a more visually appealing car, the Model A, totaled $18 million and was described by one observer as "the most expensive art lesson in history."[89] The birth of industrial design as a profession is often fixed at 1929, when Raymond Loewy redesigned the Gestetner Duplicator.[90]

Viktor was nearly 15 years younger than Raymond Loewy and Norman Bel Geddes, and nearly 25 years younger than Walter Dorwin Teague, but he entered industrial design at nearly the same time. If we choose to mark the birth of industrial design with the redesign of the Gestetner Duplicator in 1929, then Viktor started work in the field only a year later, and was beginning to make a significant mark, with products ranging from dinnerware to trucks, as early as 1933.

Unlike such figures as Loewy and Bel Geddes, Viktor was not primarily a salesman. He never went on "cold calls" to drum up new work, but waited for clients to hear about something he had done and come to him. Once clients came, however, he always was willing to try his hand at designing something new, even if he had never thought about it seriously before.[91] Because so many of his former clients were pleased with his designs, he always had more work than he could do. In general, his design activities tended to move outward in an ever-expanding web, as clients who had seen one product wondered if he would like to turn his hand to something similar. Over the course of his career, this often led him far afield from his starting point. Pedal cars, for example, would lead to golf cart lawn mowers; printing presses would lead to consoles for electronic controls; bicycle headlights would lead to flashlights, which in turn would lead to prismatic lighting fixtures, streetlights, and modular lighting systems. One of the startling things about Viktor's career is the sheer number of objects that have been produced to his designs. Unfortunately, so many records have been scattered and destroyed that an exact tabulation is not possible, but from time to time exact figures give us a glimpse into this issue. At one point, for example, Viktor came up with the notion of adding a music box to his pedal car station wagon, so that it would appeal to girls. After doing a bit of research to find out who could make such an item, he telephoned a manufacturer of music boxes. Confronted with a call out of the blue, the man at the other end of the line made it clear that he wondered whether the job would be worth his trouble. "How many music boxes do you need?" he asked. "250,000 for the first order," Viktor replied. In fact, within a year the first order had completely sold out, and Viktor had to order more.[92]

While still in art school, Viktor had an idea for a more decorative stove radiant for the Gem Clay Forming Company. The executives were skeptical, but when a salesman was finally persuaded to show prospective clients the product he came back from his first call with an order for 500,000. The company in question, Merritt and O'Keeffe, liked the design so well that they adopted Viktor's pinecone insignia as their company logo. Before he made his design, Merritt and O'Keeffe had been getting their stove radiants from several companies, but on the basis of its appeal they made Gem Clay their exclusive supplier.[93]

Many of Viktor's products were manufactured by the millions and tens of millions—just how many tens of millions is often unclear. We know that Salem China produced 15 million pieces of Viktor's Tempo dinnerware in a single year.[94] While there is no exact information about how long the pattern stayed in production, this figure was apparently typical for the average production of an Ohio pottery firm, and it suggests that his earlier designs

Viktor designed bicycles for all ages, and pedal cars that ranged from fire engines to atomic missiles. Here he sits, surrounded by examples of his inventions, in the gallery at the Institute of Art in 1959.

for American Limoges, such as Americana and Manhattan, were produced in similar quantities. Given that Viktor designed a series of such popular patterns for a 25-year period, it seems likely that at least 100 million pieces of dinnerware were produced to his designs, and it is quite possible that the actual total was three or four times that figure. In a recent interview on his work in industrial design, Viktor commented, "If we sold 600,000 of something, I felt I was on the right track."[95]

With bicycles and pedal cars the figures are equally rough and tricky to calculate because Murray Ohio's production seems to have grown significantly in the mid 1950s when the company established production facilities in Tennessee. By that time, it had the capability to produce nearly five million bicycles a year and seems to have come close to that total many times. A good guess would be that, over the course of Viktor's career, roughly 50 million of his bicycles were produced, but exact figures are not available.[96] We do know that when Viktor started with Murray Ohio, its annual dollar volume was only $2 million a year. By the time he left, some 30 years later, the dollar volume had risen to $400 million a year, and everything the company produced was made to his design.[97]

Cowan Pottery

A large proportion of Viktor's output fits into four general categories: ceramics, wheeled products, lighting devices, and printing equipment. Let us examine each of these categories in turn, starting with ceramics and his work for Cowan Pottery, established by Guy Cowan.

Born in 1884, Reginald Guy Cowan was the son of a pottery decorator who started his career in East Liverpool and rose to become the chief decorator for Onandaga Pottery in Syracuse. As a boy,

Cowan learned the fundamentals of pottery from his father, but with his mother's encouragement he completed all 12 years of elementary and high school and then enrolled in the New York School of Clay Working and Ceramics at Alfred University in 1902. There he studied under Charles Fergus Binns—"Daddy Binns"—the first significant instructor of the ceramic arts in the United States.[98]

Cowan came to Cleveland in 1908 to teach ceramics at East Technical High School, and in 1912 he established his own ceramics firm in Lakewood. His first wares were ceramic vessels with simple glazes, often based on Chinese precedents. In 1913, however, he began producing figural flower holders, to serve as centerpieces on dining tables. They proved popular, leading to further ventures into sculpture, such as bookends, lamp bases, and smoking accessories. Cowan soon found it necessary to draw on the talent of other artists both to keep up with the demand for new designs and to provide technical skills that he lacked. Over the course of a few years, a number of talented figures worked with him, if only briefly, as employees, interns, or students—including Schreckengost, Russell Barnett Aitken, Whitney Atchley, Edris Eckhardt, Thelma Frazier (later Thelma Frazier Winter), and Waylande Gregory. Schreckengost was the last designer to be hired, and he worked at the pottery only from the autumn of 1930 until December 1931. At the time Gregory and Winter were Cowan's other principal designers.

The pottery that Cowan first produced, which closely followed that of his master, Daddy Binns, began as a reaction against the "lady's china painting" of the preceding period, in which colorful hand-painted decoration was applied with no thought about the nature of the form itself. In response to work of this sort, Cowan produced simple, classic shapes, ornamented only with monochromatic glazes evenly applied in subdued colors. The most creative pieces were in the realm of little sculptures for flower holders, table ornaments, bookends, and other things of that sort.[99] These sculptures were sometimes more exciting in form, although the output of Gregory, the artist whose work dominated the firm, seldom rose above the level of a cliché. Even then, moreover, while the form might be exciting, the coloring, like that of the vases, tended to be monochromatic and bland.

Schreckengost's challenge was to find some way of enlivening Cowan's harmonious but unexciting shapes. Doing so successfully required coming up with a style of design as muscular as the shapes themselves. Viktor did it by introducing a style of decorative ornament and painting that was both powerfully geometric and boldly modern, and which possessed a cubist, machine-age character. His masterpiece of this type is his *Jazz Bowl* [128–30], with its angular black patterns against glowing Egyptian blue, but to some degree such bold modernity of approach touched all his decorative work of this period.[100]

Interestingly, in the last few months of the company's existence, and in the period just after it folded, not only Schreckengost but others associated with Cowan Pottery, such as Winter, produced their most exciting work to date. Viktor's design ability and grasp of the modernist approach was a catalyst for this creative explosion, since it encouraged others to move ahead in style and raise the quality of their work. But other factors also played a role. Around this time, two other Cleveland artists, Russell Barnett Aitken and Edward Winter, also returned from study in Vienna, bringing with them new ideas. In addition, the advent of the Depression produced a shift in attitude and moved artists away from nostalgia toward engagement with the modern age. Finally, Cowan's business problems played a positive role from the artistic standpoint, since they encouraged his employees to break out of past routines. In fact, this creative surge continued even after Cowan Pottery folded. For a decade or more after the firm's demise, former Cowan employees garnered nearly all the ceramic prizes in the May Show, and for the rest of the 1930s Cleveland was the locus of the most exciting ceramics produced anywhere in the United States.

Small Projects

With the exception of the *Jazz Bowl,* Viktor's productions for Cowan were generally modest in size, but each one contains clever touches. Even when working with pre-assigned subjects, Viktor brought an appealing freshness to his work. Significantly, his products were always somewhat constrained by the need to work with or around the other artists and craftsmen Cowan employed. For example, as has been mentioned, Waylande Gregory considered sculpture his province, so Viktor did only a little sculpture while working for Cowan, and those pieces were generally of an unorthodox sort. When

Viktor wanted a particular color effect, he had to work with the kiln supervisor, who was reluctant to try anything new. "We'll see what we can do," he would say, "but we have to keep firing at the same temperature."[101]

In the spring of 1930, Cowan began producing custom work for interior decorators, and Viktor was often given such assignments. Generally he would be given both a theme and price range, and then would sit down to make a piece that fit those specifications. In June 1930, for example, Ruth Meigs, an interior decorator with the Arden Studios in New York, wrote to Cowan proposing that he produce a table service decorated with different sports, such as golf, tennis, hunting, polo, yachting, shooting, swimming, and the like. Such subjects, she felt, would fit with the increasing popularity of "outside living," and of dining outside on terraces and loggias.[102]

Viktor responded to this suggestion by designing a series of plates with sporting scenes, which would also double as decorative plaques. His first design portrayed a fox hunt [117]. To achieve the effect of a relief carving, he first made a pencil drawing on a plaster plaque, and then painted all the areas except for the lines with black lacquer paint. Once the paint had dried, he poured clay slip over the entire surface. It stuck to the unpainted areas, the lines of his drawing, creating a raised surface in those areas. It did not stick to the painted surfaces, the background. After waiting about half an hour, he washed off the slip that had failed to adhere, creating a raised version of his drawing. From this plaster, a mold was then made from which to cast the design in clay. As the relief had a uniform height, the plates are easily stackable.

Once Cowan approved the result, Viktor made humorous sketches of other sports figures, in an exuberant stick style reminiscent of the work of the cartoonist John Held Jr. Cowan marked the figures he thought were promising with check marks, so that Viktor could compose them into scenes. Before the factory closed, Viktor produced plaques of tennis [no. 118], swimming, polo [no. 119], and golf. The full service would have included six more subjects: archery, baseball, basketball, fencing, skiing, and soccer. He had originally planned twelve, but he never did finish the last two, nor did he finish the big chop plate on which he planned to picture the umpire of a baseball game.[103]

Sports Plate: The Hunt, 1930–31. Diam. 29 cm. [117].

Sports Plate: Tennis, 1930–31. Diam. 29 cm. [118].

Sports Plate: Polo, 1930–31. Diam. 29.3 cm. [119]. These sports plates could be used either for dining or for decoration. The stick-figure style of drawing used to depict the various athletes brings to mind the work of John Held, a popular cartoonist of the period.

When he became art director at Onandaga Pottery in Syracuse, Guy Cowan made a few samples of Viktor's sports plates, such as this one with its scene of a polo match, but they were never put into full production. The Cowan Pottery plates were colored, the Onandaga versions were in monochrome.

Vase with Abstract City Scenes, 1930. H. 20.7 cm. [120]. For this vase Viktor used an experimental technique he had invented. He mixed glazes with wax to produce "underglaze crayons," which allowed him to draw directly on the clay.

Congo Vase, 1931. H. 23.2 cm. [121]. Viktor gave this vase to his friend the painter Paul Travis, who had visited Africa and was a collector of African art.

Viktor adopted a similar style of drawing, but an entirely different technique, for a commission that came in from Gump's department store in San Francisco. Gump's wanted a group of pieces for children—a cereal bowl, mug, plate, and other shapes. Viktor drew stick figures to illustrate nursery rhymes such as "Jack and Jill." This time, however, in a technique not dissimilar to his childhood football figures, he worked in crayon, mixing melted wax with underglaze colors. He admits taking the crayons home each night and guarding them carefully at the pottery so that his work of this type would not be imitated. Unfortunately, none of the pieces Viktor made for Gump's have yet been located. Two examples of this crayon technique are still extant, *Vase with Abstract City Scenes* [120], which he kept for himself, and *Congo Vase* [121], which he gave to his friend the painter Paul Travis.[104]

A third direction of experiment was that of free-flowing colors. Cowan's early experiments with glazes, often carried out with the help of Arthur Baggs, sought to create effects that were smooth, regular, and predictable. Viktor, however, sensed that irregularities could be used to create visual interest and were often even more desirable. Early in 1931, for example, just as a buyer from Gump's arrived, a batch of Cowan's red ceramics came out of the kiln streaked with unexpected brown and yellow disfigurations. Cowan viewed the batch as a loss, but Schreckengost saw the matter differently. When the buyer arrived, Viktor proudly showed him an impressively speckled example. "Do they all look like this?" the buyer asked. "No," Viktor patiently explained, "they're all different. No two pieces are alike." The buyer was duly impressed. "How much do you think Cowan is going to want for these?" he asked. In a low breath Viktor confided, "Well, I believe I can get them for you for only 50 per cent more than the usual price."[105] The Gump's buyer took them all and placed an order for more.[106]

Viktor's final experiments at Cowan used such accidental effects to create unusual colors and surfaces. In 1931, for example, using a small bisque-fired vessel as his surface, Viktor drew overlapping shapes in pencil and then colored the design with contrasting crackle glazes [122]. Each application needed to dry completely before another section was added. The result was a vividly colored map-

Flora Vase, 1931. H. 25 cm. [122]. Viktor's last pieces for Cowan Pottery, such as this vase with dripping colors, experimented with accidental effects.

like abstraction, not unlike a Fauve painting. In the sample he produced, the melon green and Egyptian blue dripped and flowed into the neighboring colors, adding to the effect. Cowan approved the results, but by that time it was too late to put the idea into production.[107]

At this time Viktor also became interested in scraping down the excess glaze from the spray booths and using it to glaze decorative tiles. This created an astonishing range of colors and textures, each one slightly different from any of the others. The few samples he made were gorgeous, but again, it was too late to implement the idea.

Two of Viktor's most modest projects for Cowan are nonetheless interesting because they anticipate some of the technical and stylistic features of the *Jazz Bowl*. The first of these is a small globular vase [123–25] that, except for the *Jazz Bowl,* is the only shape Viktor produced while working for Cowan. Viktor began with a small sphere that could be cupped in the hand and added a short cylindrical neck. Unfortunately, to Cowan, this shape seemed too stark, and he insisted on adding ungainly handles to the side. Viktor was not pleased with the result, and he completely revised the design, adding ring handles to a thickened neck, and thus creating a more unified form. Modest as it is, the final vase shows Viktor's interest in creating simple shapes of almost startling simplicity and purity. He would use this same approach when he designed the shape of the *Jazz Bowl*.[108]

The second small project, *Fish Vase* [126, 127], is a decoration of fish and seaweed that Viktor applied to Cowan's vases V-90 and V-86 using the ancient technique of sgraffito. Most commonly, the vases were covered in melon green and black engobe, although some were glazed in Egyptian blue, through which lines were scratched to reveal the white clay surface. Viktor fashioned a stencil of the motif, and in some cases other artisans executed the design. Nonetheless, no two examples of this form are precisely identical. Again, while not particularly memorable, the design shows a technique he would later exploit in the *Jazz Bowl*.[109]

Orange Globular Vase with Ring Handles, 1931. H. 15.3 cm. [123].

Egyptian Blue Globular Vase with Ring Handles, 1931. H. 15.3 cm. [124].

Yellow Globular Vase with Ring Handles, 1931. H. 15.4 cm. [125]. Aside from the *Jazz Bowl,* the one shape that Viktor designed for Cowan Pottery was this small globular vase, which was produced in a variety of colors.

Fish Vase (Egyptian blue and black), 1931. H. 14.5 cm. [126].

Fish Vase (melon green), 1931. H. 24.3 cm. [127]. These vases employ the same drypoint technique Viktor used on the *Jazz Bowl*. The design was made by hand, by scratching through a layer of colored clay to the white clay underneath, firing the piece, covering it with a glaze, and firing it again.

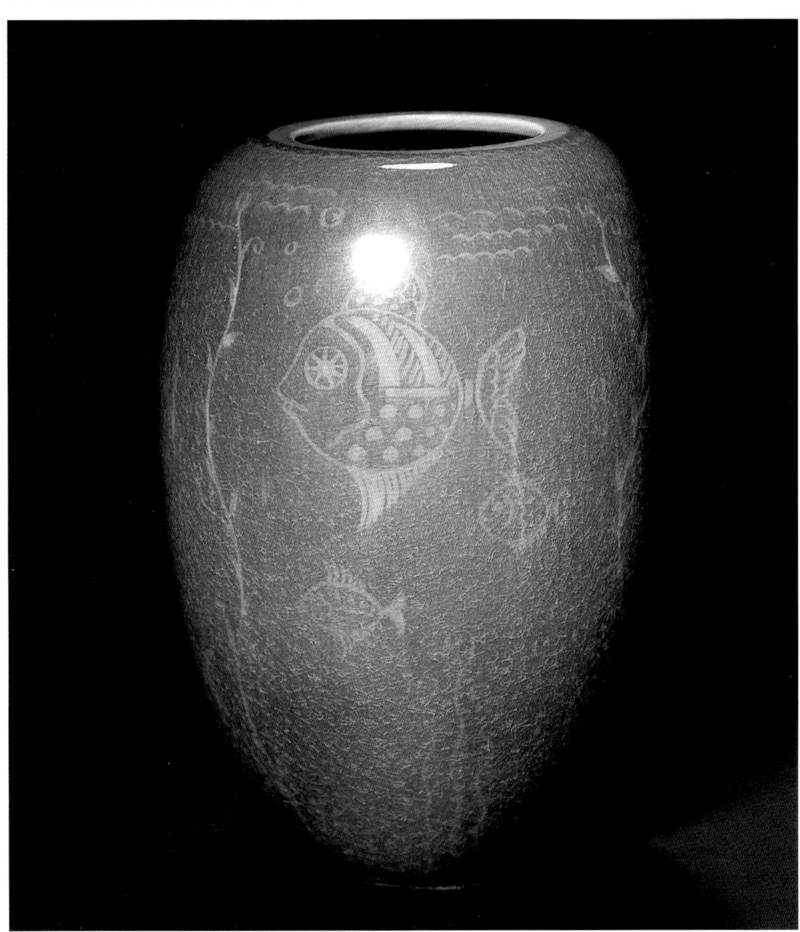

The Three Versions of the Jazz Bowl

Previous writers have not made it clear that there are three different variations of Viktor's signature piece. Each employs nearly the same decorative design, but the three are different in shape and method of production.

Viktor shaped the first *Jazz Bowl* in a pure parabolic curve—a shape that is simpler, more powerful, and more dramatic than any of Cowan Pottery's other designs. First Viktor drew the arc of this curve on a template of cardboard, having carefully calculated the capacity that he wanted. Then workers turned the shape from a large block of plaster, creating an original that served as the basis for a two-piece mold. The foot was designed, molded, and cast separately, and it was applied to the shape before the first bisque firing. In addition to satisfying Viktor's interest in pure spherical forms, the parabolic shape of the punch bowl had a practical advantage. Since it had no seams or irregularities the whole shape would fall out of the mold in one piece. Expressively, the unbroken curve suggests that the design continues upward, beyond the rim, and gives the bowl an exceptionally dynamic quality.[110]

The ornamental design was made using sgraffito—scratching through an engobe to reveal the clay beneath, creating a design in black and white. The bowl was then fired and brought back to the studio where it was sprayed with a copper-cobalt glaze. Arthur Baggs had developed this glaze to mimic the color of the mummy beads used in King Tutankhamen's tomb, so it was known as Egyptian blue.[111] The bowl was then fired again. The final result was a design in black and glowing Egyptian blue. Since the sgraffito marks vary in depth, they give a textured roughness to the surface and produce marks that sparkle with a mysterious glow. Light seems to come through the punch bowl like a stained-glass window. The vigorous roughness of the technique gives the piece a very different quality than the masterworks of French art deco, which are generally pristine and immaculate in technique.

Cowan liked the design so much that he put it into production. Accordingly Viktor made templates of the different sectors of the design. He would lay these over the bowls and scratch through the basic outlines. Then two workers in the shop would scratch out the solid areas within these

New Yorker or *The Jazz Bowl*, about 1930. H. 28.6 cm. [128].
Because each bowl was made by hand, each was drawn slightly differently. For example, the lettering on the signs varies considerably from one bowl to another. They also differ in color, ranging from greenish blue to deep indigo.

New Yorker or *The Jazz Bowl*, about 1930. H. 29.2 cm. [129].

New Yorker or *The Jazz Bowl*, about 1930. H. 29.5 cm. [130].

outlines. When they were finished, Viktor would check the work, and if he was satisfied he signed the piece. Since the stencils were small and served only as rough guides, there is remarkable variation from one *Jazz Bowl* to another. Signs that read "stop" on one read "go" on another, and the placement and detailing of elements differs considerably. Generally, Cowan did not allow his artists to sign their work, but he made an exception with the *Jazz Bowl* since it was a virtuoso piece. The signatures also vary. Some are signed on the bottom, some on the side, and some in both places. In one instance, Viktor's last name is misspelled.

Unfortunately, the purity of the shape of this first version of the punch bowl created difficulties. During bisque firing, if the bowls were placed too close to the kiln wall, the irregularity of the temperature would pull them out of round and create an irregular shape. To prevent this difficulty, Cowan proposed giving the bowl a thick lip around the rim, but Viktor protested a rim would disfigure the purity of the shape. Instead, he proposed creating a ring of clay that would rest around the lip during firing. When this was tried, it did indeed keep the bowl from warping, but Cowan thought the rings wasted valuable space in the kiln. In response, Viktor proposed using the rings as picture or mirror frames, and he glazed and gloss-fired a few examples. But Cowan did not approve this solution. Instead, a second *Jazz Bowl* shape[112] was devised, slightly smaller than the original bowl, with a flared rim so that it would hold its shape in the kiln [131]. While it carried essentially the same imagery as the first *Jazz Bowl,* this second version was slightly smaller, and the design needed to be redrawn and a fresh stencil made. Consequently, every element of the second design, although it was executed with the same sgraffito technique, is just a little different than on the original. This punch bowl did not bend out of line and fit more easily in the kiln, although it required some surface polishing.[113]

While the flared rim solved the problem of the bending, both versions were time-consuming to produce since the design was scratched through the glaze by hand. It took approximately a day to scratch the design onto one of these bowls, of either type. Consequently, Viktor designed a third and smaller version of the punch bowl, which quickly obtained the nickname *The Poor Man's Bowl,* as it was significantly cheaper to produce

Egyptian Blue Jazz Bowl with Flared Rim, 1931. H. 21.6 cm. [131]. Because Viktor's original shape for the *Jazz Bowl* had no lip, it sometimes bent out of its true shape in the kiln, if it was placed too close to the heat. Consequently, Guy Cowan designed a bowl with a flared rim. Viktor was never pleased with this shape, and only a few examples were produced.

Poor Man's Bowl, Egyptian Blue Glaze, 1931. H. 21.6 cm. [132] The original *Jazz Bowl* was expensive to produce because the decoration had to be scratched out by hand. To speed up the process, Viktor created a less expensive version. It was modeled in slight relief so that the black glaze would stick in the valleys of the design and could be scraped off the rest of the surface.

Poor Man's Bowl, Melon Green Glaze, 1931. H. 21.6 cm. [133]. Examples of these bowls have been found in several colors, including green and guava yellow.

[132, 133]. Viktor had created the initial *Jazz Bowls* by scratching through black engobe to create the design. For the *Poor Man's Bowl* he used a different approach. He worked from a plaster positive of the punch bowl's shape and carved the "jazz" design in relief, including an element that does not appear in the earlier bowls, his signature, which he ran across the label of a liquor bottle. His carving dug away the background, leaving the central motifs in relief. A plaster mold was then made from this positive, which also had a depressed background with raised foreground designs.

The cast bowls were then covered with a black engobe, and the dried engobe was scraped off the surface with a steel tool, creating a design that was black in the background areas and white in the foreground. Then came the bisque firing, followed by the application of a crackle glaze in Egyptian blue. The final result was a design with a black background and Egyptian blue foreground motifs. The bowl was much easier to produce, since the scraping process could be done in an hour or less, whereas scratching through a design in sgraffito took a full day. In addition, the shape of the *Poor Man's Bowl* was simpler, if somewhat less elegant, with nearly straight sides and a delicately articulated rim.

Some examples of the *Poor Man's Bowl* were glazed with colors other than Egyptian blue, such as yellow and melon green. According to Viktor, all the *Jazz Bowls* made under his direction were glazed in Egyptian blue. After Cowan Pottery closed, Aitken and Atchley acquired Cowan's molds and unglazed wares for the Pottery Workshop they established. Viktor has suggested that these yellow and green bowls may have been produced at that workshop. The last Cowan catalogue, however, reproduces punch bowls and other objects that were available in a variety of colors, including Egyptian green, melon green, black, and guava yellow.[114] So, it seems likely that these yellow and green punch bowls may have been produced at Cowan Pottery as well.

No one knows exactly how many *Jazz Bowls* were made. Viktor estimates that about 50 examples of the first version were produced. This recollection matches early articles on the piece, which mention that the Brownell-Lambertson Gallery was so pleased with the first specimen that they ordered 50 more.[115] The second version, with the flared

The *Jazz Bowl* tells the story of a night on the town. Starting in Times Square, at 3:30 in the morning, we pass by high-rise buildings, visit the Cotton Club and Radio City Music Hall, and relax in a cocktail lounge.

rim, seems to be more rare. Viktor estimates that only two or three examples were made. According to Viktor, the final version was made in an edition of at least 20.[116]

The Iconography of the Jazz Bowl

The design of the *Jazz Bowl* was inspired by a visit with an art school friend that Viktor made to New York one Christmas Eve, and in capsule form the bowl provides a narrative of this excursion. As we work our way around the bowl, we are told a humorous story about a night in New York. It starts with the word "dance," which floats above eight stylized faces with hats. One has a mustache, another a monocle, and another has X's for eyes—an old cartoon symbol for someone who has had too much to drink. We then pass three gas street lamps and a clock that reads "3:30." It is a safe guess that it is after midnight. Next we encounter the neon signs of Times Square. In an amusing bit of wordplay, signs reading "follies" and "cafe" stand beside street signs that read "stop" and "go." Then come a group of skyscrapers, in exaggerated cartoon perspective, with a luxury ocean liner steaming on the Hudson River behind them. We then come to the Cotton Club, and a performance by Cab Calloway that Viktor remembered, indicated by a drumhead carrying the word "jazz" surrounded by stars and bubbles. Next is a group of musical instruments, perhaps saxophones. We also visit the Ziegfield Follies in Radio City Music Hall, with its magnificent Wurlitzer organ. The story ends with cocktail glasses, complete with rising bubbles, and two liquor bottles. Inside is a sprinkling of stars and bubbles, which presumably join with the intoxicating ingredients in the bowl.

When the design was nearly complete a large circle of decoration needed to be filled in. "I had that circle there, but I didn't know exactly what to put on it, so I just put the word *Jazz*."[117] It was an afterthought, the last thing Viktor added to the design, but it ended up providing the popular name for his creation: *The Jazz Bowl*.

No other design of this period in any medium so nicely sums up the feeling of the jazz age in New York, and, in fact, while seemingly simple, the bowl has some interesting complexities. New York had been rendered in cubist fashion before, notably in a Steinway advertisement by Earl Horter (published in the March 1928 issue of *House and*

Garden) and in a 1930 textile designed by Ruth Reed titled *Manhattan*. Similar imagery also appears in the backdrop Herman Rosse designed for Gilda Gray's opening number in the 1922 Ziegfield Follies production, *It's Getting Dark on Old Broadway*.[118] It's not clear whether Viktor was familiar with any of these designs, but at least they show that art deco and urban imagery were "in the air." To the extent that a "source" for his achievement can be pinned down, it seems likely that it was Viennese. The closest match with his design is provided by the poster designs of Josef Binder, whom Viktor first met in Vienna and later entertained in Cleveland. Binder achieved his first success in Austria, and later designed covers for *Fortune Magazine*.[119] In a general way, Viktor's use of bold contrasting color, sharp angles, and modern imagery is similar, although nothing quite like it had ever appeared on ceramics before.[120]

Moreover, Viktor's design has an engaging sense of humor and irony, very different from the moralistic and humorless tone of American crafts of the previous arts and crafts movement. As Karen Lucic has perceptively noted:

> In terms of craft traditions, Schreckengost's work rebels against the norms of American art pottery of the period; its humor and satire undercut the traditional earnestness of Arts and Crafts and Art Nouveau ceramics, while its evocation of the Machine Age shuns the conventional preferences for natural motifs. Perhaps most strikingly, the buoyant iconography defies the conditions of the Depression then gripping the nation.... In thumbing its nose at laws outlawing alcohol consumption [the work] allies itself with the transgressive behavior of the social elite during America's dry years.[121]

This description is accurate, except for the snide reference to "the social elite." Let's not forget that Viktor was from a working-class background—a potter's son from the factory town of Sebring, Ohio—and that he was visiting the Cotton Club to see and hear entertainers who were Negroes—that is, representatives of the lowest caste in the America of that period, and a group that did not enjoy equal rights as American citizens. Further, the jazz that Viktor's bowl celebrates was largely an African-American creation. In fact, Viktor's *Jazz Bowl* is not celebrating the pastimes of an elite, although the elite were not excluded; instead it celebrates a distinctly American kind of blending of class lines and moral distinctions that was at once exciting and risky. Moreover, the design humorously evokes the downside of this experience as well as the positive one. The traffic signs reading "stop" and "go" can be interpreted as moral admonitions, simultaneously encouraging us to indulge and to watch out. The bottles, liquor glasses, skyscrapers, and stars, in their oddly exaggerated perspective, vividly evoke not simply the excitement of New York but the dangers of a hangover. Even the color of the bowl carries a double meaning. Though glowing and exciting, it also suggests "the blues," perhaps from the sadness of being alone in a crowd, or from being hung over after indulging too much. Part of the greatness of the *Jazz Bowl* is its realism, its lack of sentimentality, and the way it touches on the tawdriness and sadness of America as well as its excitement. In short, while seemingly simple, bold, and brash, it achieves a complexity of meaning even beyond that of most paintings while at the same time providing a wonderful visual punch.

Cocktails and Cigarettes

While the *Jazz Bowl* is the most famous of Viktor's works, it is rivaled in both beauty and the interest of its subject matter by a very similar punch bowl, *Cocktails and Cigarettes* [134]. It was this piece rather than the *Jazz Bowl* that Viktor exhibited at the May Show in 1931, where it won first prize in ceramics from a jury including the illustrious painter John Sloan. By a delicious irony, the bowl was purchased from the May Show by S. Livingston Mather, a direct descendent of Cotton Mather and other Puritan divines. With some prompting from William Milliken, then director of the Cleveland museum, Mather agreed to purchase the piece for $100, or twice the initial asking price of $50, on the condition that the design would not be duplicated.[122]

Several other pieces of the period employ similar imagery and decoration on different forms. These include a jazz design for a plate [135] and a large tray, as well as an informal piece, a pitcher with a figural design that Viktor produced as a gift for a pottery worker in Sebring when he retired. Advertisements for the Cowan studio, featuring large punch bowls, also picture at least one additional punch bowl design that has not yet been located.[123]

Cocktails and Cigarettes Punch Bowl (Party Bowl), 1931. H. 23.5 cm. [134]. Shortly after producing the *Jazz Bowl*, Viktor created a second punch bowl. It was purchased by S. Livingston Mather, a descendant of the famous 17th-century Puritan moralist, Cotton Mather.

The Rediscovery of the Jazz Bowl

The last catalogue put out by Cowan Pottery featured a number of the punch bowls Viktor had designed. In February 1933 the *London Studio* reproduced several of these bowls with a caption declaring, incorrectly, that Viktor was Viennese.[124] The *Jazz Bowl* was also mentioned in several newspaper accounts of the 1930s. After this brief burst of publicity, however, the punch bowl was essentially forgotten until the mid 1980s, when it began to be pictured in books. Diane Pilgrim and Richard Guy Wilson pictured it in *The Machine Age;* Derek Ostergard illustrated it in *Art Deco Masterpieces* (one of only two American works of art in the book); and Michael Tambini pictured it twice in *The Look of the Century*. Also around this time, Viktor began hearing of bowls that were sold at auction for large sums. Christie's in London sold one for $28,000, and since then the price has risen. The most recent one to appear at auction fetched just under $125,000. Viktor himself, however, never profited from this price increase since he gave away his own *Jazz Bowl*. In the 1940s he lent it for a party at the Rowfant Club in Cleveland, and when he asked for it back they begged to keep it just a little longer. Somehow, the bowl never made its way back home. Happy to see it in use, Viktor eventually donated it to the club.

Charger with Jazz Design, 1930. Diam. 29.3 cm. [135].

American Dinnerware

Viktor's work with dinnerware alone would be a major accomplishment.[125] He was the first designer in the country to bring a modern approach to this field, and during the Depression his designs revitalized the slumping American pottery industry. Garth Clark, a dealer and scholar of 20th-century ceramics, has stated that only four modern dinner services of any quality were made in the United States. He listed them as follows: Viktor Schreckengost, Manhattan for American Limoges, designed 1934, introduced 1935; Frederick H. Rhead, Fiesta Ware for Homer Laughlin, introduced 1936; Russell Wright, American Modern, first produced by Steubenville Pottery, designed 1937, introduced 1939; and Eva Zeisel, Museum for Castleton China Company, 1946.[126]

The list has its debatable aspects, but for a discussion of Viktor Schreckengost's career it provides a useful starting point, since it clearly places him as the first modern designer of dinnerware in this country. Indeed, Schreckengost's place can be pushed back a little earlier than 1934–35, since before Manhattan he produced Americana, another modern dinner service for American Limoges, designed in 1933 and introduced in 1934. Moreover, previous scholars have not realized that in 1932 Viktor designed the first modern American hotel and restaurant ware, Econo-Rim for Onandaga Pottery in Syracuse. While his work marked the beginning of modernism in American ceramics, Viktor's is surely the least familiar name on the list, and he is the only one of these four designers whose work in dinnerware has never been honored with a serious study. For this reason, it seems worthwhile to lay out the exact sequence of his dinnerware designs and describe each of them in some detail.

Dinnerware Design

To talk with Viktor about dinnerware is like talking with a physicist about matter, and discovering that something that we always took for granted is more complex than we ever would have guessed. We are all familiar with dinnerware and how to use it, but rarely stop to think how many factors need to be considered in its design. Does it fit comfortably in a kitchen cupboard or dishwasher? Does it stack? Is the well of the plate the right size and does the rim hold the food on the plate without spilling? Does the teapot pour without dribbling? Do the handles of the cup fit one's fingers? Are the edges of the shapes too sharp or nicely rounded? Do the edges chip? Such practical questions lead to more subtle ones of social use and style. Is this a fancy set or an everyday set? How is it made? What does it cost? How is it decorated? Does the decoration look well when the plate is turned at an odd angle? Does the decoration of the flatware look well with that of the hollowware? How does this set enhance one's home and lifestyle? Does it harmonize with and enhance the other furnishings of the home? What are this set's special selling points?[127]

Simple as such questions sound individually, it is curiously difficult to remember to take all these factors into account in one design. Fractional differences in measurement, or in the curve in the profile of a plate or cup, turn out to make a significant difference in some aspect of how a piece is fabricated or used. Moreover, for a set to be visually pleasing, all the pieces must harmonize and carry through a common element or theme of design. This requirement in itself introduces difficulties, for the qualities that make a pleasing teapot may be difficult to translate into a plate.

While we think of dinnerware as a unified set, for a ceramic designer of the 1930s it consisted of two units, fabricated in two different ways: the flatware (plates and saucers) was pressed into molds and then turned out with a lathe-like instrument called a jigger; the hollowware (vessel forms such as sugar bowl, creamer, teapot, and coffee pot) was cast in molds. To create a full line of dinnerware, including different sizes of teacups and serving dishes, required a surprising number of individual designs. Viktor's Manhattan design, for example, had about 40 different shapes.[128]

Of course, both flatware and hollowware were fabricated from clay, but the design process did not use clay at all. It began with sketches and proceeded to precisely rendered mechanical drawings. They were translated into a physical mock-up in plaster, whose shape was generally produced by being turned on a lathe. This plaster shape was then used to make the molds from which to cast the dinnerware in clay. In the process of drying, clay cast in a mold shrinks by approximately 10 percent—the exact percentage varies considerably according to the type of clay used. This shrinkage had to be precisely calculated and taken into account at the beginning.

At the time Viktor entered the dinnerware market, American manufacturers simply copied Euro-

American Limoges
Peasant Ware
Plate, 1932.
Diam. 24.6 cm.
[136].

pean models that caught their eye—generally old-fashioned ones in an essentially Victorian style. They made little effort to create a harmonious series, and in fact many of the "sets" were a pastiche of forms cobbled together from different sources. It had not occurred to them that the fussy shapes of the Victorian period might not be well suited to the hectic pace of modern life. Most of the time their idea of decoration was to add some roses.

Viktor's designs were original in three different ways: they were simpler, purer, and more "modern" in their appearance than anything produced in America before; they possessed a look that carried out a design concept in every piece and were harmonious in a table setting; and finally, the practicality and cheerful informality of design was well suited to the fast-paced lifestyle of modern America. Unlike much modern design, his creations appealed not only to the social elite, but to working, middle-class people. This was modernism of a sort that had not existed in America before, modernism for a mass market.[129]

Americana, released in 1934, was the first modern dinnerware to be mass-produced in the United States. It proved a hot seller and revolutionized the American dinnerware industry.

Syracuse China and Econo-Rim

Previous accounts of Viktor's work with dinnerware have always started with his work for American Limoges, but in fact one of his most important and original designs was created earlier, although he was never credited for it. After Cowan Pottery closed, Guy Cowan and Viktor worked together as "style and art consultants." During this period, Cowan took on commissions from Onandaga Pottery in Syracuse, and he passed many of them on to Viktor.[130]

Most of these projects were for hotel and restaurant wares, often of a specialized nature. Diners and quick eateries, for example, wanted coffee cups that cooled the beverage quickly, encouraging customers to move on and give up their seats. Nightclubs, however, wanted a cup that would keep the liquid warm for an hour or more, so that customers would linger and spend more money. Viktor obligingly designed cups to fulfill these different needs. The Statler Hotel wanted a beer mug that would not hold very much beer, since they enticed customers by offering beer for just a nickel a glass. Viktor designed a container that looks normal on the outside, but whose bottom is placed about halfway up the side of the mug, in a fashion reminiscent of a magician's false trunk.[131]

The most important of Viktor's designs of this period, Econo-Rim, represented a revolution in its field, being by far the most innovative hotelware of the period.[132] An instant best-seller, it is still being made 77 years after it was introduced. As the name suggests, the principal feature of this design was that it greatly reduced the width of the rim on plates and other flatware items, thus increasing the capacity of the well. The larger well also made it possible to serve a meal on a smaller plate, which was useful in constricted spaces, such as railroad and steamship dining rooms and hospital trays. The food covered more of the plate's surface, creating the illusion that more was being served. The design had other improvements as well. Plates, cups, and saucers could nest neatly on top of one another, making it easier to clear tables and simplifying storage. Econo-Rim also significantly lowered production costs by limiting the number of shapes. At the time, Onandaga Pottery produced more than 70 different cup designs. Yet Econo-Rim required only two coffee mugs and four teacup shapes. This reduction of shapes eliminated the need to keep changing molds and storing large numbers of molds when they were not being used.[133]

The Early Designs for American Limoges

In the reviews of the 1932 May Show, Viktor was criticized for disregarding mass production and relying on decoration alone, rather than exploring more interesting shapes. "Personally, I would like to see Schreckengost do more with shapes," wrote Milton S. Fox.[134] "He is shooting at the snob market," Robert Bordner complained, "playing to the silly cult of the unique.... It must be admitted he is pretty successful with this method. Last year, it is reported he sold $600 from the May Show."[135]

As if in answer to these criticisms, in 1932 Viktor began to focus on introducing modern design to commercial American dinnerware. In the fall of 1932, he set up a pottery studio in Sebring and began to develop ideas for a mass-produced line. Around the same time, the Limoges China Company in Sebring (later American Limoges) invited him to talk with them about creating a dinnerware design. Limoges's business had dropped off drastically both because of the Depression and because of the competition of low-cost European imports. The company desperately needed to come up with something that captured public attention to avoid closing down. For the first time they decided to hire a trained artist.

Up to that time the productions of Limoges had featured Victorian nostalgia, as in the Heirloom pattern of 1926 or Briar Rose of 1930.[136] Such designs, like those of all the other American potteries, were direct copies of European models. Viktor, on the contrary, was interested in developing a fresh, contemporary look that would still appeal to middle-class buyers. In 1932 he proposed a design, Peasant Ware [136], but the executives at American Limoges considered it too modern to put into production. Fortunately, however, they were sufficiently impressed to ask Viktor to try again, and in 1934 the company came out with Americana and Diana. The two introduced a completely new, modern look in American mass-produced ceramics, as is clear from the reactions of contemporary writers.[137] Art critic Grace V. Kelly declared that the two patterns marked the beginning of "a new era in the production of household wares in America,"[138] while another journalist warbled: "*Americana* ... is a bit hard to describe ... as it is so absolutely original."[139] "Art is about to invade our lives," another writer gushed.[140]

American Limoges Peasant Ware, 1932. [136]. The executives at American Limoges thought this design was too modern to put into production. In 1934 a few sample sets were made, and it was exhibited at the Metropolitan Museum of Art. An ingenious feature of the design is the way that the interiors of the cups and bowls are slightly ridged, to give them a handmade look.

While just slightly less effusive, the most remarkable tribute to Americana and Diana came from the most gifted professional in American ceramics of the period, Frederick Rhead, who was then chief designer for the Homer Laughlin China Company in East Liverpool, Ohio. Rhead declared that both designs achieved a perfect harmony of beautiful shape and lovely decoration. "In my humble opinion," he stated, "these two shapes constitute the most outstanding creative development by any American pottery within the last year."[141] What is most remarkable about this passage is that it came from a professional rival.

Americana and Diana proved a smashing success with the public as well. At the time they were unveiled, the *Alliance Review* reported that "the new ware, according to D. S. Albright, general manager, has brought a flood of inquiries from all parts of the country."[142] Not long afterward, the *Potter's Herald* noted that the year's business for American Limoges had "gone far beyond last year," and that "they took more orders on the opening day this year than they did in all of last year's show."[143] According to Grace Kelly, by the time of the New York show in February 1934, American Limoges had already sold its entire production and was compelled to start up another production line to keep up with the demand.[144] By July 1934, in connection with the New York ceramic show, American Limoges was advertising its "now famous *Americana* and *Diana* shapes" with their "startling new decorative treatments."[145]

Americana and Diana quickly spawned dozens of imitations, but in the meantime, Viktor did not stand still. In 1934 he produced an even more modern and striking design for American Limoges, Manhattan [137, 138], which went into production early in 1935. The service introduced a distinctly American look, which contrasted with the more old-fashioned European imports. Critics agreed that Manhattan was "one of the smartest and most outstanding dinnerware shapes of the year."[146] *Design Magazine* gave it a double-page spread, while *Creative Art* noted in the spring of 1935 that "for grace and simplicity the smooth ovoid shapes which Viktor Schreckengost has designed for Limoges deserve a place up front."[147] In recent years, ceramic historians have singled it out as one of the most distinguished modern dinnerware designs of the 20th century.[148]

In early spring of 1935 Grace Kelly noted: "When Schreckengost designed *Americana* and *Diana* last year for American Limoges, the retaining of an artist ... to do such work was more or less of an experiment, but the success of the venture was so overwhelming that D. S. Albright, general manager, made him permanent chief designer for the plant."[149] Other companies followed suit, and within a few years it became standard practice for dinnerware manufacturers to have a professionally trained designer on staff.

Early Dinnerware Designs

Most accounts suggest that Viktor's 1935 Manhattan pattern was his first modern dinnerware design, but in fact, it was his fourth, since it was preceded by Peasant Ware, Americana, and Diana. It is understandable that scholars have confused these patterns because three—Peasant Ware, Americana, and Manhattan—were essentially variations on the same concept. All three work with globular shapes, flattened a little at the top to give them a sense of stability. The three are just slightly different in their profiles, and in addition, contain interesting differences in their details.

Peasant Ware, which was made in a few samples but never put into manufacture, contains some refinements that the management at Limoges considered either not necessary or too expensive to produce. The most notable of them is that the interior of the plates and bowls contains irregular grooves, which give the pieces a handmade appearance. In addition, the shape is extremely pure, since the curved walls of the hollowware rise directly from the base of the form, without the distraction of a pedestal to sit upon. Finally, the handles of the cups, teapot, creamer, and other hollowware forms are nearly perfect circles that connect, without a transitional element, directly into the side of the vessel. The design was never put into full production, although some samples were made, and it was exhibited at the Metropolitan Museum of Art, in gunmetal and oyster white, in a dining room designed by Donald Deskey.

Americana, the first of Viktor's designs to go into production, stays close to this template, with several significant changes. The grooves on the interior of the plates and hollowware were eliminated. The pieces sit on a hexagonal platform and several, such as the sugar bowl and teapot, have hexagonal handles. (The hexagonal shape provided interesting decorative opportunities, since the sides of the hexagon could be painted in an alternating pattern.) The cups are no longer perfect

American Limoges Manhattan Shape Meerschaum Pattern (working model), 1935. [137].
Garth Clark, historian of American ceramics, has listed Viktor's Manhattan as one of the four most distinguished modern American dinnerware designs of the 20th century. It is also the earliest of the four. When Viktor began designing for American Limoges, output had dropped to one-third production. Within a year, it was back to full production and American Limoges had started renting kilns from another company to keep up with demand.

circles, but have a flat "push-in" element at the base of each handle. This feature allowed the cups to be jiggered rather than cast, with the handle then attached to the vessel form as a separate piece. An attachment at the base of the handle made it easy to press the handle into the side of the vessel with one's thumb to create a firm join.

Manhattan, generally regarded as a slight improvement on Americana, goes back to some of the ideas explored in Peasant Ware. Once again, the grooves on the inside of the forms were eliminated. The flatware is almost the same as Americana, but the rim is a little narrower—a move toward eliminating the rim altogether. The hexagonal base was replaced with a more harmonious and less distracting circular one. The handles of the cups and other forms were simplified in shape. Some of the forms, such as the sugar bowls, have handles that are turned sideways, which creates an interesting variation of design. In the serving plates, Viktor introduced rectangular lugged handles that give a nice dramatic emphasis to the shape and distinguish them from the dinner plates. This became a device he used very effectively in later patterns as well, notably in Triumph of 1937.

American Limoges Manhattan Shape Plates, 1935. Diam. approx. 24 cm. [138]. Viktor's bright, bold, cheerful decorative schemes were strikingly different from the Victorian designs of the past. The Flower Shop pattern was so popular that within a year 38 imitations had appeared, from places as distant as Czechoslovakia and Japan.

Red Sails H

Metropolis

Garden of Eden Blue

Flowers

Diana was not quite so austerely modern as Americana, but represented a sort of art deco classicism. Vertical rather than globular in feeling, it had panels fluted in a fashion similar to a Doric column, modulating the sides of the hollowware shapes. (These flutes created a hexagon, which is no doubt why Viktor used a hexagonal base for Americana.) The handles continued the theme of vertical uplift, and rather than ending in a stump, they ended in spiral knobs similar in feeling to the volutes of a Corinthian capital. Although clean and modern in feeling, the design contained a hint of classical architecture and thus was appropriately named for the chaste Roman goddess of the hunt, Diana. The most successful decoration for the shape was a pattern of platinum stars with black trim, which retained the simplicity and purity of the effect, but gave it added sparkle.

At the time he released Manhattan, Viktor also began putting considerable effort into devising varied decorative schemes for it and other wares. During this period, many modernist designers opposed all forms of decoration, and for years the Museum of Modern Art in New York showed only dinnerware in pure white. In the commercial market, however, developing different decorative schemes was not simply a concession to popular taste but a commercial necessity. Each of the major department stores wanted its own dinnerware pattern—one for Marshall Field's, one for Carson Pirie Scott, and so forth. This practice forestalled price wars, since no one can undercut your price if you're the only one who carries an item. It was too expensive to customize the shapes by making special molds for every store. Thus, it was essential to develop a large repertoire of interesting and varied decorative schemes.[150] By February 1935, for example, when Viktor first displayed his Manhattan shape at the Ruth Coulter Gallery in Cleveland, he had already devised about 60 decorative treatments, and he developed many more over the remainder of the 1930s. For Cleveland alone, he designed patterns for four major department stores: Halle's, Higbee's, the May Company, and Sterling Davis. Perhaps the two most striking such designs were Flower Shop and Animal Kingdom, both of which were created with decals [141].

Despite the success of Viktor's modern shapes, the executives at American Limoges kept pushing for a traditional look, particularly in the decorative treatments. Since women purchased most dinnerware, these experts insisted that decoration should include flowers. Many designers would no doubt have thrown up their hands in despair, but for Viktor the challenge of working in a narrow range served as a creative stimulant, like writing poetry within the confines of a sonnet. What the people at Limoges had in mind were flower patterns of a Victorian sort, but Viktor recognized that flowers can be produced in more than one way.[151]

The result was one of his most delightful designs, Flower Shop [138], which features bold stencils of flowers and flower pots, set on ledges that are indicated with a single zigzag line. The background was a lush cream white, with a bright rim of solid red acting as a frame. While it takes a moment to recognize the fact, the design closely follows the principles of the Wiener Werkstatte, which also produced many designs of colorful geometric shapes resting on a clean white surface.

At a time of national worry and depression, the informality and bright colors of the design struck a cheerful note. The design proved wildly popular: Higbee's sold 28 boxcars filled with it. At the time Viktor began designing, American Limoges was running only one-third of its kilns, but on the strength of Flower Shop it went back into full production. Indeed, within four months they began to rent kilns from Sebring Pottery to keep up with the demand.[152] So much of Flower Shop was produced that too much selenium red collected in the kilns and the plates started to develop dark spots. Consequently, the kilns had to be remodeled, with additional vents. Within a year, 38 imitations of Flower Shop were being produced, in places as distant as Czechoslovakia and Japan.[153]

Another popular pattern was Animal Kingdom [139], which Viktor created early in 1936 to give a fresh look to the Manhattan shape and which he patented later in the year.[154] The design featured animals in bright red—including a mule, an elephant, a goat, a cow, a rooster, a pig, and a squirrel—each accompanied by a star. As intended, it proved a crowd pleaser, and at the time of the Pittsburgh Glass and Pottery exhibition in February 1936, Gimbels created a window featuring the pattern, which was constantly surrounded by interested spectators.[155]

In this period, however, decals were printed in Germany, and obtaining them took time and entailed extra expense. Consequently, Viktor often devised alternative methods of decoration that were quicker and cheaper. Several patterns used simple bands of color, creating effects curiously

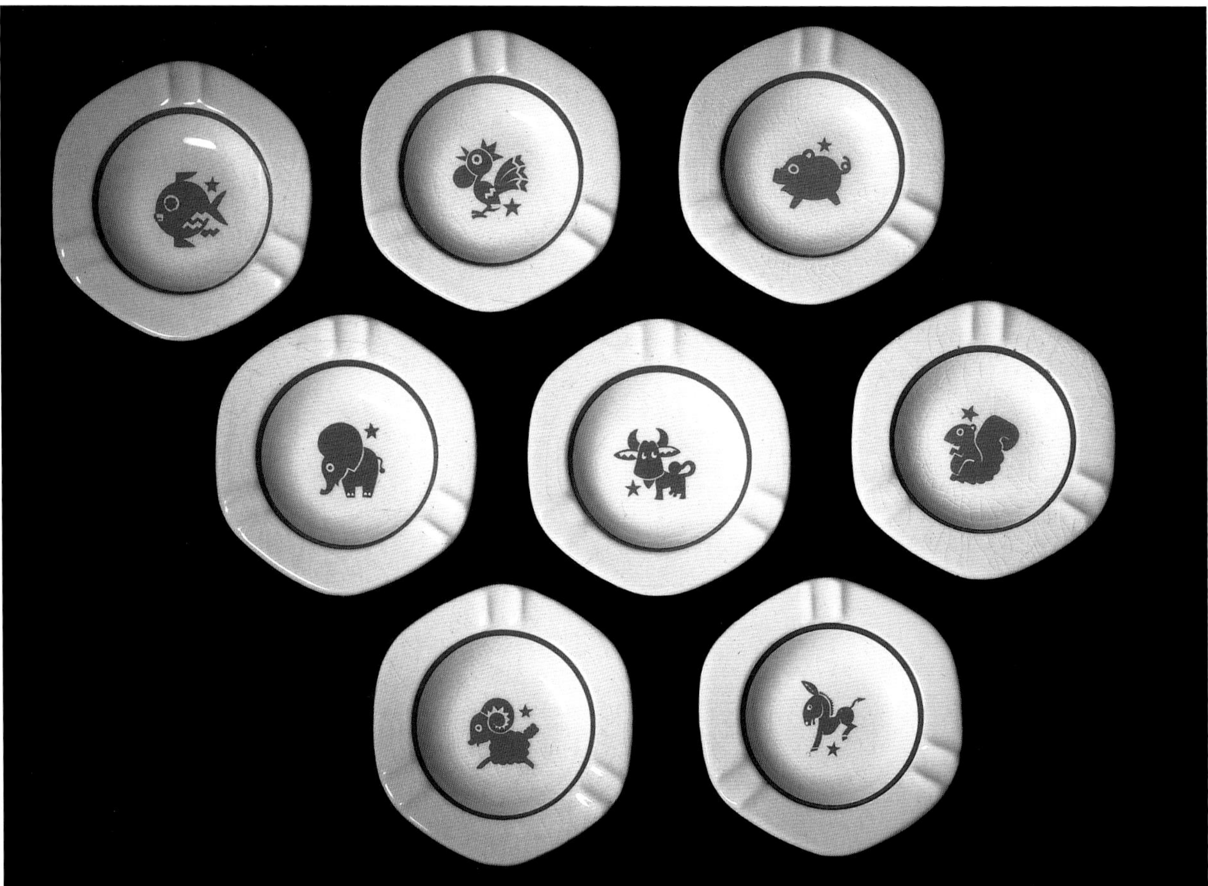

American Limoges Manhattan Shape Animal Kingdom Pattern Ashtrays, 1935. Diam. 11.8 cm. [139].

Animal Kingdom, along with Flower Shop, was one of Viktor's most popular early patterns.

similar to the target paintings created in the 1960s and 1970s by the color-field painter Kenneth Noland. The trick was to get effects that were rich and intense but also subtle. In addition, Viktor devised patterns such as Evening Star and Joan of Arc, which were produced by rubber stamps that printed designs in gold and platinum. Perhaps most stunning of all were treatments employing intense colored glazes, such as Meerschaum or Mazzarine blue (the latter used with lemon coin gold to intensify the effect).[156]

American Limoges Snowflake Shape Blue Plate, 1935. Diam. 28 cm. [140].
This party plate updated Victorian designs.

Snowflake and Embassy

By August 1935 Viktor had released two new shapes, both more historical and less modern in approach. Snowflake [140], very Victorian in feeling, contained a band of snowflakes in relief running around the rims of the plates and saucers, and sprinkled over the sides of the hollowware forms. Plates and saucers had decorative indentations, and the handles of the hollowware had bends and curlicues. Embassy, perhaps his least successful pattern of this period, was not an original design, but rather an attempt to take the shape of a platter already produced by Limoges and translate its indented outline into vertical hollow-

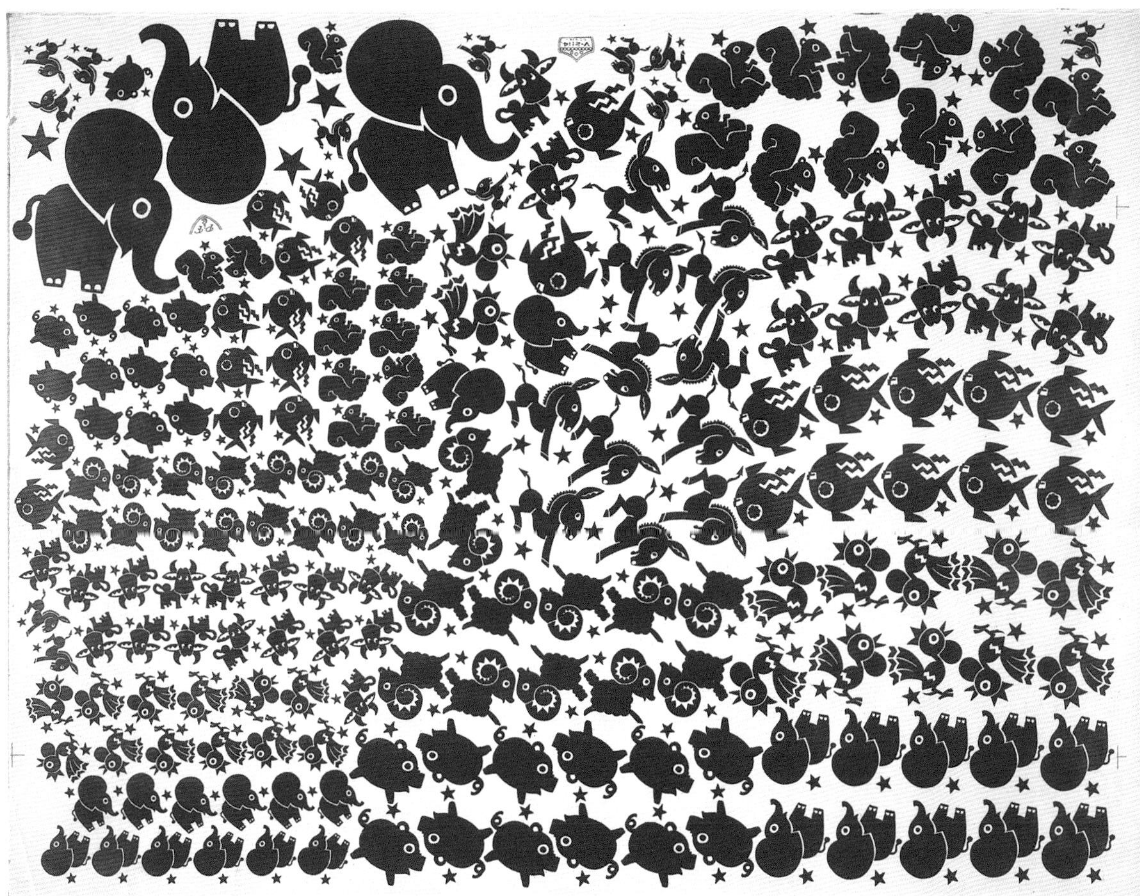

Animal Kingdom Uncut Decal Sheet, 1935. H. 57.5 cm. [141].

ware forms. The resulting pattern is a curious compromise between straight and curved forms, with almost flat side panels separated by indentations and fluting. While less than entirely successful, the game of trying to harmonize round and square led naturally into Viktor's Triumph shape, which along with Manhattan was probably his most successful design of the 1930s.[157]

The Embassy pattern of 1935 was built around existing shapes.

Triumph and Victory

In September 1937 Viktor produced Triumph [142], one of his finest designs, which used a wide band of close-set ridges for the rim of the plates and the base of the spherical hollowware pieces. Triumph, largely inspired by the desire to use ridges in order to reduce the need for color decoration, produced a decorated piece with less expense. For the sake of color, a few decals or color touches were still applied, but the horizontal ridges made it easier for the decorator because they provided clear visual definition of the shapes. Essentially, the hollowware was made by combining two forms: a lower one with straight sides and ridged indentations, which served essentially as a base; and an upper one that curved out just slightly to create globular shapes reminiscent of the Manhat-

Manhattan shape, Port | Blue | Zenith H | Eclipse

American Limoges Plates, 1935 and 1937. Diam. approx. 24 cm. [138, 142]. Some of Viktor's most striking designs featured simple bands of colors.

Triumph shape, Twinkle Twinkle T | Tone T Pink-Royalty Blue | Tone Yellow

tan pattern. When colored bands were added to the shape, they were painted in the ridged indentations that guided the brush. They were also designed to run underneath the handle, rather than into it. The upper globular portion contained areas suitable for applying decals, such as the Flower Shop design.[158]

The immense appeal of the design comes from its dynamic combination of curved and straight lines, a theme that continued in the handles of the cups, teapot, and coffee pot. The plates continue the idea of banding with ridged indentations that run around the perimeter. A final clever touch is the highly original handle on the lid of the sugar bowl, a rectangular form that sits neatly upon it like a chimney on a curving roof. Perhaps more sophisticated than Manhattan, Triumph combines purity of form with a dynamic play of straight and curved elements that brings to mind the work of architects such as Frank Lloyd Wright.

Shortly after creating Triumph, Viktor began designing for Salem China as well as American Limoges. Both companies belonged to Frank Albert Sebring, and he was eager to have designs that were distinct from each other, but extremely similar. Viktor's first pattern for Salem, Victory [144], was very similar to Triumph, but used vertical rather than horizontal ridges. It was much less successful visually, and the design, while competent, has none of the visual magic of Triumph.

Jiffy Ware

In 1942, American Limoges introduced Viktor's Jiffy Ware [143], an oven-proof commercial line designed to take up a minimum amount of space in a refrigerator. To accomplish this, the pitchers and containers were made with straight sides so that they could be pushed right up against one another, and the containers were designed to be nested and had lids that were recessed to facilitate stacking. The lids could also be taken off and used independently, as hot plates or ashtrays, for example.[159]

American Limoges Jiffy Ware Space-Saving Design, 1942. [143]. Designed with flat sides, Jiffy Ware took up less space in a refrigerator than other wares of the time. The lids were recessed to facilitate stacking. They could also be used independently, as hot plates or ashtrays, for example.

Candlelight and Symphony

Viktor's early patterns were strikingly modern in effect, and articles and advertisements generally pictured them either in white or with simple, geometric decorative treatments. In the late 1930s, however, emphasis in the dinnerware industry as a whole gradually became more conservative and more pictorial, and, reluctantly, Viktor was forced to backtrack a little from the modernism of his earlier work.

In January 1940, for example, Viktor produced Candlelight for American Limoges, a formal dinnerware pattern intended to compete with the imports produced in Czechoslovakia and Japan. It was self-consciously old-fashioned in look, although in subtle ways it had modern features. The hollowware forms all had an hourglass silhouette, reminiscent of a Victorian lady with a bustle, which is particularly striking on the teapot. Nonetheless, some of the designs were ingeniously modified to suit modern needs. Oddly, the most original shape in the lineup was the one that initially looks most ordinary, the plate, which has an edge that curves up. This creates the illusion that the walls of the form are thin and delicate, although in fact they are not. Indeed, this curious effect was noted in an article of the time, which observed that the plate shape "is very low, with practically no well, and appears as thin as imported china."[160] Overall, Candlelight created the illusion of expensive vessels made of pure porcelain but used cheaper ingredients and was considerably less expensive.

Early in 1942, Viktor introduced a similar shape for Salem China, Symphony. It modernized Candlelight, dispensing with the hourglass silhouette and returning to less fussy globular forms, adding lugged handles to the serving dishes, and giving even greater upward flair to the rims of the bowls and plates. Viktor has described the design as a "lightening" of Manhattan, with a more traditional, less streamlined look.[161] This time, however, all the decorative schemes were essentially old-fashioned: Victorian Rose, Lansdown, and Sheffield. Victorian Rose proved most popular.

The change to more pictorial decoration came about in part because technological advances made it possible to create images with shading and more delicate colors. It became possible, for example, to either gray down colors to make them more subtle or lighten them to pastel tones. Colors

American Limoges and Salem China Coffee Pots and Lots, 1937–38. H. approx. 22 cm. [144].
Lining up a group of Viktor's early coffee pots reveals the originality and variety of his shapes.

From left to right: American Limoges Triumph with Bermuda pattern; Triumph with Flower Shop; Ranch with charcoal matte glaze; Ranch with constellation glaze; Salem China Victory with Godey's Print decoration.

could also be shifted away from the primaries to more exotic hues such as blue-green, lemon-yellow, and salmon. Perhaps the happiest result of this trend was that Vernon Kilns in California persuaded the painter Rockwell Kent to recycle some drawings of his Eskimo mistress, Salamina, into a striking art deco design for a plate. But generally speaking, these designs were nostalgic and clichéd, featuring Victorian floral motifs or colonial buildings that jarred with modern sensibility.

Clever, Merchandising Minds

Around this time Viktor began to attend women's fashion shows to get a sense of what the popular color harmonies would be for the next year. He also began to meet with designers in other fields to develop schemes that would harmonize with other table products, such as linens and glassware. Unfortunately, the move toward fully coordinated color schemes ended up significantly compromising the modernity of Viktor's designs. In 1938 the Carson Pirie Scott department store created a complete line of household products that were both affordable and entirely compatible in their colors and decorative schemes. The concept was to allow a couple of modest income to achieve the kind of harmony in their home decor that had previously only been available to the very rich, who could afford an interior decorator.

A few years later, under the name Regency House, this concept was franchised to 50 different stores from coast to coast.[162] To achieve harmony of style, all the products followed standard color schemes and were all designed in the Regency style, based on "authentic sources of the Regency era."[163] For manufacturers, of course, it offered an opportunity to sell their wares through 50 major department stores at a single stroke.

Given the assignment, Viktor performed the task with admirable good cheer, rather as if he were asked to produce a set for a period play. He created a watercolor of flowers titled *Regency Bouquet* that was unveiled as a decorative plate by American Limoges in September 1940.[164] This bouquet marked the beginning of what might be termed the "floral phase" of Viktor's dinnerware design, when seemingly every pattern that was not historical in reference contained flowers in one guise or another. In 1942, for example, he created National Bouquet, a design based on a watercolor he had made combining all the state flowers in a single bouquet. It was followed by designs of each of the state flowers, with one flower on each plate. Other patterns of the period included Abundance and Laurel Wreath, while Old Virginia, released around July 1942, featured six Schreckengost sketches of buildings in Williamsburg, Virginia, reproduced in soft brown or deep rose. It was possible to reproduce these watercolors more illusionistically than ever before thanks to a photolithographic decal process developed by DuPont.

Guns and Roses

Discussing the need for modern design, which had sounded persuasive just a few years before, was wasted breath. The curtailment of European imports produced an incredible boost for U.S. manufacturers. American Limoges, for example, totaled 75 percent ahead in orders in 1942 as compared with the same period only a year before.

As late as his article in *China and Glass* of August 1940, Viktor wrote optimistically of the forward progress of modern design.

> The trend in dinnerware is modern, but you may not be conscious of it.... Modern does not mean that a thing must be radical, angular, queer looking, stunty, wild colored, slashy, shiny, and streamlined. It is quite the contrary. It is basically simple, pure, fills its functional requirements to the highest degree, respects the laws and qualities of the materials, uses color and ornamentation to enhance and give variety to beautifully proportioned forms and areas.... Modern is not something that you can put your finger on; it is a way of thinking.[165]

By December 1940, just three months after making this hopeful assessment, Viktor published a more pessimistic assessment of the state of American dinnerware in an essay for *Ceramic Industry*. While the war had disrupted foreign imports and created a flood of orders for local factories, he noted that the benefits for the designer were very mixed. For with such an unselective market, there was little incentive to come up with anything new. As he wrote:

> It has always been my belief and still is that the real chance for the designer comes not in a flush market, but rather in those lean years when competition is keen. In the current flush market, however, the public seemed satisfied with an endless flood of old-fashioned floral designs: It seems to simmer down to this: many

> buyers want bigger and better roses at lower prices. Not a very inspiring thought for the designer.[166]

He concluded by asking whether the quality of current productions would really hold up in a competitive world market once the war was over. Once international competition returned, he maintained, American ceramic companies could only compete if they modernized in two respects. First, they should adopt updated technologies of manufacture to cut labor costs and make production cheaper. Second, they should develop imaginative designs that would distinguish U.S. products and give them a unique national character. "After the war," he asked, "will the buyer continue with the American manufacturer, or will it be the same old squeeze play all over again?"[167]

The Changing Language of American Dinnerware

Viktor's patterns of the early 1930s, particularly Americana and Manhattan, opened up the field to a modern approach. Because of their unexpected success, within a year or so other designers began producing "modern" wares. While many of these products were uninspired copies of Viktor's designs, generally with some element misunderstood, a handful of gifted designers produced original and interesting work. Of them the most notable were Frederick Rhead, Russell Wright, and Eva Zeisel. Their designs, along with Viktor's, changed the character of American dinnerware. Indeed, by the time World War II had ended, Viktor was often picking up ideas from their work and integrating them into his own style.

The work of Frederick Rhead was closest to that of Viktor. Rhead's last position, as chief designer for Homer Laughlin Pottery in East Liverpool, encouraged him to try his hand at production dinnerware. Inspired by the use of color in automobiles and household contraptions, he decided to try creating dishes in the same spirit. The result was one of the most successful dinnerware patterns of the 20th century: Fiesta Ware—the first American dinnerware to stress the notion of mix-and-match. Looked at closely, Fiesta Ware is remarkably similar to the Peasant Ware that Viktor unsuccessfully tried to push into manufacture three years earlier, or to Americana or Manhattan with banded decoration. The major difference between the two designs is that rather than using contrasting color bands, Rhead glazed his plates in a single tone, cleverly choosing delectably hedonistic and child-pleasing ice-cream colors of vanilla, lime, and orange and lemon sherbet.[168]

Toward the end of the 1930s, a slightly different approach to modern dinnerware design came into vogue, which employed forms with a less regular, more fluid, more biomorphic quality. Ideas about decoration also shifted, to stress either monochrome glazes (whether white or colored) or asymmetrically placed designs scattered across the surface like fallen leaves. The American pioneer of the fluid approach was Russell Wright. His greatest commercial success came in 1937, when he turned his attention to ceramics and created a line of dinnerware titled American Modern. One major selling point of this product was simply its title, which acknowledged that large numbers of Americans were eager and ready to embrace modern design. In addition, however, Wright's shapes and colors broke with past practice. He abandoned strict geometry to embrace more flowing, biomorphic shapes, reminiscent of the work of the surrealist sculptor Jean Arp. In addition, rather than using ornament, Wright covered the whole surface with a single tone of delicately speckled glazes in unusual, slightly sour colors with names like seafoam, granite, and coral.[169]

Somewhat later than Wright was Eva Zeisel, whose work provided a direct link with European modernism and who brought European refinement to American dinnerware design. Born in Budapest and largely raised in Vienna, Zeisel came from a wealthy and cultured Hungarian family. Before coming to the United States she designed for porcelain factories not only in Hungary, Austria, and Germany, but in revolutionary Russia as well. Like Wright, Zeisel's shapes often have a biomorphic quality, but they were more elegant and generally aimed at a more upscale market. Her most famous design, Museum of 1942, was commissioned by the Museum of Modern Art. It is an elegant pure white service, closely modeled on German prototypes.[170]

Postwar Designs for Salem China

When Viktor returned to dinnerware design after the war, the terrain of the American dinnerware industry was going through seismic shifts. Most of the Sebring potteries folded just before and after World War II. Viktor did not go back to American Limoges because it had changed management and its products had become cheap looking. The company was subsisting chiefly on "novelty ware," garish giveaway pieces for drugstores, restaurants, and movie houses. Viktor's last experience with American Limoges was blackly comic. He did some special plates for favored customers of the firm but the executive he was working with scrambled the addresses, joining the names of the recipients with companies that were their business rivals. Rather than creating good will, the plates were sent back with angry letters, and the executive in charge of the project was fired. To Viktor's embarrassment, while he no longer worked for the firm, they continued to produce many of his early patterns with garish and completely inappropriate decoration.[171]

Viktor did continue designing for Salem China, where he served as art director through the mid 1950s. None of his postwar designs had quite the same impact as his first designs for American Limoges, which changed the face of the American dinnerware industry. Indeed, the entire dinnerware field had become more sophisticated by this time, and skilled designers such as Wright, Zeisel, or his own brother Don were turning out excellent designs. Yet, Viktor's best postwar designs show a wonderful process of creative growth. While still classic in feeling, they are somewhat freer in form than the prewar work and show ingenious adjustments to make them cheaper to manufacture and more functional in use.

This postwar work for Salem moved in two directions. First, Viktor began using more freely formed shapes, in keeping with the trend toward biomorphic form instigated by Wright and Zeisel. Second, he developed a new decorative approach. Rather than using neat, geometric patterns, he made much use of watercolor motifs, which were freely splashed across the surface. This development was partly an outgrowth of his own extensive work in watercolor just after the war. It also reflected a lifestyle that was more casual and informal than even a decade before, prizing spontane-

Salem China Ranch Pattern Dinnerware, 1951. [145]. The various pieces of this patio ware can be stacked in different ways, and the covers can be used as both dishes and lids.

Salem China Plates, 1950s. Diam. approx. 26 cm. [146].
Many of Viktor's postwar ceramics featured floral designs in cheerful colors. One of the most popular patterns was Parsley, a plate that was always elegantly garnished.

ity, freedom, and bold colors. The effect of these designs often closely resembles the dress patterns and decorative fabrics of the period, and indeed, part of the concept was that plates and other ceramic forms could play a major role as interior decor in an otherwise simplified and stripped-down setting. Most of these patterns featured flowers and plants. One of the most clever designs, and a big seller, featured sprigs of parsley, so that the plate would always look garnished [146]. Not all the designs used vegetation. A pattern titled Good Morning, with a crowing rooster, was also extremely popular. Another popular decorative pattern was Christmas Eve, designed in 1950 and produced continuously for just one year short of half a century, only going out of production in 1999. Because it was introduced so early, Salem was able to register the name "Christmas Eve" as a trademark. In general Viktor's designs possess a feminine quality, but a striking exception was Primitive, a pattern that Viktor created for his Free Form shape of 1955 [147]. It featured animals and running cavemen with spears, and was specifically intended to appeal to men. At once sophisticated and strikingly masculine, it is certainly one of the most unusual and interesting designs of the decade. Though it looks like a cave painting, Viktor made the drawing.

The first of Viktor's postwar shapes, Tempo of 1948, was one of the most beautiful, despite the fact that most of the features distinguishing it from his earlier designs were made so that the ware could be produced more rapidly, with less skillful workers. Elegant but inexpensive, it was made of ivory-toned semi-porcelain and intended for daily use, which no doubt explains why it is difficult to find today.

In many ways Tempo represented a return to Viktor's favorite globular forms in Manhattan, but with many adjustments to make it both more functional and cheaper. The spout of the teapot, for example, was considerably more massive and simpler in form, making it easier to cast. Similarly, the plate section provided heavier support on the shoulders, creating a sturdier shape that was also less likely to warp during firing. The plates had low broad rims, which reduced chipping, both in manufacture and in use. The hollowware forms curved gently inward, which also helped prevent chipping and retain heat, keeping food warm for a longer period. Handles and lugs were ample in size for a safe grip, even with hot pads.

The smooth, low plates had small ridges at the shoulder to keep the food on the plate. Viktor told Dorothy Grafly in 1949 that, as a result of unskilled labor, "All edges had to be protected from chipping. Delicate handles and knobs were out, but knobs could be made large enough to put decoration on the surface."[172] He also made sure that the lids were interchangeable from one hollowware form to another. If you broke one, you could substitute another. While some advertisements show Tempo in pure white, for the most part it was sold with underglaze and overglaze decorative patterns, such as the popular Strawberry Patch (applied with overglaze lithograph) or geometric designs such as Dalton, a banded decoration in lemon, coral, lime, or azure combined with soft gray.[173]

Somewhat less successful was Lotus Bud of 1950, which reflected Far Eastern influence and was largely conceived as a body for colorful, freely brushed floral decorations that loosely evoked Chinese ink painting. The shapes struck a balance between historical and modern. The short rim on the plates was a modern form, while the fluted base on the hollowware provided a historical note, somewhat simplified in treatment. The delicacy of some of the detailing, such as the fluting on the hollowware, was devised in a conscious effort to create a contrast with the boldness of the blobby floral decorations.

Ranch and Flair of 1951 go back to a purely modern look and continue this process of smoothing out the shapes one step further than the Tempo design. The plates do not have conventional rims, but simply arch upward in a careful sweep, which serves the same purpose without ever breaking the line of the curve. Ranch uses traditional round forms, but Flair introduced an ingenious oddity: the whole surface of both plates and hollowware forms is designed around a rounded square. Through ingenious shaping of the mold, Viktor was able to create this effect with a standard jigger, at no extra cost.

Viktor's last major design of the 1950s, the Free Form shape of 1955, was one of his most pleasing and original designs, and a high point of his career. As the name suggests, all the pieces were free-flowing and unusual in form, with a biomorphic fluidity somewhat different from his earlier

Strawberry Patch Garden Windblown Flair Fantasy

Salem China Free Form Shape Primitive Pattern Dinnerware, 1955. [147]. One of Viktor's most unusual and playful shapes, Free Form is also practical. The tripod feet of the teacup are designed so that it will never drip. The teapot always pours perfectly thanks to the extended lip at the bottom of the spout. Loosely based on cave paintings, the Primitive pattern ornamenting this set was specifically intended to appeal to men. Viktor began the design process with sketches in pastel.

work that may reflect the influence of Zeisel and Wright. In addition, Viktor had been pursuing a similar line of thinking in his ceramic slab forms, and the hollowware of Free Form explores a similar repertoire of canoe-like shapes. Two features make Free Form strikingly different from Viktor's earlier designs. First, rather than having attached handles, in one way or another the handles and grips form an integral part of the form, though they are expressed in creatively different ways. The creamer, for example, has indented thumb and finger grips on either side rather than handles, while the handle of the teapot is a sinuous tail-like extension. In addition, the Free Form shapes have an even more interesting feature. All the hollowware pieces rest on tripod supports, creating visual interest but also improving the function of the teacup in a thoroughly practical way.

The design of the teacup was patented, for it represented the first significant improvement in teacup design in at least a century. Most teacups have a flat, banded bottom, which creates a suction between the cup and saucer, and makes them pick up the least drop of liquid and spill it in some inconvenient place. Viktor's cup has tripod feet that do not pick up liquid even if the saucer is filled.

Royal Crest Dinnerware, about 1950. [148].
This elegant postwar design features gourd-like shapes with playful, contoured handles. Many of the pieces have indentations that serve as finger grips. In a resourceful bit of detailing, the saucer curves out to hold a piece of cake. While a few test sets such as this one were made, the design was never put into full production.

Indeed, at the 1955 dinnerware show in New York, Viktor devised a machine to lift the cup across a white tablecloth from one tea-filled saucer to another, and over the course of the show, not a single drop fell on the cloth. The spout of the teapot also showed an ingenious practical enhancement, a projecting lower lip. Standard teapots with a tubular spout will drip if there is a backflow, but Viktor's design eliminated such dripping.[174]

In addition to his work for Salem China, around 1950 Viktor produced one of his most creative designs for Royal Crest in California [148]. The elegant but whimsical design, in pure white, features biomorphic gourd-like shapes. The handles are flowing, sinuous curves. Many of the pieces have whimsically indented finger grips. In a clever bit of detailing, the asymmetrical saucers curve out slightly on one side to hold a piece of cake. Unfortunately, while a few test sets were made, the design was never put into full production.[175]

Don and Paul Schreckengost

Along with Frederick Rhead, Russell Wright, and Eva Zeisel, two other figures produced remarkable ceramics in the 1930s: Viktor's brothers, Don and Paul.

Don, Viktor's youngest brother, was an outstanding athlete who played semi-pro baseball and nearly pursued sports as a career. He also sang in a trio, the Makers of Rhythm, which performed on the radio under the sponsorship of Energetic Shoes. In the end, however, ceramics won out. After graduating from the Cleveland Institute of Art, Don took a job as chief designer for Salem Pottery. From Salem, he went on to teach ceramics at Alfred University, and then, after Rhead's death, became chief designer for Homer Laughlin. At the age of 87, Don is still active in the ceramics field, currently serving as chief designer for Hall China and Summitville Tile.[176]

One of Don's greatest designs was produced just after he joined Salem, in 1934. One day the Henshaw Color Company in Cleveland brought him an unusual lustrous orange glaze, made chiefly from uranium. At the time, the pottery at Salem was ranked in five categories, the lowest of which was "lump"—ware that had bent out of shape in the kiln and was considered worthless. Don suggested taking a stack of lump, glazing it with uranium, and calling it Hillbilly Ware. Salem did so, and it sold out immediately. Encouraged by this success, Don began sketching designs for the new color, trying to come up with something bright, fresh, and casual. He quickly came up with an unusual three-cornered shape he called Tricorne [149] and designed a jigger to fabricate it. Frank Sebring Jr. was so impressed by the design that he insisted Don patent it.[177] Well more than half a century later, the pattern still looks daring and has won a place as a classic of American art deco design.

Don's work is often confused with Viktor's, but at least biographical dictionaries list his name. The middle brother, Paul, pursued a career that was virtually invisible. Like Don, Paul played semi-pro baseball and attended the Cleveland Institute of Art, but he did not graduate. Instead, he returned to Sebring, married, and raised a family of nine children—five boys and four girls. To support them he worked as a mold-maker at the Gem Clay Forming Company and earned a reputation in the trade as the most skillful such artisan in the United States. In his spare time, in his basement, he produced a great deal of free-lance work, most of it unsigned and uncredited. He was particularly adept at creating animals and figures, such as a well-known panther-shaped lamp, often found in flea markets. In addition, he produced items every Christmas for Gem Clay to serve as gifts for special customers. Because these objects were intended to be unusual, Paul's designs were among the most audacious of the 1930s. His most famous design was one of these Christmas creations—a dramatically streamlined teapot of 1938 [150], featured at *The Machine Age,* an exhibition organized by the Brooklyn Museum in 1986. Along with Viktor's *Jazz Bowl,* it has become one of the most sought-after ceramics of the 20th century.[178]

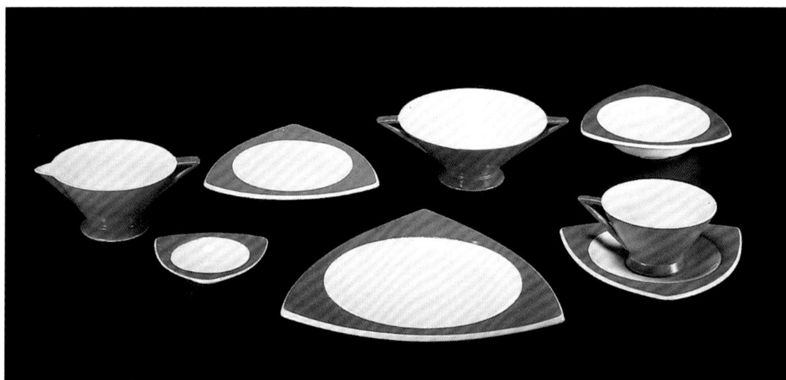

Don Schreckengost (born 1910). *Salem China Tricorne Shape Dinnerware Set,* 1933. [149].
Viktor's brother Don was also a noted ceramic designer. In 1935 he came up with this striking Tricorne shape as well as the machines to fabricate it. The orange uranium glaze adds to the modernity of the effect. Sixty-five years after it was created, the design still looks futuristic.

Paul Schreckengost (1908–1983). *Gem Clay Forming Company Teapot,* about 1938. [150].
Paul Schreckengost worked chiefly as a mold-maker for the Gem Clay Forming Company, but he also designed items every Christmas as gifts for special customers. Paul's creations were among the most daringly styled of the 1930s. His most famous object is this teapot, which looks like a space ship about to take off.

Steel

Another broad category of Viktor's work in industrial design is that of wheeled products made of steel. He first produced work of this type for the White Motor Company of Cleveland, for which he designed trucks, but his happiest experience was with the Murray Ohio Manufacturing Company, for which he designed bicycles, lawn mowers, juvenile vehicles, and fans for more than 33 years. His work with Murray in turn led to a consulting contract with Sears, Roebuck & Company of Chicago, then the nation's largest retailer, to advise Sears on its product line, with particular emphasis on bicycles, lawn mowers, fans, and lawn furniture.

Trucks

As has been mentioned, in 1932 Viktor produced one of his most widely imitated industrial designs, the first cab-over-engine truck. To develop the design he began with one-quarter scale plans, moved up to full-size drawings, and then worked on constructing a mock-up of plywood. Making everything work proved surprisingly complicated. For example, when the driver was lifted up and brought five feet forward, could he still see the traffic light? Not unless you changed the shape of the windshield, by sloping it backwards. How could the driver get into the cab? Even the headlights proved difficult. Initially, Viktor embedded the headlights in the fender and also put a step there so that a man could step up into the cab. It turned out that Pierce Arrow had already patented a headlight that was part of the fender. So Viktor simply cut a hole into the front of the fender and put a regular headlight behind it.[179] A quirky feature of Viktor's design is that the door hinges in the back rather than the front, so that the front fender could be used as a step for getting into the cab. While logical in concept, many drivers disliked this feature, and it eventually disappeared from use.[180] White Motors first presented the cab-over-engine design in a dairy truck because it wanted to take advantage of the Dairies Industrial Exposition held in Cleveland in October 1934.[181] When the design proved popular with trucks, in 1937 White began producing buses based on the same concept.

The development of the cab-over-engine truck has sometimes been termed "the greatest development in truck transportation."[182] Viktor's role in creating this product, however, has never received

By fitting the engine under the cab, Viktor added five feet to the cargo space. With the extra freight, truckers could pay off the rig in a year.

serious attention in the general literature on trucks. Indeed, many accounts of the company completely omit this key innovation, although they devote considerable space to the attractive but much less important designs of Alexis De Sakhnoffsky, who applied streamlining to the company's products in the late 1930s.[183] This reticence, in fact, dates back to the period when the design was introduced. For various reasons, the executives and the marketing department at White failed to grasp the most significant aspects of the design and did not promote it properly. In fact, the saga of the cab-over-engine truck provides an interesting instance of how a company can fail to capitalize on a major breakthrough because of poor management and faulty vision.

White Motors had its origins in the White Sewing Machine Company, founded by Thomas White in 1886. His three sons became interested in making trucks and manufactured their first vehicle in 1906. The business was hit hard, however, by the Depression, and the company passed out of the White family's control after Walter White was killed in a car accident in 1929. By 1931 sales had dropped to a quarter of their level during the 1920s, and the company desperately needed to come up with a new product. Viktor's inventive design for the first cab-over-engine truck was produced during this difficult period.[184]

By 1934 when Viktor's truck was introduced, White was fighting for its survival as a company. In 1932, under an unpopular president, Ashton Bean, White Motors merged with Studebaker, only to have its own assets seized a few months later when Studebaker went bankrupt. White did not extricate itself from this crisis until February 1935. In the meantime, the workers unionized, and in 1935, just as Viktor's model was being introduced, they went out on strike. Under a new president, Robert Black, the strike was settled and the company gradually stabilized its affairs. Because of the management confusion of 1934–35, the company missed the opportunity to advertise its new product the way it was to promote Sakhnoffsky's less significant designs a few years later.[185] In addition to its management difficulties, White Motors was clearly dominated at the time by engineers, who became so absorbed in the technicalities of engine construction that they did not grasp the significance of a revolutionary concept.

To cut eight inches off the height, Ray Spiller and the engineers at White had developed a special engine, the horizontally opposed (or "HO") 12-cylinder engine, called the "pancake 12." Essentially the layout was that of a V-type engine in which the angle of the V opened to 180 degrees, so that the cylinder banks were horizontal and opposite to each other. In the final design, the floor of the cab was unobstructed by any sort of box or protrusion, yet the overall height of the unit was only slightly more than that of a conventional truck. The proximity of the engine to the cab created a heat problem, but that was solved for the most part by exhaust manifolds on the underside of

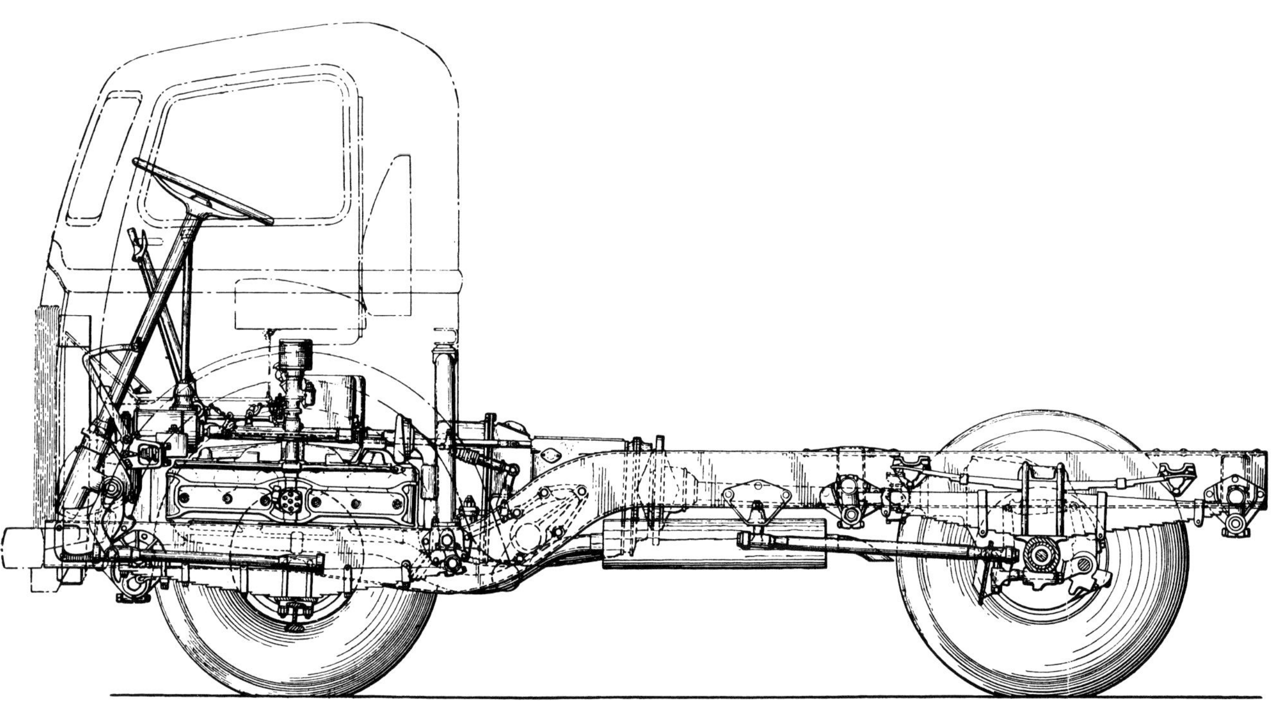

the engine, fan airflow, and insulation between the cab and engine.[186]

White's advertisements provide detailed descriptions of the pancake engine used in the truck, but they do not strongly emphasize the more important cab-over-engine concept, with its obvious economic advantages. Their slogan for this latter feature, "Underslung Power," made it sound like a jockstrap. In fact, despite the loving attention devoted to it by White's advertising department, the pancake engine proved to be flawed. Very soon it became apparent that the cylinders wore unevenly, in large part because the "splash" system of lubrication used at the time did not provide equal lubrication to both cylinder banks.

Finally, there was one major awkward feature of Viktor's design, namely that the engine was difficult to get to. Access to the engine was normally achieved through hinged and removable floorboards. To make it possible to carry out major repairs, the engine, accessories, and instrument panel were mounted on a subframe that could be removed from the front as a unit. Neither of these methods was entirely satisfactory because the first did not provide full access to all the working parts and the second was time-consuming and difficult.

In the end, the pancake engine disappeared, while the blunt-nosed cab-over-engine concept survived, although modified to be used with conventional engines, which created a slight increase in height. The difficulty of gaining access to the engine was finally resolved in 1949, when White introduced the first electric-powered tilt-cab mechanism, which tipped forward the entire front cab unit and made the engine available for service in 30 seconds.

Getting access to the engine was a problem in the first cab-over-engine designs. The problem was eventually solved with an electronic mechanism that tilted the cab forward.

At the time he developed his design, Viktor registered a patent on it.[187] But the wording was inherently weak, and he has never collected royalties on his invention. After noting that Viktor had created "a new, original, and ornamental Design for a Motor Vehicle Cab," the patent merely claimed protection for "the ornamental design for a motor vehicle cab as shown." By making a few changes to the "ornamental design" other companies were able to use the basic concept with impunity.

Patent law is based on the concept that something is added—a gizmo of some sort that contributes to the operation of a mechanism. The cab-over-engine truck, however, was based on the principle of taking away—of removing the front end from the vehicle. Like a Zen master, who thinks not of the form of the vessel but of the emptiness it encloses, Viktor's contribution was to make empty a space that had formerly been filled. Placing the driver over the engine was not in itself a patentable novelty, since patent law does not allow one to patent basic principles, and the placement of the motor had never before been viewed as a major issue. The concept was revolutionary, but patent law has no place for Zen masters.

The Murray Ohio Manufacturing Company

Four or five years later, however, Viktor established a relationship with Murray Ohio that was more successful than the one with White Motors. His abilities were obviously a key factor in bringing this about, but credit should also be given to the executives at Murray, who when they found that Viktor had a knack for making winning products, gave him free rein. As had been the case with dinnerware and trucks, it was a crisis in sales threatening the survival of the company that led management to turn to Viktor. What was different about Murray was that even when the crisis ended, he was allowed to continue playing a leading role.

Founded in 1919, Murray Ohio was an extension of a Detroit company that did metal-stamping for the automobile industry. In 1925 the president of the company, C. W. Hannon, bought a controlling interest in the stock and made Murray Ohio an independent concern. For years the company produced fenders, bumpers, gas tanks, and other sheet metal parts for the independent automobile manufacturers in Cleveland, including Jordon, Peerless, Franklin, Rolland, Hupmobile, Cleveland, and Sheridan.

Because demand for automobile parts went through unpredictable swings, Murray turned to toy manufacture in 1923. As Frank Gwinn, a member of Murray's board of directors, declared: "There will always be babies born!"[188] Yet, for years, toy production remained a sideline. This situation shifted in 1936, when Murray received a large order from Sears, Roebuck to produce bicycles and wheeled toys. Around this time, Japanese and German competition in the toy field dropped off, as they shifted their energy toward war work.[189] This was fortunate for Murray Ohio, since the surge in demand for bicycles and other toys occurred at exactly the same time that its core automotive business evaporated. Over the course of the 1930s, every one of the independent auto companies in Cleveland went out of business. Viktor arrived at Murray at just this moment of change and proved remarkably adept at responding to the company's needs. Within a few years, aside from defense work, virtually every product produced by Murray was something that he had designed.

One of the little mysteries of Viktor's career is how he made the shift from being the man who had never designed a bicycle but would like to try, to being the man responsible for every product that Murray produced, and who played a role only rivaled by the CEO in shaping the direction of the enterprise. Neither Viktor nor the executives at Murray Ohio seem to have intended this to happen, but very quickly it became apparent that Viktor's design abilities went beyond the surface look of things. He had a grasp of mechanics and the cost factors of manufacture and shipping; he was adept at working with sales staff and engineers; he saw a project through from beginning to end; he was remarkably persuasive; he was a good listener; he had a shrewd political sense; and even when under intense pressure he always acted like a gentleman. People enjoyed working with him and he produced a nice-looking and commercially successful product. While still at work on his first bicycle, he began taking on other projects.

Viktor was also entrusted with giving sales presentations to Murray's most important clients, such as Western Auto and Sears, Roebuck. Indeed, in 1938 Viktor persuaded Sears, then the nation's leading retailer, to make Murray its leading bicycle supplier. He did this not only through smooth talking but through ingenious design. Taking the existing elements that Murray was manufacturing—frames, seats, handlebars, fenders, and so forth—he devised 42 different bicycle designs, with different looks and color schemes. The buyer from Sears was delighted and took it to his superiors. Shortly afterward, Murray received a contract to produce Sears' basic bicycle line.[190] After winning over Sears, Viktor moved on to other companies, such as Firestone, Goodyear, Western Flyer, Western Auto, J.C. Penney, and F.A.O. Schwartz.

From Pottery to Pedal Cars

In 1949 an article in the *Plain Dealer* noted that a company in Cleveland, Murray Ohio, had just become the largest producer of toys for Santa Claus in the world, and that the person chiefly responsible for this situation was a young designer by the name of Viktor Schreckengost. As the article reported:

> While Santa Claus may direct this vast operation from the North Pole, it is Schreckengost who, in collaboration with the sales and engineering staff, designs, sketches pastel visuals, and carves mock-up plastilene models for wood patterns and dies, with one eye on the toy market and another on the aesthetics of good design and functional sturdy construction.[191]

Viktor's first pedal car designs date to 1938, but the great surge in demand took place after World War II. Since Germany and Japan had been bombed flat, American manufacturers had a field day. With faultless timing, Murray cut back on its defense work and filled the slack by returning to the manufacture of bicycles and pedal cars on a scale even greater than before. Items rolled off the assembly line on a scale comparable to that of the leading Detroit automakers.

The shift from pottery to pedal cars was less great than it might seem, since in the 1930s car designs were first shaped in clay—a special sort of clay, mixed with wax, which was lighter and a little more malleable than that used for ceramic work.[192] After making initial sketches in charcoal or pastel, Viktor created a full-scale clay model, finished with shellac and color. This model was then turned over to the engineering department, which estimated the manufacturing cost. The next step was to construct a wooden model with working metal parts. That was followed by a working metal model, which was used as a basis for establishing final manufacturing costs. During this process, experts were consulted at every step, for instance, to make adjustments to the turning radius or to shorten a dimension by an inch or so to make it fit better in a carton for shipping. When the metal model was satisfactory, final engineering drawings were made from it, dies cast, materials stocked, and production arrangements established. The factory began turning out its models in July for the forthcoming year. In creating his designs, Viktor consulted with car designers in Detroit to guess what cars would look like two or three years ahead.

The term "ergonomics" had not yet been coined, but one of the pathbreaking features of Viktor's designs is that he did research to make his cars fit the bodies of children, which have different proportions than adults. "We did extensive accumulation of information on the size of kids," Viktor recalls. "Leg lengths, arm lengths, weights, and so forth. This was long before [industrial designer Henry] Dreyfuss made his materials available. We took basic vehicles to children's homes, hospitals, and playgrounds, and had the various sizes ride them. In return for this privilege, we gave the institutions many models for permanent use."[193] The data gathered from measuring children was condensed into cardboard cut-outs of children's bodies that were used to test the fit of the prototypes. Pedal cars and airplanes required a particularly exact fit. Velocipedes, scooters, and wagons allowed a much greater range.

Despite their small scale, Viktor's toys had to create the illusion that they were real automobiles. In interviews over many decades, Viktor has always stressed that his primary challenge in designing pedal cars was to appeal to a child's imagination. "We wanted kids to think that they had a little one just like dad had."[194] Viktor noted that he used a "shorthand approach."[195] For example, the wings of a pedal pursuit plane had to awaken the child's imagination but still be narrow enough to go through doors. "You just have to suggest the existence of things like wings and propellers. The child's imagination goes on from there. But there must be enough suggestions for a toy to look authentic."[196] His Comet and Torpedo pedal cars were not copies of any particular automobile, but were "a composite of all modern cars."[197]

His basic premise was that it should be possible to develop good design for low-cost products. "It is just as easy," he noted, "to conceive a smooth, attractive wrap-around bumper or smartly styled crown fender as an awkward, clumsy model."[198] In developing a successful design, he noted that "Form is everything."[199] The trick was to develop a simple, basic shape, which could then be altered in a few details from year to year. While, of course, pedal cars did not actually rush forward at lightning speed, creating a streamlined design helped foster that illusion.

The aerodynamics of wind-tunnel research are of no value in toys because high speed is not a factor. However, the growing child is fully aware of modern forms such as the racy appearances of jet planes and rockets. The juvenile imagination works wonders. A boy conceives himself traveling at breakneck speed, as a pilot, because of the clean, sweeping, floating lines of his vehicle. It is only necessary to plant this illusion in his mind. He will let it grow.

Small details often played an important role in creating a convincing effect.

> Children have a keen sense of authenticity. The smallest detail is important. The bell on the fire truck model, for example, is not just an ornament but has all the characteristics of a genuine fire bell. I know because I crawled over and around Cleveland Fire Department equipment to be certain of the design. The rolled flange or flared edging gives the particular pitch and quality.[200]

Fire Chief Car (Child's Pedal Car), first issued about 1965. H. 45 cm. [151].

In use for 35 years, this fire engine has been passed along to children of three families who live on the same street in Cleveland.

MURRAY O. M CLEVE. O.
PURSUIT

Pursuit Plane (*Child's Pedal Car*), first issued 1941. H. 64 cm. [152].

Pursuit Plane (*Child's Pedal Car*), first issued 1941. H. 64 cm. [153].

The earliest pedal airplanes looked like orange crates, with wings held on by baling wire. Viktor simplified this confusion into an appealing Brancusi-like egg shape. To cut costs, he made the pedals by bending the front axle. The wings were short enough to fit through a doorway, and the propeller turned as the machine moved forward.

Despite the importance of authentic detail, sometimes it was important not to be too true to life, and the fire bell provided an interesting instance of this fact. Viktor noted that he had been careful to muffle the tone of the bell so that it would strike an acceptable balance between pleasing its young user and irritating the rest of the family with its incessant clang.

Viktor noted that the needs of the parent should not be overlooked and confessed that once he had gone astray on this point. He built an imitation gasoline tank with the idea that it could be filled with water and give the child an extra element of play and illusion. But children spilled so much water in houses while filling the tanks that the idea had to be discarded.[201] Color was "a variable tool," and also, when appealing to children, not difficult to choose. "Fire engine red, the more dazzling the better, has been found by all odds the most attractive to children."[202]

As with bicycles, a major factor in the design was to find ways to reduce the shipping rates. As Viktor recalls: "On the little autos, we were able to reduce the size of the bulk by one-third by removing the windshield and placing the wheels in the seat area. Rails and ladders fit flat under the body. Steering wheel and shaft lay along the bottom."[203] It was also possible to get a reduced rate by shipping so-called mixed lots, since in theory a railroad car could be packed more tightly if the boxes were of different sizes.

Viktor's first toys were produced to use up surplus steel. When Murray stamped out fenders they had 30-inch circles of prime steel left over—known in the trade as "wasters"—that they were paying money to haul away. If they could make a product with this material, not only would the material cost nothing, it would save hauling money to boot. Viktor promptly designed a series of children's toys shaped like small cars, buses, and trucks [165]. The most elaborate was a little locomotive, about 25 inches long, that a small child could sit on and push forward. Coming out of the smokestack was a handle so that he could steer while he moved along. From such small toys, Viktor moved on to wagons and pedal cars.

Schreckengost's little red wagon [154] is an example of a design that looks simple but contains a number of interesting features. Children's wagons of this sort were initially used in the country to haul

Super De Luxe 4-Ball Bearing Wagon, first issued 1961. H. 40.1 cm. [154].
At first, it appears ordinary, but Viktor's little red wagon had a number of innovative features, including rolled metal edges, ball bearings for each wheel, and a handle bent so that a child sitting in the wagon could use it to steer.

milk, and their traditional dimensions were established by the need to hold two milk cans. Viktor's wagon holds strictly to this size, which would have been familiar to his buyers. It also turned out to be just about perfect for most household tasks, such as hauling stacks of Sunday newspapers or pulling two small children.

Yet while its dimensions are traditional, Viktor ingeniously took advantage of the malleable qualities of stamped metal to create an effect quite difficult to achieve with boards. The contours of Schreckengost's red wagon have rolled edges, which were still a novelty in this period. The contours are also subtly tapered, for the sides are thicker and taller in the front and lower and thinner in the back. This tapering creates a flowing sense of streamlined movement, and the rolled edges provide handholds. The width of the sides, in fact, is perfectly scaled to the hands of a nine- or ten-year-old child.

The wagon also contains two mechanical improvements. The first is a ball bearing for every wheel, which provides a smoother, more cushioned ride. The second is something taken for granted today, but which seems to have been Viktor's invention. The front handle is curved, so it can be used not only to pull the wagon, but, when bent back, as a steering mechanism for a child sitting in the wagon.

Clever as it is, however, Viktor's little red wagon pales in comparison to the Champion pedal car [155], which remained Murray's top-selling pedal car from 1938 until the mid 1960s. It completely revolutionized the pedal car field. Pedal cars began as toys for the rich and were originally assembled as perfect miniature replicas of automobiles. Over time, to bring the price down to a mass-market level, details were simplified and the number of stampings reduced. At the time Viktor designed the Champion, however, it was still customary to build pedal cars the way automobiles were made, with a chassis attached to a metal

Champion (Child's Pedal Car), first issued 1938. H. 36 cm. [155]. Viktor's first pedal car revolutionized their design. Earlier cars were constructed like real automobiles, with a chassis welded to a frame. The Champion was stamped out in a single piece, except for inserts at the front and back that could be changed to create different types of vehicles. The resulting cost savings made pedal cars affordable by the middle class.

frame. Viktor's major breakthrough in the Champion was to recognize that this form of construction was not necessary for a toy. Instead, the Champion was stamped out in a single piece, and then folded into its final shape. Shrewdly, he made the front and back of the Champion separate pieces, so it was easy to customize the grille and back end of the car, or to change it from a sedan into a truck, fire engine, or station wagon. The simplified manufacture and reduced cost of the Champion completely altered the sociology of pedal cars, since it made them affordable to middle-class and working-class families.[204]

Despite its more economical construction, the Champion was also more exciting than rival products because of its dramatic streamlining. Cleverly, Viktor created the illusion of an automobile without literally copying one. Nearly all of Viktor's early cars, for example, have large, bulging front ends and then become smaller toward the back. In their overall form they are more like an airplane or a fish than an automobile. This shape creates the illusion that the front, where the pedals are located, is a site of incredible power, whereas the rear end is just a streamlined blur.

The most popular version of the Champion had "dip sides"—a streamlined bulge, roughly in the shape of an airplane fuselage, that ran along the bottom of each side. In some curious way this device evokes both running boards and streamlined contours. In fact, all Viktor's early pedal cars, when viewed from front or back, show a gradual inward contour of the body from the wheelbase—a look that he once described as a "tumble home" effect. This slight curve both makes the car more stable and is aesthetically pleasing.[205] Overall, Viktor's design for the Champion is unlike any car ever made, although it does resemble somewhat the visionary "concept cars" of the period, such as Raymond Loewy's unexecuted proposals for Hupmobile.

Indeed, it is remarkable that we recognize these strangely shaped devices as cars at all. The trick of pedal car design, Viktor discovered, is that if the front grille is shaped like that of an automobile, the mind will accept almost any shape at all for the body itself. Paradoxically, the front grille cannot be too literal. It needs to be slightly exaggerated—a cartoon version of the front end of a car. Indeed, Viktor often provided this grille with face-like qualities. For example, the dump truck, fire truck, and station wagon that he loosely based on the 1938 Buick, have come to be known as the "sad face models" because the front grille seems to frown.

Even more visually striking than the Champion is Viktor's Pursuit Plane of 1941 [152, 153]—surely the most beautiful metal pedal toy ever fabricated. Before Viktor, pedal airplanes had looked like orange crates, with wings held on by baling wire. Viktor's Pursuit Plane simplified this confusion into a Brancusi-like egg shape. The propeller turns as the machine moves forward. The short wings were designed to fit through a normal doorway. While the shape is unlike any airplane that ever flew, the design conveys a completely convincing illusion of being a real plane. Even the name of the product, Pursuit Plane, was the result of careful thought. "We did not want to emphasize war and violence," Viktor recalls. "We wanted to say, 'it's fast, man.'"[206]

The design has several clever mechanical features. Ingeniously, the pedals were created simply by bending the front axle, which significantly cut production costs. Unlike most pedal cars, the front wheels do not turn, but instead the steering is handled by a cable that leads to the back wheel. This was a possible source of confusion, since the rear wheel has to turn in the opposite direction of the one you wish to go. So, to go right, the wheel must turn left, to go left it must turn right. In order not to confuse the kids, Viktor covered the back of the fuselage with a cross member that hid the wheel from view. The design proved an immediate hit and it was turned out in the tens of thousands. In 1941 an article in the *Cleveland Press* reported that the busiest section of the Murray factory was the one devoted to the Pursuit Plane, and a closely related design, the R.A.F. Spitfire.[207]

The appeal of the Pursuit Plane design is suggested by the degree to which it has been reproduced. Hallmark, for example, now sells a miniature model that costs about $60—more than the original full-scale toy. In 1994, F.A.O. Schwartz produced a full-scale replica, in a limited edition of 250, with an impressive retail price of $4,500.

An interesting and ingenious offshoot from pedal car design was Viktor's baby walker of 1951. More precisely, it was a two-purpose design, since it could be used indoors as a walker and outdoors as a stroller. The trade name for the product, the Murray-Go-Round, was derived from the fact that one of the wheels could be locked, so that a child could still move but would stay in one place, merely rotating around a single point. Sev-

Viktor's stroller was lower and more stable than a traditional baby carriage, and also doubled as a walker. It was christened the "Murray-Go-Round" because one wheel could lock, making it possible for the vehicle to turn in a circle but preventing it from rolling away.

eral things were original about the product. While it resembled a traditional baby carriage, it was lower, more stable, and took up less space. The chassis was made of sturdy, lightweight hydrogen-brazed steel. A spring-mounted wood and steel carriage was then suspended at three points. The steel frame provided both strength and lightness, while a low center of gravity provided stability. The device rolled easily because of its ball-bearing wheel assembly. It could be used to pull both packages and children, since it had a removable foot tray and package carrier, as well as an adjustable chrome handle. The finishes were non-toxic, acid-proof, and came in two decorative schemes, high-luster peacock blue or cherry red and ivory.[208]

Flat-Face Pedal Cars

Viktor's Champion dominated the pedal-car field until the 1950s, when he received his first serious challenge from Brook Stevens, an experienced car and motorcycle designer who is now best known for coining the term "planned obsolescence." Over the course of his career, Stevens participated in the design of 41 different automobiles, for companies ranging from Cadillac to Volkswagen. He also conceived the Oscar Mayer Wienermobile, with its hot-dog-in-a-bun styling concept.

In 1957 and 1958, using his experience in automobile design for guidance, Stevens took on the task of designing pedal cars for AMF (American Machine and Foundry), which had purchased the Junior Toy and Binghamton pedal car lines in the 1950s. In that two-year period, Stevens and his firm produced 17 pedal cars that introduced a fresh, flat-faced look. While less sculpturally appealing than Viktor's two-decade-old Champion, the styling of Stevens's models was definitely more up-to-date than Viktor's model, which evoked automobiles that were no longer current, such as the Chrysler Airflow.

Murray had to respond or slip out of fashion, and so in 1959 Viktor produced a flat-face pedal car design, and Murray completely retooled its plant to produce it.[209] Viktor quickly recognized that the advantage of this approach was that it allowed one to use the side of the car as a billboard, thereby changing the look of the car at minimal cost. The Murray flat-face design was ultimately adopted to the Fire Chief [151], Super Sport 8, Fire Chief Battalion No. 2, Speedway Pace Car [156], Maverick, Radio Sports Car, Gilmore Racing Car, and Circus Car. Thus, Murray effectively fended off the challenge from AMF and remained the world's leading pedal car producer until the company finally abandoned the business as no longer profitable in 1973, one year after Viktor's retirement.[210]

Throughout the 1960s, Viktor came up with inventive schemes for pedal cars, although none had quite the commercial success of the Champion or the flat-face designs. One of the most delightful is the so-called Tot Rod of 1962, which essentially removed the cover of a pedal car to reveal its pedals and frame.[211] A few years later, in 1962, he encased a very similar frame to create a racing car.[212] One of the most delightfully eccentric designs was for an atomic missile, although it was never a big seller, probably because it was just a little too large to fit in a corner of the garage.[213] He also created a juvenile tractor and various boats with toy outboard motors.[214] The boats were completely open at the bottom, but so powerful was the spell of their illusion that at least one tot pedaled one into the family swimming pool and nearly drowned. This accident led to a lawsuit against the Murray Company that was eventually dismissed.

While most pedal cars were used by boys, Viktor put some thought into developing something different for girls. The result was a turquoise station wagon. As Viktor recalls: "It had an open area in back so kids could haul things around, and it had

Speedway Pace Car (Child's Pedal Car), first issued 1959. H. 36 cm. [156].
Viktor's flat-face cars responded to changes in design since the 1930s and countered competition from the AMF toy company. He used the side of the car as a billboard, thereby changing the look at minimal cost.

Viktor's riding lawn mowers were fun and safe, and quickly put competing brands out of business.

a Swiss music box that played *Whistle While You Work*. Murray got permission from Walt Disney to reproduce the song. We also made a pink and white ice cream truck—girls loved it."[215]

Not only are many of these creations beautiful designs, but they connected with the mind-set of everyday Americans, with their daily lives in both work and leisure. Someday perhaps someone will write a study of these seemingly simple little toys, exploring their deeper meanings and using them to unlock the aspirations and fantasies of this period.

Lawn Mowers

While his later pedal cars were all successful products, Viktor's major breakthrough of the 1960s was to realize that what he had learned from designing pedal cars could be extended to another field of design, lawn mowers. Since men are just larger versions of boys, he reasoned, a riding-type lawn mower would appeal to adult fantasy in much the same way that a pedal car appeals to children. Around 1969–70 he began to design both the Murray and Craftsman riding lawn mowers, which in slightly modified form are still being produced by Murray. Curiously, no foreign company has come up with a comparable product, so they are still shipped in considerable quantity to Europe.[216]

Essentially, Viktor devised two types of riding mower. One was the "big man's toy," which looked like a tractor. The other was modeled on a golf cart, so that you could look out the front and see what you were mowing. To promote this second design, Murray got a professional golfer, Jack Nicklaus, to sponsor the machine and developed the slogan: Mow your lawn like a pro! Despite this seemingly persuasive appeal, and the fact that the golf cart mower was the more practical of the two, the tractor has always done better in sales. For some reason, men (who are the main customers for such machines) feel that it is a manly thing to sit on a tractor.[217]

Other companies entered the riding-mower market at about the same time as Murray, but failed because of bad design. Following the pattern of a push-mower, their machines put the blades out in front of the driver, where they looked and were very dangerous. Buyers who wanted to keep all ten of their toes, which turned out to be nearly everyone, purchased Viktor's mower instead.

Bicycles

Along with pedal cars and mowers, Viktor's main focus at Murray Ohio was on bicycles. In the public mind, however, Murray does not occupy a place as large as other bicycle makers, such as Raleigh, Schwinn, Columbia, and Evinrude, or even some of the smaller lines such as Shelby or Monark. There are several reasons for this, but certainly the principal one is that Murray generally hid its brand name behind other labels, since its bikes were marketed chiefly through the major retail outlets such as Sears, Roebuck & Company, Western Auto, and later through K-mart, Wal-Mart, and other discount stores. The Murray bike for Sears, for example, was marketed under the brand name J.C. Higgins, which honored the firm's first accountant, Mr. Higgins, but was also deliberately designed to sound like J.F. Spaulding, a firm with a high reputation for quality sporting goods. At the height of his career, Viktor was designing bikes under 108 different labels and had seven assistants at Murray customizing the different lines. Under Viktor's leadership, Murray became the largest maker of bicycles in the world, but this fact was not easily discerned by the general public, since its product names were so diverse.

The length of Viktor's tenure as the lead designer for Murray appears to be without parallel in bicycle history. Other designers produced an interesting bicycle or two and then moved on to other activities. Viktor remained in the foreground of bicycle design for more than 30 years, from 1939 to 1972. During this period he consistently kept the company at or near the forefront of bicycle design, producing much of the cutting-edge design of the period and also catching on to hot trends so quickly that Murray never lagged behind the competition.

Blind Welding

Murray's success was due not simply to the good looks of its products but to improvements in manufacturing. Viktor's first step after leaving the navy was to introduce new techniques, developed during the war, so that bicycles could be produced more cheaply. In 1941, Murray had obtained a contract to manufacture Oerliken magazines, artillery shells used for anti-aircraft guns. The Oerliken had charges arranged side-by-side in a spiral configuration, so that they would fire off sequentially in all directions, like a string of firecrackers. The product required hundreds of careful welds. Only one company, National Cash Register, seemed to know how to make a magazine of this sort, but it was making only a few a day. With help from General Electric, which fabricated a suitable furnace, Murray devised a more efficient way to produce them, which blind-welded the pieces together in a single step. The technique was to embed a plug of silver or copper as solder at the joints, place the whole canister in a hydrogen atmosphere, and run an electric charge through it. The charge would race through the metal and create a weld wherever the pieces were pressed together. With this technique, production of Oerliken magazines soared from a few dozen to about 1,500 a day.

When Viktor came back to Cleveland on furlough during the war, C. W. Hannon walked him through the plant and showed him the blind-welding technique. "Think about it," he said. "Could we design a bicycle like that?" Once Viktor left the navy, in 1947, he worked with the engineers to build completely new manufacturing equipment, and he devised a system by which the crank, seatpost, top frames, and front fork were all welded at one time. This method created a stronger weld, since the pieces were not under tension from being pressed together, one by one. In addition, it was significantly quicker. The most significant time-savings came in the clean-up, since by the old method cleaning up the excess flux and solder took as long as the welding process itself. The hydrogen reduction chamber process required no cleaning at all. Once a frame was welded it could immediately be sent down to be dipped in the paint tank. The technique revolutionized the bicycle industry. Indeed, Murray's frames were so much cheaper than those of other manufacturers that for a time it constructed bicycle frames for rival companies such as Schwinn, which would then add on a few parts to make a distinctive product that could be sold under the company's brand name.

This process of developing techniques for single-step welding encouraged Viktor to analyze carefully how bicycles are assembled and led to additional advances in bicycle assembly. For example, in May 1953, Viktor and another employee of the Murray Company, Gilbert B. Hahn, submitted a patent for "Knockdown Bicycle Construction," which showed how to produce a bicycle that could be broken down into small parts so that it could be packaged in a small container and "correctly assembled by a distributor or purchaser in a fool-proof ready manner."[218] Whether consciously or unconsciously, this patent was surely related to Viktor's thinking about the process of single-step welding, being in essence an application of the same principles in reverse. Essentially, the design made it possible for the front forks, as well as the wheels, fenders, and handlebar, to be disassembled. Doing so reduced the size of the carton by one-third and through a quirk in shipping guidelines achieved an even greater proportional reduction in the cost of transport. The design was practical, however, only for small bicycles because the cost reduction for shipping a large bicycle was not as significant and taking apart a larger bicycle was inherently more cumbersome.

The desire to simplify construction also led Viktor to a design for a tricycle that used exactly the same parts for both boy's and girl's models.[219] Changing from the boy's to the girl's model could be accomplished simply by turning over the top crossbar of the frame, and the only difference in assembly was that the head had to be pierced at a different point and a different angle. This particular tricycle design also had another clever feature not mentioned in the patent. Since it was chain driven, it was easy to adjust the power ratio and make a girl's model that was a little easier to pedal than the boy's version. The design proved so popular that in the late 1950s Murray continued to manufacture it in Cleveland, even after they moved the bulk of their business to Tennessee.[220]

Murray's Move to Lawrenceburg

In 1957 strikes and labor difficulties forced Murray Ohio to relocate to Lawrenceburg, Tennessee, just outside of Nashville. The company used the move as an opportunity to make operations larger and more efficient.[221] The Tennessee plant contained 40 acres under a single roof and was capable of production on a scale unattainable before. Tons of raw material were hauled to the plant to produce about 250 miles of steel tubing every 24 hours. Fifteen thousand bicycles rolled off the assembly line every day, adding up to well over four million in a year.

While necessary for the company's survival, the move made Viktor's life considerably more frantic. He continued to work for Murray for 16 years after the move. From 1957 until 1972, Viktor commuted to Lawrenceburg every other week to super-

Tricycle, first issued 1964. H. 78 cm. [157].
Tricycles such as this one outsold those of the competition because of ingenious features such as the double step on the back. The extra step made it easier for a small child to climb up to the seat and also provided a ledge for a friend to stand on.

vise the design office there, headed by one of his former students at the Cleveland Institute of Art, Ed Harris, and to meet with management. He had 11 designers working full time, each responsible for maintaining a relationship with a different company. Generally, he would fly to Nashville and be picked up by a helicopter that would take him to the plant.[222] To appreciate Viktor's work it is helpful to understand his place in the history of bicycle design.

The Origins of the Bicycle

The bicycle originated in the early 19th century as a two-wheeled walking tool, or "hobbyhorse," and around the 1830s was outfitted with pedals. Since early bicycles had no gears, they had enormous front wheels, which maximized the force of the pedaler. Unfortunately, it also produced an unbalanced design, which easily flipped forward, resulting in "headers." This problem was finally solved in 1886 when the English machinist James Starley came up with the idea of using sprockets and a chain to transmit pedal power to the rear wheel efficiently.

The result, the "safety bicycle," with two wheels of equal size, was nearly impossible to tip over backward or forward. This basic design was further perfected with a series of inventions, such as safety brakes, hollow steel tubing, the lever-tension wheel (which tightened all the spokes at one time in a single movement), and pneumatic tires with rubber inner tubes and canvas coverings. In the 1890s, at least one-third of all the patents filed at the U.S. Patent Office were bicycle related.

Safety bicycles transformed cycling from an exotic amusement into a craze, which was rapidly picked up in all levels of society. Two million bicycles were sold in the United States in 1895 alone. The mobility possible with the bicycle brought startling social changes, in many ways similar to those created by the automobile just a few years later. Courtship patterns shifted, since men could now travel 15 or 20 miles in a day rather than five or six. Couples found that they could perfect their "rhythmic sense" by cycling together. Sometimes couples even eloped, using bicycles to make their getaway. Women threw aside their long skirts and corsets to adopt bloomers and other modern fashions.

Then, almost as suddenly as it had appeared, the bicycle craze evaporated, in large part because of the development of a bigger and more powerful rival, the automobile. Between 1900 and 1905 the sale of bicycles dropped to less than one-quarter of its former level.[223]

The Motorcycle Look of the 1930s

Fortunately, this slump did not last forever, and Viktor came to bicycles at a time when sales had begun to climb, after stagnating for 25 years. If the 1890s was the first great bicycle age, the 1930s was the second. For despite the hardships of the Great Depression, bicycles sales surged. The reason for this growth was a change in how bicycles were used, which opened them up to a new and ever-expanding market. Whereas in the 1890s they were sold as a form of adult transportation, in the 1930s they were chiefly sold to children. The standard features of a bicycle—two equally sized wheels, a gear mechanism, pneumatic tires, brakes, and a diamond-shaped frame—were developed in the 1890s. But there was still room to refine them, to add additional accessories, and above all, to explore issues of styling for its own sake. The result was a renaissance in bicycle design, this time focused not simply on basic mechanical features, but on issues of styling and design.

In the 1930s a different approach to bicycle design evolved: the "motorcycle look." During the 1920s, many bicycle companies also made motorcycles, and it was natural to carry over to bicycles some of the features of motorcycle design. In addition, since children handle bicycles roughly, it made sense to develop a sturdier bicycle frame and wider tires. Children also like to imagine things, and one aspect of 1930s bicycle design was to introduce an element of fantasy that had not been present before. Children liked streamlined features, which made their bikes resemble motorcycles and airplanes. They were fond of extra gadgets, such as loud horns and flashing lights. Viktor's bicycles play delightfully with all those features.[224]

The 1939 Mercury

Viktor's first bicycle, the Mercury [158], was designed in 1939, when the motorcycle look was at its peak. In many ways it adopts this look, but differs in its elegance and sophistication. The classic "motorcycle" bicycles, such as the Schwinn Aerocycle Streamliner and the Elgin Blackhawk, are powerful but bluntly clumsy designs. The very elements that are intended to look streamlined

Murray Mercury, first issued 1939. 175.3 cm from front to rear tires. [158].
This elegant bicycle was first exhibited at the 1939 New York World's Fair. Its most unusual feature is the use of sculptural elements for the head, tank, and chain guard. They convey a feeling of speed and bring to mind the streamlined trains, cars, and luxury liners of the time.

convey an unwieldy sense of gravity and weight, and create the impression that the machine requires a motorcycle engine to propel it rather than a child. Indeed, during the 1930s some bicycle manufacturers resisted the bulky tank and heavy frame of the Aerocycle and Blackhawk, viewing them as heavy and impractical, and attempted to create a streamlined look without those elements. For example, the 1936 Huffy Streamliner and the 1936 Monark Silver King Flo have no such tank and employ lighter framing elements. But these bicycles also do not possess the mystique and romantic excitement of the Aerocycle and the Blackhawk.[225]

Viktor's 1939 Mercury strikes a delicate balance between the visual power of massive motorcycle forms and the practical imperative to create a bicycle that was a little lighter in construction. Having been trained as a sculptor, it was natural for Viktor to turn toward sculpture to achieve this end. Every piece of the bicycle feels considered and sculpturally shaped, but his most dramatic contribution was to introduce three streamlined elements of pure sculpture in chrome for the head, the tank, and the chain guard. While all three are visually similar, in fact they were produced in different ways, for the design on the head was die cast whereas the forms of the tank and chain guard were stamped from metal sheets. All three were chrome-plated. Viktor first made these elements in clay, and then a skilled metalworker at the Murray plant, Tony Tucci, fabricated them in metal.

Viktor registered a design patent for each of these elements.[226] The linear simplicity of the patent drawings enables one to read the form and essential message of each of these elements even more clearly than in the dazzling shininess of the bicycle itself. While all these forms are a little ambiguous, they each contain at least a suggestion of representation. The head on the front of the bike closely resembles the prow of an ocean liner, and is quite similar to a famous poster by Cassandre from this period advertising the *Normandie,* the greatest of the art deco luxury liners. The designs of the tank and the chain guard bring to mind one of Raymond Loewy's streamlined trains.[227] All three

J.C. Higgins, first issued 1948. 175.3 cm from front to rear tires. [159]. This bike is a light-weight version of the motorcycle look that was popular at the time. Careful thought went into designing every accessory. One of the most appealing features is the double-beam batwing headlight.

forms evoke modernity, the power of modern machinery, speed, and luxuriousness (although, of course, the Mercury was comfortably priced, for a middle-class market). Since they are attached to a functional object, none of these elements has ever been considered as part of the history of art, but they are among the finest works of American sculpture of their period. While other cycles (such as the Elgin Blackhawk) had chrome-plated functional elements, such as the mud guards, wheel hubs, and handlebars, it appears that no one before had made such use of purely decorative ornamentation in chrome.

The J.C. Higgins

Imitation is the most sincere form of flattery, and Schwinn quickly responded to Viktor's Mercury with one of the most successful bicycles in its history, the memorably titled Black Phantom. It directly copied the streamlined train motif on the tank of Viktor's Mercury, with the proud addition of the word Schwinn splashed across it. Despite Viktor's design patent, the copy of this element is literal and precise, with only the addition of some scalloping at the bottom to make the form more wing-like. (The wing metaphor was probably suggested by the wing-like shape on the front fender of Viktor's creation.) The Black Phantom, however, failed to follow through this streamlined motif in the design of the head and chain guard. Overall, the detailing is less elegant than Viktor's design, but the black color and the arresting titles were strokes of genius. They gave the bicycle a phantom-like allure that clearly appealed to some dark quality in the minds of little boys. The design was a runaway best-seller and brought impressive profits for the firm.[228]

Schwinn, however, was not the only company to be closely watching its rivals, for Viktor's first major postwar bicycle, the J.C. Higgins model for Sears [159], was largely inspired by Schwinn's most popular bicycle of the period, the B Series Hollywood of 1941.[229] In a sense it was a backward step for Viktor, since the Hollywood had a heavier frame and larger tank than the Mercury, and was a more straightforward application of the motorcycle look. What distinguishes the J.C. Higgins is its refinement of detail, a vast improvement over its model.

The front vertical member of a bicycle is known as the fork because it comes down from the handlebars in the shape of a two-pronged fork, one prong on each side of the front wheel. Both bicycles dramatically featured a spring fork on the front wheel, a mechanism to cushion the ride. This device had been developed some time before, but it was still being perfected. To make sure that prospective buyers noticed it, both bicycles made the front spring as large and prominent as possible.[230] In a rather ungainly fashion, Schwinn placed the spring of the front fork in a horizontal position. Viktor, however, positioned it vertically, so that it resembles a beehive. This more effectively suggests how it functions mechanically and also creates an interesting visual echo of the inverted beehive springs cushioning the seat. While the Schwinn bicycle runs the fork directly into the front axle, that of Viktor's bicycle hovers some distance out from the wheel, in a fashion both visually intriguing and suggestive of an additional element of cushioning.

In other respects also, Schreckengost's detailing is superior. The Schwinn Hollywood breaks the line between tank and luggage carrier with a slight hump, creating an awkward camelback look that breaks the streamlined flow of the design. Viktor made the luggage rack a high unbroken horizontal, so that the forward sweep of its line is not broken, and the bicycle seems to rush forward. Similarly, the Schwinn chain guard is stumpy, whereas Viktor's is visually extended by the addition of a fender support, giving it a much more sweeping, energized line.

The crowning glory of Viktor's bicycle is the headlights. Schwinn shaped its headlight like a taillight, whereas Viktor dramatized the front end with twin rocket-ray bat-wing headlights, a lighting device on which he held a patent.[231] With shrewd appreciation of the psychology of a child, Viktor notes: "Kids could count them. If you had two of them, you had twice as many." Rather than relying on mundane tail reflectors, he mounted twin ray lights on the back end as well, which projected colorful beams of red light out the back to contrast with the twin white beams shooting forward. The genius of the design was that it achieved an appealing harmony of overall shape, yet also had innumerable selling points because of its carefully conceived accessories.[232]

The Supersonic Look

The J.C. Higgins proved an extremely popular design and it was continued in production in only slightly modified form until the end of the 1950s. In the meantime, Viktor introduced an even more exciting look than motorcycle streamlining. Perhaps

Sears Spaceliner, first issued 1965. H. 97 cm. [160]. In the 1960s, Viktor dramatically lightened his bicycles to create a supersonic look. The double bars in the frame made it possible to create very thin metal tubes and to run an unbroken line past the seat bar. Viktor also reduced the size of the tire, creating a new standard in the American bicycle industry.

his most original contribution to bicycle design was what might be termed the "supersonic look" of the 1950s, which pushed the concept of streamlining to a new level of daring and technical sophistication.[233]

Space-age streamlining was in many ways an outgrowth of the earlier streamlined motorcycle look of the 1930s, but it translated the concept into a more modern idiom. Most significantly, Viktor replaced the heavy tank characteristic of the motorcycle look with slender "jet sweep" tubing, creating an almost weightless look reminiscent of the weightlessness of modern architecture, such as Frank Lloyd Wright's Fallingwater, in which ceilings and floors seem to float on air, in defiance of the forces of gravity. As has been noted, the motorcycle look contained an inherent contradiction, for while the forms were fluid, they were also massive, creating a bicycle that was actually much heavier than desirable. Viktor's space-age streamlining retained the fluidity of the earlier bicycles combined with a breathtaking lightness of form. There had been gropings in this direction even in the 1930s, for example in the Huffy Safety Streamliner of 1936 or the Monark Silver King Flo of 1936. These early efforts in this direction, however, were curiously awkward and lack a clear sense of forward movement. Viktor successfully mastered these difficulties, both because of his superior grasp of how to create beautiful lines and through a series of technical enhancements.

The modification that made the supersonic look possible was an idea that Viktor patented in 1953, that of using twin tubes on a bicycle frame rather than one.[234] This idea had two visual advantages. First, it allowed him to create a continuous line that ran across the seat support. Early bicycles tended to break the rhythm of the design at this point, notably in the Schwinn company's designs, which almost always stressed an awkward camelback look. Using a continuous tube rather than joined tubes created a modern sense of flow and grace. Second, having two tubes rather than one made it possible to reduce significantly the thickness of the tubing, making the bike look almost inconceivably light when seen in profile. Viktor first employed this technique on the Fleetline series of bicycles in 1954, but he refined it to the greatest extent in the mid 1960s.

In addition, as has been noted, one of the chief reasons for the heavy motorcycle look was the shift to a sturdier tire. In the mid 1930s, such tires needed to be thick, with a rim at least two inches wide. By the 1950s, however, this was no longer the case. In the Fleetline series, Viktor brought down the tire size to a 1¾-inch rim, which soon became the standard of the industry. Having made these two fundamental steps, Viktor reviewed the other structural elements of the bicycle to carry through the theme of miraculous lightness.

As mentioned, this process reached its culmination in the Sears Spaceliner of 1965 [160], a bicycle that repays close study for the extraordinary refinement of its detailing.[235] In the Spaceliner, the spring fork does not come down directly to the wheelhub, but floats alongside it, creating a weightless effect. The hubs themselves are not solid, but sparkling red plastic jewels. Because of the bounce of the spring fork, the mudguard on the front wheel is higher than that in back. While this difference serves a practical purpose, it also creates a visual illusion that makes the bicycle look eager to rush forward. Throughout the design, the bars of the structure are shaped with admirable subtlety and skill. To cite a single example, the bar that connects the carrier with the seat takes a slight upward bend as it moves forward to join the seatbar, making the bicycle itself seem about to "lift off."[236] Finally, Viktor redesigned the accessories—the lights, horn, and other gizmos. They are no longer tacked-on attachments, but visually merge with the tank, so that nothing interferes with the supersonic flow of the design.[237]

The Eccentric Look

In their way, the Fleetline and Spaceliner series achieve a perfection of bicycle design that has never been equaled. Perhaps what is most remarkable about Viktor's design career, however, is that he never became imprisoned within his past achievements, but continued to move forward. His final phase of bicycle design took place when he was entering his 60s, just the age when painters such as Rembrandt and Titian developed their famous old-age styles. Paradoxically, however, Viktor's work did not age but instead increasingly emphasized qualities we associate with youth and childhood—such qualities as fun, playfulness, and lack of self-consciousness. Like children's drawings, they are unconventionally fresh and astonishing. These bicycles can be generally grouped under the rubric the "eccentric look."

In the mid 1960s, Murray began getting orders from the West Coast for tiny front forks with 14-inch wheels. To learn how they were being used, Viktor made a trip to California. He found that kids were transforming regular bikes by replacing the standard front wheel with a small one borrowed from a child's tricycle. This made an unbalanced bicycle, which did not have much speed but which was perfectly suited for doing wheelies and acrobatic tricks. Along with other manufacturers such as Schwinn, Murray began producing "kooky bikes" to fill this market. Viktor's design patents show that he produced bicycles of this type from about 1967 to 1969.[238]

Perhaps the most striking of the series was one of the last, the "supercharged" Murray Mark II Eliminator [161]. Advertising copy boasted that this "revolutionary new custom drag bike" was "the raciest machine yet to hook the surface," and for once the hyperbole of advertising seems an under-

The Murray Company boasted that its supercharged Mark II Eliminator [161] was "the raciest machine yet to hook the surface." The tiny front wheel and oversized rear wheel give the bike the aura of a powerful dragster; they were also ideal for doing wheelies and acrobatic tricks. The Texas Longhorn handlebars, banana seat, and upthrust sissy bar add to the effect.

statement compared with the machine itself. At once space age and Rube Goldberg, everything about the bike looks funny and slightly out of proportion, from the curving pretzel handlebars (sometimes known as Texas longhorns) to the lemon yellow banana seat and upthrust sissy bar in the back. Nonetheless, despite the profusion of apparently eccentric features, everything about the machine sends an expressive message about force and forward motion with uncanny clarity.

The basic image of the machine is that of a powerful dragster, kicking up the dust with its enormous rear wheel as it drunkenly reels forward. This is expressed through the oversized rear wheel, the diminutive front wheel, and the curve of the upper transverse bars, which convey the impression that the frame has crumpled through the force with which the rear wheel rushes ahead. As the advertisers noted, this was a machine to "move you out front and keep you there."

Significantly, every mechanical element also reads as a metaphor for something exciting about the ride. The horizontally coiled spring of the front fork seems to slam forward like a clenched fist and evokes speed and excitement, while the even more overscaled vertical springs of the sissy bar suggest the unbelievable kick and bounce with which the machine rides. Even the logo of the Mark II, a demonically fanged and hooded cobra burning rubber on the asphalt, conveys a sense of excitement and makes us regret that Viktor never finished those monumental sculptures he sketched out for the serpent building at the Cleveland zoo.[239]

To even sit on such a machine, let alone pedal it, looks excitingly risky, and thus appealing to children. The strongly articulated handlebars in front and sissy bar in back, however, provide at least modest reassurance to worried parents. Moreover, despite its funky character, the machine is also almost perversely elegant. The neatly placed silver, orange, and yellow bands on the black frame, for example, suggest the decoration of one of Viktor's teacups.

In its fundamentals, the Eliminator series explores an approach to design almost exactly opposite that of the Fleetline and Spaceliner series. Whereas the Fleetlines and Spaceliners are sleekly elegant and ethereal, with much of the mechanics hidden under the sleek streamlined skin, the Eliminator series allows everything to hang out, as if, like the rock star Madonna, it were wearing its underwear on the outside. The wires that run to the Shamano gear mechanism are not hidden inside the frame, but dangle loosely from stem to stern; the spring fork is studded with oversized bolts and sprockets, which formerly were discretely hidden; the sissy bar is articulated with enormous springs; and the gear shift, with its overscaled levers, becomes a fearsome statement in its own right, sitting like a speedboat on the wavy ocean of its crossbars.[240] Even the red taillight flaps from the banana seat like a loose shirttail. Wires, springs, screws, sprockets, and other elements, all serving some solemn and mysterious but often inscrutable purpose, enliven the effect.

Sadly, the kooky bike craze came to an end around 1974, when federal regulators began to crack down on bicycles that caused headers because of their front disc brakes and unevenly sized wheels. Fortunately, Viktor had retired two years before. Thus, he ended his career in bicycle design on a high note, with a machine whose exuberant playfulness and overall funkiness are unlikely to be surpassed any time soon.

The Campus Compact

If the Mark II Eliminator pushed eccentricity to the limit, another bicycle by Viktor shows that bending the standard can sometimes also serve a practical purpose. The concept that inspired the Campus Compact [162] is one that was never fully implemented in this country, although it has been successfully applied in parts of Europe. The notion was that colleges, hospitals, and other large complexes would purchase hundreds of bikes that they would provide as free transportation within their campuses. Such bikes needed to be used by both men and women, young and old. Thus, it was necessary to drop the frame as low as possible and provide ample luggage racks. Inherently, these requirements made it difficult to pursue a purely streamlined form, but rather introduced an element of visual syncopation.

In fact, Viktor's solution was curiously similar to the Eliminator series. Both have eccentric proportions, although the Campus Compact has wheels that are the same size. Nonetheless, despite their many similarities of overall form, they communicate a very different idea—the Eliminator looking racy and risky, the Campus Compact comfortable and safe in a way. This contrast nicely corresponds to the difference between a madcap, reckless youth and an absent-minded professor.[241] That would be clear even from the form itself, but to underscore the point, Viktor chose to ornament the Campus Compact with bands of a rich brown, evoking wood paneling and leather-bound books, with just a splash of silver to give the potentially dowdy effect some life and richness.

Sending a Message

Viktor astutely recognized that people ride bicycles not only to go places, or to get the fat off their tummies, but to intensify their relationship to the world through which they move and make a bold fashion statement about how stylish or distinguished they are. While his bicycles work nicely as functional objects, the way in which they speak to and capture fantasies in psychological terms lifts them above the crowd. Their look distills a lifestyle. Whether we are roaring forward in the comfort of Raymond Loewy's streamlined train as we ride the 1939 Mercury; soaring cosmically on our rocket-powered Sears Spaceliner; wearing our underwear on the outside as we do wheelies on our Mark II Eliminator; or reading Kierkegaard as we pedal thoughtfully on our Campus Compact, in each case the look of the machine communicates a fantasy about its purpose. As Viktor once wrote: "Children want to imagine an object as more than what it is."[242] The comment penetrates to the essence of Viktor's approach to design, but it should be rewritten to include not just children but all of us.

Cabinets, Fans, Chairs, and Toys

In addition to pedal cars, mowers, and bicycles, Viktor worked on many other projects for Murray. In 1938, while just starting work on his first bicycle design, he proved his usefulness by designing some metal cabinets.[243] A few years later he displayed his practical ingenuity in creating a lawn chair that could be made with just two pieces of stamped steel [163]. Most of the design came easily, but he ran into difficulties when he tried to visualize a perfectly comfortable seat. Unable to draw one out of his head, he decided to do some research. So he took the bottom of a barrel, put eight inches of soft clay on the top, and covered it with a sheet of plastic. Then he stood beside it out

Campus Compact, first issued 1968. H. 101.6 cm. [162]. This unisex bicycle was intended for university campuses, so Viktor dropped the frame as low as possible.

Lawn Chair, Beverly Hills Model, first issued 1941. H. 83 cm. [163].
At Viktor's request each employee of the Murray Company sat, in turn, on a mound of soft clay covered with plastic. The resulting impressions gave him the shape for the seat of this chair.

at the Murray plant and gave anyone who would sit on it a chit for a drink. Before long, 428 fannies had molded the clay into a contoured shape. He then took the clay to the shop, took sections off it, and made the dies. "It's the most comfortable chair you've ever sat in," Viktor gloats.[244]

Viktor also designed electric fans, which in an age before air conditioning were almost a necessity for the American home. When placed in an upper room, such a fan could lower the temperature of a home by a good 15 degrees.[245] Viktor's work with fan design pursued two lines of thinking, one primarily visual, the other practical. His first step was to simplify the visual appearance of Murray's fans by creating less fussy stampings for the end panels and changing the pattern of the wire screen.[246] In addition, he designed fans that were mounted on wheels [164], making them easy to move without heavy lifting. This was particularly welcome for women, who often had difficulty lugging around heavy objects. Unlike Viktor's bicycles and pedal cars, his fans do not call attention to themselves but blend into the background. But that was just the point, and from a commercial standpoint, they were equally successful designs. Sears, for example, sold roughly 50,000 of Viktor's 1954 fans for $50 apiece, raking in the tidy sum of $2 million.

In the early 1940s, Viktor redesigned the Murray logo, interlocking the M and O in a more dynamic fashion.[247] Shortly after the war, he also designed the interior of the Murray showroom in New York. The central pillar could not be removed, so he used it as the fulcrum for a circular space, with curving platforms on which bicycles and pedal cars could be displayed.

Sears, Roebuck

Since Murray designed bicycles for Sears, Viktor became closely involved with the company and made many visits to its Chicago headquarters to discuss various products. Not long after the war, Sears offered Viktor a position as its top designer, supervising a staff of 60. Viktor, however, did not want to run a business but to make designs, so he declined. He did accept a consulting role, which entailed spending one day a week looking over the Sears line of bicycles, mowers, lawn furniture, and similar items.[248]

Viktor recalls coming through the drafting room at Sears one day when a team was working on the design of some kitchen cabinets. Sears had a policy that nothing had to be assembled by the customer, that each product was ready to use when it was shipped. Unfortunately, in this case a handle was sticking out in a way that made the whole cabinet too large for the standard box and thus more expensive to ship. To solve the problem, Viktor took out a compass and drew a six-inch circle around the center of the two doors. "Depress it one-half inch and put the handle flush," he told them.

A little later, as he was on his way out, the president of the company called him into his office. "Vik, you were in the drafting room," he said. "I hope I didn't interfere with anything," Viktor replied. "No," he said. "I appreciate what you did with that circle around the handle. There's a check for $500 which you can pick up at the desk on the way out." Viktor remembers thinking it was pretty good pay for drawing a circle, but he did not fully appreciate the significance of his little gesture. Not long afterward the motif reappeared as the insignia for the Sears Cold-Spot refrigerator.[249]

Mobile Adjustable Fan, first issued 1963. H. 81 cm. [164].
Once wheels were added, moving a fan around the house was no longer a chore.

Lights and Lighting Systems

When Viktor and his brothers were boys, they constructed toy automobiles, using wheels they gathered from the dump, scavenged from old baby carriages and similar vehicles. They devoted great effort to duplicating all the features of a real car, but a problem they never solved was how to make working headlights. They tried using a candle, but found that if they had no glass in front of it, the forward motion blew it out, and if they covered the front with glass, the lack of oxygen smothered it. Try as they might, they never did work out a satisfactory solution. At some level this failure must have haunted Viktor, and it may explain the extraordinary thought he put into the headlights of his bicycles. In Viktor's bicycles the lights are not simply an extraneous add-on but an integral part of the design.[250]

His first bicycle headlight was a streamlined form called the "rocket ray" that he designed for Murray and that was manufactured by Delta Electric, which produced it in large and small versions. It was such a striking design that Delta sold it across the entire bicycle industry. Shortly after the war, he expanded on this idea when designing his J.C. Higgins bicycle for Sears, mounting two rocket rays on a wing-like shape to create a headlight cluster popularly known as bat-wing headlights.[251]

The success of these bicycle headlights led to a series of commissions to design flashlights for Delta. The most original of them was the Buddy Light, shaped like a square container rather than a tube, with a metal handle like a lunchbox. Just $4\frac{1}{4}$ inches high, it required the usual two batteries, but held a much larger than standard light set in a reflector $2\frac{1}{4}$ inches across. The product sold by the tens of thousands. Viktor continued to design flashlights for Delta well into the 1960s. One of the more interesting products was a flashlight for the Boy Scouts. With help from DuPont, he found a luminous material for the handle that would pick up enough light during the day to make it glow. As a result, you could find it at night. "When do you need a flashlight?" Viktor asks rhetorically. "When it's dark."[252]

Viktor also explored a different aspect of lighting systems in a series of designs for the Holophane Company. A major problem in a lighting fixture is that a bare bulb will create a blinding glare when you look at it directly but will not distribute the light evenly through a room or an outdoor space. Holophane's solution to this problem was to use prisms to control the diffusion of the light. Since prisms bend rays of light in a geometrically predictable fashion, the spread of the light can be calculated and controlled with great precision. Working closely with engineers, Viktor designed fixtures suitable for lighting a variety of indoor and outdoor spaces. Viktor's back door and garage are still lighted by Holophane fixtures and lenses.[253]

To broaden Holophane's product lines, Viktor also designed a series of serving plates using industrial glass. The line was marketed under the name Verlys of America.[254] His first design was embossed on the inner surface. After this first trial,

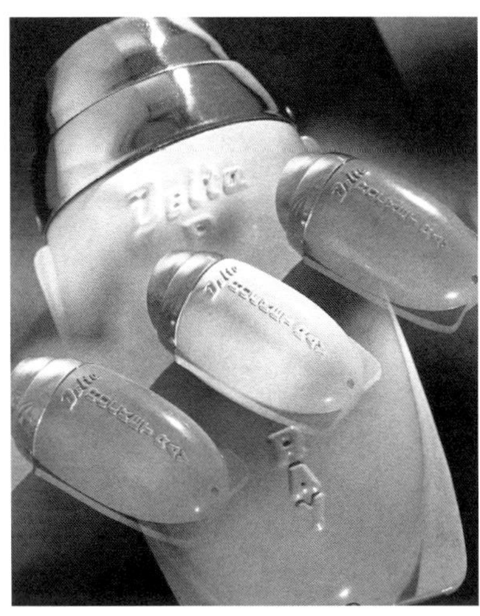

Viktor's Rocket Ray headlights were made in various sizes. Their success led him into the design of flashlights.

Viktor's Buddy Light cast a larger beam than a traditional flashlight.

By means of prisms, Viktor's Holophane fixtures controlled the spread of light and prevented glare.

however, it occurred to him that he could achieve the same visual effect by embossing the glass from underneath, which created a container with a smooth serving surface, making it easier to use and clean the vessel.[255]

Toward the end of his career, Viktor worked with General Electric at Nela Park in Cleveland to develop modular ceiling units that could create a completely luminous surface and that could be modified to direct the light in any direction—up, down, or sideways.[256] These units were four-foot squares, lit by a bent neon tube and equipped with a series of lenses and reflectors to control the spread of light.

Printing Equipment

Viktor also played a major role in modernizing printing equipment, introducing a look that is now standard for printing equipment of all types, from photocopy machines to high-speed presses. He produced his first printing press for Chandler Price in Cleveland around 1938, but most of his designs were produced for Harris-Seybold after the war. In 1946 he got a call from Ray Spiller, with whom he had worked on the cab-over-engine truck. By that time, Ray had become chief engineer for Harris-Seybold. "I've got another chicken coop on my hands," Spiller reported.[257]

Spiller's phone call led to Viktor's first commission for Harris-Seybold, the redesign of a sheet-fed printing press. When this project was finished in 1948, Viktor's clean-lined design persuaded the executives there to put him in charge of all their products. In this period, Harris was expanding rapidly, and each time it acquired a company, Viktor redesigned the equipment.[258] By 1962 the work had become so extensive that Viktor approached his former students Hugh Greenlee and Roy Hess and worked out an agreement to create a firm—Schreckengost, Greenlee, Hess—specifically to handle the account.[259]

Over the years, both alone and in partnership, Viktor designed offset, sheet-fed, and web presses, cutters, perforators, electronic typesetting equipment, computer peripherals, computer monitors, broadcast equipment, and computer interface systems. Many of the machines he worked on had tens of thousands of working parts, but one would never guess their complexity from the cleanness and clarity of Viktor's designs.

The design of printing presses had changed little since the 19th century. These noisy, inky, greasy machines had open working parts that were both dangerous and messy, since the ink spilled out everywhere. Since presses were generally black, it was hard to see the ink and keep the machines clean. Viktor's first printing press for Chandler Price, a cylinder halftone press, enclosed existing machinery in a handsome two-toned gray steel case, which protected the moving parts, kept the press clean, and safeguarded the operator. The case was hinged, however, to provide easy access to the working parts. To make the press easy to use, the controls were all clustered together in one area on the operating side and highlighted with vermilion and plated chrome. The sheet came out onto the delivery table printed side up. In addition to making the press easier and safer to use, the steel case also made it easier to move and install without damage. Viktor recalls that the president of Chandler Price was distressed by the cost of the sheet-metal required to cover the machine, but stopped complaining when orders for the machine started pouring in. The company sold only about 50 of their previous model and more than 1,000 of the Schreckengost design.[260]

Viktor's first designs for Harris-Seybold followed the same general principles, although because the press was considerably larger and more complicated than the one for Chandler Price, it took several stages to produce a completely modern design. The first step was to encase the sides with sheet metal, providing protection for the operator. The casing was hinged to allow access to the working parts, and the top of the press was left open. In

In his first printing press for Chandler Price, Viktor enclosed the working parts in sheet metal. The press was cleaner, safer, and easier to use than earlier models.

later versions of the design, Viktor broke up this casing into modular units, which looked more elegant and made access to the inside of the machine even easier.

A bolder step was to shift the color of the press from black to white. This served a practical function, for the least bit of ink or grime would show up as a blemish on a pristine white surface. For the first time, it became possible to keep a printing press truly clean. This change also transformed the social role of the operator, who became an expert technician rather than a mechanic. Photographs record that when the presses became white, the clothing of the operators also changed from greasy blue coveralls to plain white attire. Viktor even made white drains for the oil, and put a brass plate on each press with the name of the operator, as a way to encourage printers to keep their machines spotless.

The principle of neatly enclosing a press in a smoothly shaped box led naturally to the notion of creating a portable printing press, completely enclosed in a smooth-sided shipping case. Such a press was of obvious value to the military, since it could be used to print maps in advanced areas, such as the site of a battlefield or training maneuvers. After coming up with the idea, Viktor made a drawing that Harris-Seybold sent to the three services. The rendering was so convincing that the air force telegraphed back: "Ship immediately." As it happened, Harris had yet to build a single press of this type, but with such encouragement they immediately rushed it into production. Air force, army, and navy all ordered units, and eventually more than 1,000 were sold.[261]

The patent for this project was one of the most detailed of Viktor's career and included three pages of closely spaced type describing every detail of how the press and shipping case should be constructed. The case was designed so that it not only protected the press in transport, but also served functional purposes. One end of the box contained a unit for developing offset plates, including a developing tank and storage tank for chemicals. The other end held a combination cabinet and bookcase for storage, as well as a desk for examining and using the final printed product.[262]

Viktor's success on these first projects led to additional commissions from Harris-Seybold to design cutters, perforators, and other equipment for the printing industry. The toughest job turned out to be removing the little dots of paper created by the perforators—tons and tons of them. They eventually worked out a viable method using a powerful suction pump. As he had with his printing presses, Viktor devised casework for these varied machines that was both good-looking and practical. He also devoted careful thought to improving operator safety. Many workers had lost fingers in the plant's huge papercutters. Viktor's simple but effective

When Viktor began designing presses for Harris-Seybold, their machines were dangerous because their working parts were exposed (left). He sheathed the machinery in metal, making the presses safer, and changed their color from black with brass fittings to white with chrome (right).

solution was to make it necessary to press two buttons, spaced far apart, to bring the cutter down. If the operator's left and right hands were both on the buttons, they were at a safe distance from the machine's blade.

At the end of his work with Harris-Seybold, Viktor designed huge high-speed presses for R.R. Donnelley & Sons in Chicago, which printed magazines such as *Time* or *Life* or catalogues for companies such as Sears, Roebuck in editions of a million or more. The largest presses required double-eight colors, that is, 16 colors printing at once—all the regular inks, plus the exotics such as copper, blue, gold, and silver. Any small loss of time cost large sums of money, and thus, well-conceived design was critical.

As usual, Viktor began with careful research. Someone mentioned that if he met with a printer, he should ask to see his shins. So he did so with an old printer and found that his legs were marked with scars and bruises all the way up the front. "How come?" Viktor asked. Because every elevation on the press was a different dimension. If something was out of whack on press three, they would have to run up and down steps of different heights, constantly banging their knees. The first thing Viktor did was to set a module so that every dimension was the same. Wherever you were on the press, you knew that the risers would be the same height.[263]

In addition, he made the more radical breakthrough of electronic controls. Instead of requiring printers to run down the line checking adjustments, Viktor developed a control console for the master printer, with a television screen providing information on every color and a telephone system to talk to the assistants down the line. From the social standpoint, this shift in design is fascinating, for it transformed the printer from a blue-collar worker, rushing from place to place, smeared with oil and ink, to a manager and supervisor sitting at a console, reading gauges, adjusting dials, and making phone calls.[264]

When Viktor introduced such control systems on large presses, they alone cost more than $250,000, but it was the only way to solve the problem. The president of Harris-Seybold gave Viktor a vigorous tongue-lashing when he learned of the expense, but as had occurred so often before, Viktor had intuitively grasped the direction of the future. Harris-Seybold eventually sold its entire printing division to Wittenberg, a German company, so that Harris could focus exclusively on electronic control mechanisms. They even changed the name of the company to Harris Controls.[265]

Viktor's high-speed presses for R.R. Donnelley & Sons in Chicago printed 16 colors at once and were regulated with sophisticated electronic controls.

Influence as a Teacher

In addition to his own productions, Viktor has reshaped the field of American design through his influence as a teacher. Viktor's teaching at the Cleveland Institute of Art clearly began as a financial fallback. It provided him with a secure fiscal base, a set of useful artistic contacts, and a place to show his work. The security of his teaching position enabled him to survive and thrive in Cleveland during the 1930s, when a number of his most talented rivals in ceramics, such as Russell Barnett Aitken and Whitney Atchley, were obliged to move elsewhere. By the 1950s, however, Viktor's salary as a teacher provided only a tiny fraction of the income he derived from his industrial work. Yet he continued teaching throughout this period—evidently because it was fun, indeed almost a form of relaxation, which allowed him to think about industrial design from a different perspective. While Viktor had less time to prepare for his classes than some of the other teachers, this was counterbalanced by his mastery of his field and the range of his experience. His classes also provided an endless stream of recruits to hire as assistants. With one exception, all his assistants at the Murray Company were graduates of the Institute of Art, which sometimes left the lone outsider with the feeling that he had stumbled into the wrong class reunion.

In developing his program, Viktor's models lay in Europe, in schools such as the Bauhaus and Kunstgewerbeschule, which had developed theories of "abstract form" that took art training out of the confines of specific handicrafts and allowed one to design for any medium. Viktor's program also stressed such ideas. The first class his students took dealt with the relationship of abstract forms, and those lessons provided the basis for everything that followed. From this foundation, the teaching progressed toward the specific challenges of designing for different techniques of production.

Schools such as the Bauhaus or the Kunstgewerbeschule, while they may have preached about mass markets and mass production, were essentially theoretical. Neither school effectively connected with industry. For Viktor, the rough-and-tumble business of getting products produced was a critical aspect of the creative process. His program was without parallel in the degree to which it connected with the real world of business and manufacture at every juncture.

For one thing, the entire faculty maintained active careers in industrial design. Indeed, he insisted that his instructors teach only three days a week. In his classes, Viktor took his students on tours of factories to see how furniture, dinnerware, and bicycles were made. For the student critiques at the end of each term, Viktor brought in hard-nosed business types to serve as jurors. Students soon learned that creative flights of fancy needed to be grounded in practical reality and that good design needed to be combined with factors appealing to popular taste. If they had difficulty with verbal presentation, Viktor would send them to a speech class to better their skills. Finally, because Viktor networked constantly with figures in industry, he was able to place his students in good jobs. Those who passed through the design program at the Institute of Art invariably landed in jobs that paid four or five times as much as the graduates of other programs of the school.

The program boomed in the period after World War II. The classes Viktor taught varied from year to year. For the most part he centered on his own design interests of the moment, but did so in a way that touched on larger issues of design. His class on toy design, for example, focused on designing children's vehicles, like those he produced for Murray. The larger issue that he addressed, however, was that of designing for people with highly specific needs.

In some cases, Viktor used a class as a vehicle for exploration and experiment. In the 1960s, while putting electronic controls on his presses for Harris-Seybold, it occurred to him that such controls could be applied to musical instruments as well. Specifically, he became interested in improving the design of the harp. A traditional harp needs to be tuned to a particular key and cannot change keys without being completely retuned. Viktor reasoned that it would be more sensible to design a harp that could be retuned with the push of a button. Unfortunately, after designing such an instrument, he learned that classically trained harpists were not interested in such shortcuts. They preferred the old way, and so Viktor set the project aside. The direction of his thinking, however, was prescient. Today, four decades later, the creation of instruments equipped with electronic controls has transformed the music industry.[266]

Those who studied with Viktor agree that not only was the content of his classes fascinating, but that he was an extraordinary role model. Students

John Nottingham, shown here on a Schreckengost tractor, went on to study with Viktor. In partnership with his classmate, John Spirk, Nottingham has revolutionized American toy and appliance design.

were in awe of his intellect as well as his easygoing manner, air of confidence, elegant clothes, and fast cars. One of his former students, Joe Oros (class of 1939), has confessed that he not only listened to what Viktor said, but began to study how he dressed and the way he gestured, to figure out why he was so persuasive.[267] Viktor's training at the Kunstgewerbeschule had been strictly disciplined and rigorous, but in his teaching, in keeping with the psychology of American youth, he was always wonderfully casual and informal in approach. What pushed his students to work hard was not an authoritarian manner, but the penetrating nature of his seemingly casual questions, which immediately showed up the weakness of anything ill-considered or poorly designed.

Unlike many other major figures in modern design, Viktor's approach is not easily reduced to a single formula. He never focused on a single area of design, but viewed the task of designing anything as a logical process of asking questions. Giuseppe Delena (class of 1978) recalls of Viktor that "his teaching style was never to pontificate or to dictate, but rather through a series of almost casual questions, to make the students succumb to some very serious thinking."[268]

Delena still vividly remembers Viktor's dinnerware assignment. He started off thinking that nothing could be simpler than designing a cup, a saucer, a plate, and a creamer. Think again. As Delena recalls: "After I had done a few sketches, Viktor would come around with his most congenial smile and nonthreatening manner and start asking questions. 'Is this an elegant set or an everyday set? If it's an everyday set how are you going to communicate that visually? Should your lines be thin and flowing or should they be more definite and geometric? Look at your sections. How thick should your coffee cup be? Why? Can you design the shape to retain the heat?'"[269]

At times the questions would let up for a few seconds and Viktor would pick up a pencil and effortlessly sketch different cups in cross-section and perspective. Then he would return to his questions. "Can you stack the cups? How are you going to do it? Bottom to bottom? Lip to lip? What's the right dimension for the handle? What is the cost of this dinnerware going to be? Who will buy it? Why? What color is it going to be? What are your selling points?"[270] "To this day," Delena comments, "when I work on a design project, I ask myself the same questions. When I look at the bodyside sec-

Viktor's student Joe Oros designed the Ford Mustang and other classic American cars. His wife, Betty Thatcher Oros (far right), was the first woman automotive designer ever hired by an American firm.

tion of a car I remember the coffee cup section, and I look for just the right balance, curvature, stance, and feeling."[271]

During his 70 years of teaching, Viktor has instructed nearly 1,000 students. They include the first woman ever hired full-time by an American automotive company and the first African American to graduate from the Institute of Art. Over the years his students have produced billions of dollars of successful products for American industry.[272]

One major stream of graduates flowed into the automotive industry. (Today the Institute of Art is considered one of the three top schools in automotive design.) During the early years of the design program, a key figure in the success of its graduates was George Walker, who was not one of Viktor's students, but an earlier graduate of the school. Walker, a former pro football player, began his career as a fashion illustrator, turned to making advertisements for cars, and eventually moved to Detroit to be closer to the automotive industry. Walker's big break came just after World War II, when he was invited to compete with the in-house staff to produce a design for the 1949 Ford. He won the contest, and in 1955, after a few more years as a consultant, became Ford's first chief of design, a position he held until his retirement in 1961.[273]

The figure chiefly responsible for Walker's successful 1949 design for Ford was Oros, whose scheme was put into production with only slight changes. From 1946 to 1955, Oros contributed as a consultant to all Ford's cars and trucks, including the memorable Thunderbird. In 1955 he became the chief stylist at Ford. One of his triumphs was the 1964 Mustang, one of the most successful designs in automotive history. Oros served with Ford in a series of design roles until 1974. In a recent note to the school he noted: "If I had the chance to redo my career, I would want to be involved with design, repeat the Cleveland Institute of Art, and marry the same girl."[274]

The girl in question, Oros's wife, Betty Thatcher (class of 1939), also studied with Viktor. After graduation she took a job with the Hudson Motor Company, where she worked on the interior and upholstery of the 1942 and 1943 models, as well as the design of instrument panels, front ends, and other elements. When she married Joe Oros in 1943, she resigned her position at Hudson, since at that time fraternizing with staff from another company was grounds for dismissal. Her brief stint at Hudson marked a milestone, since Betty was the first woman designer ever hired to work full-time by a major American automotive company.

Still another distinguished early graduate was Theodore Ornas (class of 1939), who worked for a series of firms designing everything from alarm clocks to luxury yachts. In 1951 he became chief designer for International Harvester, where he pioneered the concept of the sport-utility vehicle in such models as the Travelall of 1952, the Lodestar medium-duty truck of 1961, and the Scout of 1962. In addition, Ornas made major innovations in the design of large trucks through the use of lightweight materials and standardized components that greatly reduced production costs.[275]

Ed Jaquet (class of 1954) created the first "image boards" to define division identities for Ford and was the first Big Three auto designer to focus

Jerry Hirshberg created Nissan's design studio in San Diego.

Hugh Greenlee (left) and Roy Hess, partners in the firm of Greenlee-Hess, designed an amazing range of products and worked with Viktor in the design program of the Cleveland Institute of Art.

on child safety. Richard Avery (class of 1958) worked in styling and design for Ford, and then moved on to become director of design for Chris Craft Boats. To his surprise, shortly after he left Ford, one of his concept designs was purchased from Ford by Nissan, and became the sporty Nissan 240Z.[276]

Jerry Hirshberg (class of 1963) worked with General Motors until 1980, when he was hired away to create a design studio for Nissan in San Diego. He has developed a series of award-winning cars, such as the Pulsar NX, the Pathfinder, the Hard-Boy pickup trucks, the J-Feri, the Bluebird, and the Quest minivan. He also designed electronic equipment, motels, yachts, and vacuum cleaners. One of the most visible figures in the design world today, he has frequently been featured in Nissan TV ads.[277] Other graduates who are currently active include Robert Barnes (class of 1968) and Bruce Young (class of 1978), who design for Ford; David Ross (class of 1984) and Pat Murray (class of 1984), who work for General Motors; and Joseph Dehner (class of 1988), who works for DaimlerChrysler.

Still another stream of graduates have focused on consumer products. Perhaps the most notable of these figures are Roy Hess (class of 1948) and Hugh Greenlee (class of 1949), who created a design partnership in 1953. The Greenlee-Hess firm was always a small one, never employing more than five people, but it produced an amazing range of products, including industrial equipment, radios, televisions, computers, hand tools, ski poles, welding equipment, boats, recreational vehicles, and consumer packaging. For 34 years they maintained a relationship with Ohio Rubber Company, which employed them to discover uses for rubber products. In 1965, three years after creating their firm, both Greenlee and Hess began teaching in the industrial design department of the Institute of Art, where they continued Viktor's tradition of combining teaching with an active career in industrial design. Over time, both Greenlee and Hess served as chairman of the department.[278]

Still more successful than Greenlee-Hess has been the design firm of Nottingham-Spirk. In 1972, John Nottingham and John Spirk turned down design offers at Chrysler and Huffy Bicycles to create their own design firm, which has since grown to a staff of more than 50. Over the years they have produced hundreds of successful products, which have completely transformed several companies. When Nottingham-Spirk started working with Little Tikes, the company made plastic bedpans for hospital use as well as a small toy line. Nottingham-Spirk recognized that the same technology could be used to create large plastic environments for children, something that had never been done before. They went on to design hundreds of products for Little Tikes, whose sales grew from $1 million to more than $500 million. In the mid 1980s Nottingham-Spirk came up with the idea of producing a molded plastic playhouse. At first the idea was rejected because "toys over $100 don't sell in the spring," but when the idea was tested it proved an instant success, and the Little Tikes Playhouse is now the best-selling house in the world. They recently created the Cozy Coupe line of juvenile vehicles, the best-selling car in the world. Other Nottingham-Spirk products that are number one in their field include the Swivel Straight Christmas Tree Stand, which will hold a Christmas tree straight in less than one minute; Spin Pop, the first product in the new category "interactive candy"; a series of household cleaning products for Dirt Devil, including the number one corded hand vacuum cleaner; and the Spin Brush toothbrush, now the best-selling toothbrush in the United States. Nottingham-Spirk has also devised product identity programs for Elmer's Glue-All and Manco "Duck" Tape®; packaging for Procter & Gamble, Nestlé, GE, Kraft-General Foods, and others; and innovative products for Newell-Rubbermaid, Anchor-Hocking Glass, Playtex, Gillette, West Bend, Sony Electronics, Picker Marconi, Diebold, Reliance Electric, and many other firms. Over the years the firm has been awarded more than 200 patents and has produced more than $10 billion in products. Several former employees have gone on to toy companies such as Mattel and Hasbro, and as a consequence the Institute currently sends more graduates into toy design than into the automotive field.[279]

The Way to Work

In 1996, in a review of an exhibition of Cleveland art, critic Steve Litt wrote that "the story of art in Cleveland hasn't always been a happy one" and that the display "arouses mixed emotions." The problem he noted was "the tension between art and commerce," which often led to an uneasy compromise. In the same review, however, Litt stated that "Schreckengost emerges as a hero of the show—a creative thinker whose work reconciles the warring sides of the city's artistic personality without compromise."[280]

Indeed, Schreckengost's career at once exemplifies and transcends the story of the Cleveland School. As has already been hinted, some of the key aspects of Viktor's career are typical of Cleveland artists, including his interest in the minor arts such as watercolor and ceramics, his links with the modernism not of Paris but of Austria and Central Europe, and the way that nearly everything he did is somehow connected with industrial processes and industrial design. Exactly what it is that so often lifts Schreckengost's work to a level above the crowd is difficult to put one's finger on, and surely varies from instance to instance, but two notable characteristics are its technical inventiveness and its lack of sentimentality.

Take the *Jazz Bowl* as just one instance. Certainly its basic technique of sgraffito is an old one, but Viktor's particular combination of sgraffito with a jazzy, somewhat Viennese poster-style of decoration, and the way he covered the whole thing with glowing Egyptian blue, was unique. Taking simple methods, almost as old as pottery itself, he came up with a look that was completely new. Moreover, the spirit of the bowl was unprecedented, a breath of fresh air in a conservative and even stodgy medium. As has already been discussed, the piece is striking for its rejection of the pieties of the Arts and Crafts movement and for its bold engagement with urban life, including issues of alcohol, race, and sexual morality. For Viktor, a key device in avoiding sentimentality has been humor, since humor invariably looks at things in more than one way and is based on our sense of a disparity between things as they should be and things as they really are. The narrative presented in the imagery of the *Jazz Bowl* is essentially a humorous one.

While much Cleveland art feels cautious, that of Schreckengost continues to engage and challenge us. In his review of the Cleveland show, Litt singled out Schreckengost's *Jazz Bowl* as an object that "rocks," that "quickens the pulse," and that "embodies the go-go energy of the jazz age and the desire to lift utilitarian objects to the level of high art."[281]

Intriguingly, in Schreckengost's career, the things that presented limitations for other Cleveland artists, such as the emphasis on minor arts, became a source of creative opportunity. For example, the minor arts allowed him to maintain a kind of playful creativity that probably would not have been possible in other media. Looking over Viktor's work, one of the most striking things that is evident is his willingness to take on any challenge, whether making a painting or monument, designing a bicycle or printing press, creating masks for a party, or decorating a drumhead. While he proved shrewd at making a good income, even in the heart of the Depression, many of his activities, such as his extensive work in stage design, seem to have been carried out for the pure fun of it.

In periods like the Italian Renaissance such versatility was taken for granted. Artists such as Leonardo da Vinci took on such projects as festival floats and party costumes with the same energy with which they painted frescos and altarpieces. Much of modern painting, sculpture, and assemblage, however, has been carried out in an atmosphere of high seriousness that precludes such playful involvement with real life. Mark Rothko, for example, backed out of a commission to make paintings for a restaurant because he insisted that his work be experienced with silent reverence, which precluded such human needs as eating or conversation. Moreover, it has been taken for granted that "real" artists do not get involved in the marketplace. Would anyone have accepted Jackson Pollock as a painter if he had also made covers for the *Saturday Evening Post*? While Viktor's career has surely been modern, it has followed an entirely different course than that of the artists who are most praised in art history books and celebrated in exhibitions. Viktor is a famous artist in the sense that nearly everyone alive is familiar with something that he did, but his name is unfamiliar outside a small circle, and the overall shape of his career is virtually unknown.

Singling out the most notable traits of Schreckengost's work is curiously difficult, for one of the ongoing themes of his career is his incredible versatility, his ability to break through the boundaries of one field into another. His work with stage lighting made him think differently about the design of refrigerators; his sculpture in clay made him give a vitality and sensuality to pedal car design; his skill as a cartoonist made him realize how to make monumental sculpture that would read well from a distance. Nonetheless, it seems worth attempting to summarize some key aspects of Viktor's work.

The last major surviving figure from what might be termed the "first phase" of American industrial design, Viktor has been actively engaged in every stage of its development. During his lifetime, industrial design has grown from zero to a major factor in the world economy, and nearly every item of daily life has taken on a new form, material, and method of manufacture. Trained in Vienna under the shadow of Josef Hoffmann, Viktor served on committees and worked alongside the founding figures of modern industrial design, including Raymond Loewy, Norman Bel Geddes, Donald Deskey, and Walter Dorwin Teague. Along with these figures, he played a major role in creating the profession of industrial design as we know it today. Through his students at the Cleveland Institute of Art he has helped reshape the world in which we live. Tracing Viktor's life serves well as a vehicle for tracing one of the most significant changes in human history.

As the son of a potter, Viktor grew up with clay. He was certainly the most versatile, and in many ways the most interesting and significant American artist in clay of the early 20th century. He created the first modern mass-produced American dinnerware, Americana of 1933–34. He designed the *Jazz Bowl*, a masterpiece of American art deco, in 1931 for Eleanor Roosevelt. He was the leader of the first significant school of ceramic sculpture in America and developed a style that brought out the unique capabilities of clay as opposed to other mediums such as stone or bronze. Some of his pieces, such as *Apocalypse '42,* look funky and startling even today. In 1946, in his slab forms, Viktor was the first potter to break away from wheel-thrown vessels and consider vessel forms as works of pure sculpture. Viktor's monumental sculptures for Lakewood High School and the Cleveland zoo were the most ambitious examples of architectural terracotta in America in the 1950s. Over the course of his career, Viktor has worked with turned, cast, carved, and molded forms, often exploiting the technical qualities of clay in untried ways.

Although particularly gifted in clay, Viktor developed the conceptual skills to design in any medium, from light to steel. He proved enormously successful in creating commercially successful products in the fiercely competitive world of industrial design. In an interview of 1949, Viktor declared that industrial design provided the sculptor with an "unlimited field," asserting: "Subject matter really makes no difference whatever. You apply the same basic principles in the shaping of a figure as in the designing of some industrial object."[282] One of his first designs, the blunt-nosed cab-over-engine truck, has been hailed as "the single greatest innovation in truck design." In addition, over the course of his career Viktor designed bicycles, as well as children's pedal cars, lawn furniture, lawn mowers (including the first golf-cart lawn mowers), flashlights, streetlights, and an array of other products. Perhaps his most beautiful designs are his bicycles, in which he progressed from the motorcycle look of the 1930s to space-age streamlining. This style of design employed new technical improvements to pare down the bicycle frame to unprecedented lightness and visual grace.

Viktor's industrial designs are invariably beautiful in formal terms. Indeed, in several instances, such as his Americana and Manhattan dinnerware, this purity of form was his chief goal. But this formal beauty is only one part of a clarity of thinking about form that runs much deeper. For example, Viktor was always extremely skillful in devising ways to fabricate a better product more cheaply. His Champion pedal car of 1938, for example, was made by stamping out the chassis of the car in a single piece, rather than welding it to a frame. Moreover, by adding units to front or back it could easily be transformed into another sort of vehicle, such as a fire engine or a dump truck. What is more, the streamlined look of the car made it more exciting visually than those of the competition. In bicycles Viktor was the first to develop a method to weld the whole frame in a single step, using a hydrogen brazing process. Murray's bicycle frames were so much cheaper to produce that for a time the company was selling bicycle frames to Schwinn, its main rival.

Viktor's enduring success in design, however, was based largely on something more subtle and psychological—his grasp of what he liked to term "human factors," a concept that really has two parts.

In the first place, Viktor was a pioneer in the field now called "ergonomics," that is, in making machines that fit the body, and serve the psychological needs, of the operator. His printing presses, for example, introduced a variety of features we now take for granted that improved comfort and safety, such as enclosing the moving parts and devising understandable operating mechanisms, often through the use of electronic controls. His power mowers were the first in the industry in which one's toes were well protected from the mower blade.

In the second place, Viktor was a genius at thinking up what he termed "sales points," features that made his product either better or more visually exciting than that of his rival. He had a particularly good grasp of the psychology of children. His bicycles always had better headlights, louder horns, and brighter and more exciting colors than those of the competition. Sometimes in looking at his designs you can almost hear a child saying, "Dad, I want this one."

Viktor's interest in such features often led him to move outside the sort of reductive, formal design associated with the Bauhaus and the Museum of Modern Art, even to stretch the limits of good taste. Invariably it resulted in exciting and commercially successful products.

While there are some other rivals for this title, Viktor founded what many consider the first modern program of industrial design in the United States at the Cleveland Institute of Art. His contribution was to take many of the modern approaches toward design pioneered in Vienna and at the Bauhaus and transform them to suit the realities of American business and American popular culture. His students have played a major role in industrial design, particularly in the toy and automotive industries, and have produced literally billions of dollars of successful products. Probably every adult alive in the United States has handled products designed by Viktor or one of his students.

Viktor has never exactly retired. When he was hired by the Institute of Art in 1930 at the age of 25, he was the youngest teacher in the history of the school. Now 94, he still teaches part time. Last time I visited him the school had just mailed him a contract for next year. Back problems and a ruptured disc forced Viktor to give up ceramic sculpture in the early 1970s, but he continues to paint and keeps up a hectic schedule of social engagements and lectures.[283]

As he nears the century mark, Viktor can observe that several of his early designs have become classics. His most famous single work remains the *Jazz Bowl*. Cowan Pottery produced only a handful of them, and starting in the 1970s they began to show up at auction, fetching higher and higher prices each time they appeared. First one sold for $10,000, then $20,000, then $50,000. Major museums started to acquire them. The Fogg Art Museum at Harvard featured their Schreckengost bowl on a note card, while the High Museum of Art in Atlanta featured theirs on a large color poster. A *Jazz Bowl* now costs more than $100,000, and the price is rising.

To Viktor, however, these museum pieces and "one-off designs" represent only half the story. He has always loved to balance such museum pieces with industrial design for mass production to an audience of thousands or even millions. "I get a kick out of seeing the influence of my toys on kids growing up. I'm sure they had more of an effect, much more, than going to the museum once a year."[284] He recalls with pleasure one morning when he drove to work and between his home and the art school counted 32 things he had designed—including exhaust fans, lawn mowers, tractors, trucks, children's toys, and lighting fixtures for the streetlights. "It was just as exciting to me," he notes, "as going to the art museum and seeing one of my paintings."[285]

Industrial design requires teamwork and persuasion. In this photograph of a design conference at Murray Ohio in about 1939, Viktor (foreground) goes over every detail with salesmen, engineers, and executives.

Notes

1. Milton Wider, "Sketches a la Noah: Schreckengost, Rained In, Caricatures His Plight," *Cleveland Press* (23 September 1939), p. 5; see also Eleanor Clarage, "Main Street," *Plain Dealer* (12 September 1939).

2. Dorothy Grafly, "Viktor Schreckengost: Sculptor of Form in Space," *American Artist* (May 1949), p. 54.

3. Ibid.

4. Louise Bruner, art critic for the *Cleveland News,* commented of these aerial views: "There have been airplane views of the earth before, but almost always the artist adds an obvious cloud to confirm his point of observation, just as others add an umbrella to show it's raining. Schreckengost disregards such props and substitutes such scientifically accurate reporting that a pilot can look at one of his water colors and describe the weather and estimate the elevation." See Louise Bruner, "Schreckengost Succeeds in New Artistic Medium," *Cleveland News* (24 January 1948). Quote taken from Grafly "Viktor Schreckengost," p. 54.

5. Grafly, "Viktor Schreckengost," p. 54.

6. Ibid.

7. Ibid.

8. Polly Parson, "Young Art Patrons Acquire May Show Objects," *Cleveland News* (7 June 1948), p. 14.

9. Glenn C. Pullen, "Wilder Farce Lampooned at Eldred Hall," *Plain Dealer* (31 October 1940).

10. William McDermott, "*Murder in the Cathedral* Presented by University Players at Eldred Hall," *Plain Dealer* (18 October, 1939), p. 18.

11. Jack Warfel, "Eldred Theater Opened at Reserve," *Cleveland Press* (18 January 1939)

12. Ibid.

13. From a playbill for the Eldred Theater, 5–9 November 1941 (Schreckengost scrapbook).

14. William F. McDermott, "Saroyan's *Jim Dandy* Has Premier at Eldred Hall and Audience Is Still Wondering," *Plain Dealer* (6 November 1941); Arthur Spaeth, "The Play," *Cleveland News* (6 November 1941).

15. "Divorce and Million Won by Mrs. Millikin," *Plain Dealer* (4 February 1952); "Actress's Big Exit Missed by Press," *Plain Dealer* (5 February 1952).

16. William F. McDermott, "Marta Abba Returns to Stage in Fine Performance of Sardou's *Divorcons*," *Plain Dealer* (21 August 1941), p. 15.

17. Albert E. Prudence, "Marta Abba Excellent in French Comedy," *Cleveland Press* (21 August 1941), p. 12.

18. Dorothy Grafly, "Viktor Schreckengost," *American Artist* (May 1949), p. 53.

19. Unrecorded interview with Viktor Schreckengost (21 March 2000).

20. According to an e-mail message from Patricia Leathem (30 November 1999), Viktor's stage work with Barclay Leathem ended when Henry Kurth came to the Eldred Theater and became responsible for creating the sets.

21. Grafly, "Viktor Schreckengost," p. 53.

22. Ibid., pp. 51, 53.

23. "Akron's 'Rubber Ball' to Play Up Synthetic Fabrics and Materials," *New York Daily News Record* (21 November 1939), reprinted from *Akron Beacon Journal* (?) (17 November 1939).

24. See *Akron Beacon Journal* (18 November 1939).

25. See "Akron's 'Rubber Ball' to Play Up Synthetic Fabrics and Materials."

26. From 1937 to 1939, Viktor won a first prize at the May Show every year, as well as two special awards. In addition, in 1938 he won first prize in sculpture at the Ceramic National in Syracuse; in 1939 he won the Charles Fergus Binns Medal from Alfred University for "outstanding contribution to the ceramic field"; and in 1940 he won a certificate of honor from the Philadelphia Art Alliance for the "finest piece of sculpture" in an exhibition at the Philadelphia Museum.

27. Agnes Helmquist, "Trio Blazes Trail in New Art Here," *Cleveland News* (24 May 1932).

28. Ross Anderson and Barbara Perry, *The Diversions of Keramos, American Clay Sculpture 1925–50* (Syracuse: Everson Museum of Art, 1983), pp. 74–80; interview with Aitken's wife, Irene (21 February 2000).

29. See Anderson and Perry, *Diversions of Keramos,* pp. 50–72; *Painted Mask* (Cleveland Museum of Art) is reproduced on p. 65.

30. The piece was featured in *House Beautiful* with a caption noting: "Simple though this form of pottery is in theory, its actual difficulty is in the very sureness and swiftness of line necessary to its design. Its technique defies any but the artist. The mark once made cannot be changed. Viktor Schreckengost, a new name in American ceramics, and an artist whose signed work made its first appearance at a recent exhibition, uses this ceramic method with complete assurance.... He is very young yet ... the quality of his work already placed him in the artist-potter group. It is so promising now that one may look for a deeper and richer expression as he grows in his own experience." *See House Beautiful* (November 1932), p. 312.

Similarly, Milton S. Fox singled out the plate for special praise in "May Show Exhibition Reveals Unusual Work" (unidentified Cleveland newspaper, c. May 1932, Schreckengost scrapbook), characterizing Viktor as "a brilliant designer" and noting: "His pieces have that smartness which one associates with extremely 'modern' interior decoration. One would hardly expect to see such vigor and boldness of attack in pottery."

31. For his giraffes (mother and baby), he used a slightly different technique but again allowed the natural clay to show through. He made the animals out of reddish clay and, while the clay was moist, took a small, pointed wooden tool and carved in the pattern of the hide. The two creatures were then fired in the kiln to 1600° F. He next "painted" the feet and outlines around the spots with a hard white glaze made of tin. Then he fired the piece, with its added white glazes, a second time. While in one instance he used an engobe and in the other a tin glaze, both share the principle of creating the pattern by allowing the color of the clay to show through. Viktor's technique for the giraffes was described in detail in an article addressed to children. See Katherine Gibson Wicks, "How Clay Figures Are Made," *Cleveland Press* (11 January 1939).

As early as 1938 Ray Bruner commented on Viktor's use of natural clay, noting: "In making his ceramics, he tried to let the material itself give the proper color and texture without adding too much to obscure it. He believes that if something is made of even a cheap pine board the wood itself should not be hidden. If something is made of metal, the full quality of the metal should be revealed." See Ray Bruner, "Art," *Cleveland Press* (2 July 1938). As another critic noted when he exhibited his group of zebras: "We are aware of the material from which the zebras are modeled; for the craftsman has not tried to conceal its native textural quality, nor has he tried to achieve a 'finished effect.'" (Unidentified newspaper clipping, Schreckengost scrapbook.)

One of Viktor's favorite games with children is to try to draw an animal in the simplest possible manner, often with just a single line. For example: "Start with a squiggly line and see how quickly they can guess what animal it is. Of course it's a pig with a little wiggle of a tail. That's all you need." (Undated interview.) His animals in clay often play with these distinctive qualities and similarly try to evoke them in the simplest possible manner.

32. Vally Wieselthier, "Ceramics," *Design* 21 (November 1929), p. 101.

33. See Cornelia Curtiss, "Many Roles of an Artist's Wife," *Cleveland News* (29 March 1948).

34. Barbara Perry, ed., *American Ceramics: The Collection of Everson Museum of Art* (New York: Rizzoli, 1989), p. 184.

35. Interview #7, p. 15.

36. During Viktor's childhood in Sebring, the Ku Klux Klan was an active presence, and photographs exist of Klan members burning crosses just outside of town. When he was a child, Viktor witnessed a Klanner in a white sheet blowing a bugle from the tallest building downtown, to summon a gathering of the Klan. Viktor's parents, however, would have nothing to do with these gatherings, and to a child the faceless costumes seemed immensely sinister.

37. "In Pygmies' Trap, Saved by Boots," *Plain Dealer* (18 September 1928).

38. Ibid.

39. For a biography of Travis, see William H. Robinson and David Steinberg, *Transformations in Cleveland Art 1796–1946* (Cleveland Museum of Art, 1996), p. 239. Interview #1, pp. 12–13; Interview #4, p. 9.

40. When the Austrian poster designer Josef Binder came to Cleveland, he was fascinated by the African-American waitresses at Stouffer's restaurant and, with Viktor's help, hired one of them to model for him.

41. In 1931 the *Decorative Arts Yearbook* of the Studio Ltd., London, reproduced two of Viktor's thrown heads from Vienna, *Chinese Head* [69] and another head, now lost, as well as a jackass in bright red pottery and the piece called *Nigger Harmonies* (later retitled *Harlem Melodies* [76]). See Richard J. Powell, *The Blues Aesthetic: Black Culture and Modernism* (Washington, D.C.: Washington Project for the Arts, 1989). According to an article in the *Cleveland Press* (19 March 1932): "His Negro dancers, and his trio, bring a sharply Viennese note to Cleveland ceramic sculpture."

42. Bessie Smith, quoted in Paul Oliver, *Screening the Blues: Aspects of the Blues Tradition* (London: Cassell & Company, 1968), p. 66.

43. The piece was technically ingenious. Since it pushed the size limits of Viktor's kiln, he made it in two sections, both as large as possible, one for the flames and the other for the figures. "It wasn't to belittle that I used the brass halos," Viktor commented, "I couldn't afford gold." Marlene S. Hamann, "The Ceramic Sculptures of Viktor Schreckengost," master's thesis (Syracuse University, 1983), p. 37.

44. On 13 February 1938 Viktor took part in the *African Art Exhibit* with Paul Travis and Daniel Bozo. The Antioch Baptist Church Young People's Chorus sang at the opening.

45. In "Metropolitan Buys Figure" (7 November 1942), the *Cleveland Press* reported that the Metropolitan Museum had purchased Viktor's group *Shadrach, Mesach, and Abed Nego*. In reviews of the 1930s, Viktor's renderings of African-American themes were consistently praised and were viewed as good-humored in their approach. In 1939 the *Bulletin of the Cleveland Museum of Art* noted: "Viktor Schreckengost's five first-prize pieces in CERAMIC SCULPTURE show real power, whimsical humor and rare distinction in the choice and successful use of suitable glazes." It then praised *Smoked Ham* in which "six little pickaninnies enjoy a ride on the broad back of a magnificent porker." See CMA *Bulletin* 26 (1939), pp. 61–62.

According to W. H. Cunningham in the *Cleveland News,* "Schreckengost is a good cure for anyone who attends the show under the misapprehension that the art there must be observed in high-brow seriousness. Probably the two best examples of his humor are the pieces *Smoked Ham,* a tremendous pig with six pickaninnies riding on its back, and *Androcles and the Lion,* in which the lion is about as fierce as Ferdinand the Bull." At the May Show in 1938, after Viktor won the top award in ceramic sculpture, William Milliken noted: "He has never been more delightful than in the gay humor of *Black Sheep* or in the sculptural dignity of *The Creatures God Forgot.*" See CMA *Bulletin* 25 (1938), p. 81. Grace V. Kelly declared of the 1939 May Show: "Ceramic sculpture, always a class of compelling interest in the May show, holds to its well-earned reputation this year.... This is particularly true in the case of Viktor Schreckengost, whose *Smoked Ham, Naama, Androcles, Keramos,* and *Mother Earth* are rollicking delights, and always the center of crowds who respond to their whimsicality and imagination, as well as to those who understand their merits as sculpture and the excellent quality of their glazes." See "Young Artists Swell Ranks of Water Color Exhibitors at Museum's May Show," *Plain Dealer* (14 May 1939), p. 16-B. In 1946, Grace V. Kelly noted that while the sculpture section was smaller than usual, the ceramic sculpture was up to par, and went on to praise "a Negro man and woman delightfully stylized, petitioning, 'Oh Lord, Please Take Away the Darkness.'" See Grace V. Kelly, "Sculpture Shows Decline, but Ceramics and Pottery Hold Up Well in May Show," *Plain Dealer* (23 May 1943), section D.

Schreckengost's *Birth of Boogie Woogie* was shown at the *11th National Exhibition of Ceramics* in Syracuse in November 1946. See Ben Wolf, "American Ceramists Display Their Craft at Syracuse Museum," *Art Digest* 21 (15 November 1946), p. 31.

46. Interview #8, p. 22.

47. Ibid.

48. "With World War II, the golden age of ceramic sculpture in Cleveland came to an end almost as quickly as it had risen." See James Stubblebine and Martin Eidelberg, "Viktor Schreckengost and the Cleveland School," *Craft Horizons* 35 (June 1975), p. 53.

49. Grafly, "Viktor Schreckengost," pp. 50–51.

50. "For the Ceramist, a New Technique," *Craft Horizons* 8 (August 1947), pp. 58, 59.

51. Herman Millman, "New Pottery Technique Developed by Schreckengost," *Cleveland Press Magazine* (31 May 1947). Despite the controversy they stirred, a number of the hewn forms won awards. The first was bestowed by the noted Japanese-American painter Yasuo Kuniyoshi, who served as judge of a show at the Ten-Thirty Gallery in Cleveland in September 1948. He awarded Viktor the first prize of $50 in ceramics for *Samara,* a bowl that was hewn rather than turned. Two years later, in 1950, Viktor won the $100 pottery prize at the 15th National Ceramics Exhibition in Syracuse for *Oblongata* [88] and *Sappan* [83]. Around the same time, one of Viktor's hewn form pieces, *Cassia,* was acquired by the Walker Art Center in Minneapolis.

52. Reproduced in *Akron Art Institute Bulletin* (November 1931); *American Magazine of Art* (November 1931); *Arts and Decoration* (November 1931); *Bystander* (12 December 1931); *Creative Art* (December 1931); *Crockery and Glass Journal* (November 1931); *Design* (December 1931).

53. See Georges-Marie Haardt, *La Croisier Noire* (Paris: Librarie Plan, 1927); reproduced in Richard J. Powell and David A. Baily, *Rhapsodies in Black: Art of the Harlem Renaissance* (London/Berkeley: Hayward Gallery/University of California Press, 1997), p. 26.

54. *Jeddu* [95] was reproduced in the *Cleveland Bystander* (9 May 1931), *Cleveland Press* (4 July 1931), *Chicago American* (1 November 1933), and *American Magazine of Art* (September 1931), p. 202. Robert B. Harshe, the director of the Art Institute of Chicago, invited Viktor to show it in its *Forty-fifth Annual Exhibition of Painting and Sculpture*, 27 October–11 December 1932, at the Art Institute. Viewers of the time sensed something tragic in Schreckengost's piece. Walter R. Agard, for example, stated: "His Negress is a strong face, suavely modeled, with just enough stylization to save it from too great naturalism. The linear rhythm is fluid; the balance of headdress and base is finely planned; and the tragic longing on the face is portrayed with sensitiveness and power." See Walter R. Agar, "Cleveland's Artistic Appreciation of Africa," *American Magazine of Art* 23 (September 1931), p. 203.

55. In 1934 Viktor was invited to show *Mangbettu Child* [96] at the *Century of Progress Exposition* in Chicago. At the time the honor was announced the piece was on view at the Pennsylvania Academy of the Fine Arts. "Considering the thousands of artists in the United States, it is a great honor to the few selected and invited to show their works. Selections were made without knowledge of any of the artists that they were being considered. The invitation was a pleasant surprise to Schreckengost." See "To Exhibit Art Work in World's Fair: Viktor Schreckengost Among Few Artists Given Show Space," *Alliance* (Ohio) *Review* (5 February 1934).

56. While mostly white porcelain, they were painted with colorful bands, using a new kind of paint for porcelain that had just been developed by DuPont. In the end, Viktor found the process of creating cast sculpture constrained the freedom of his work. Consequently, he preferred directly modeled figures in clay. As he later stated: "But the more I worked in clay with bronze in view, the more I realized how much spontaneity was lost between the two. As a sculptor I wanted materials that could be worked directly in permanent form." See Grafly, "Viktor Schreckengost," p. 50.

57. "Sebring Potters Honor Memory of Founder of City and Many Potteries," *Potter's Herald* (East Liverpool, Ohio) (2 June 1938).

58. Grace V. Kelly, "Sculptor Finishes Trophy; Federal Project, Student Exhibition Opens This Week," *Plain Dealer* (26 February 1939), Women's Magazine and Amusement section. See also "Official Program, 11th Annual Miami All-American Air Maneuvers," 6–8 January, Miami, Florida (Schreckengost scrapbook); *Christian Science Monitor* (10 January 1941).

59. Ibid.

60. Christina Corsglia, "Viktor Schreckengost's 'Four Elements' for the 1939 World's Fair," *Ars Ceramica*, no. 6 (1989), pp. 57–65.

61. Earth: a body of Indiana black-bird clay with a dark brown engobe over it. Water: red clay with a soft green engobe face and touches of red, white, brown, and green engobe. Air: red clay with a white engobe face and touches of red, white, brown, and green engobe. Fire: a natural red clay with touches of white, brown, and soft-green engobe in the head and eyelids.

The ornament of each head was decorated with clear glaze and a turquoise glaze made of white clay with copper oxide. Because of the rich color of the clay, the transparent glaze, when applied to areas without engobe, fired to a bright red.

62. Interview #8, p. 34; Interview #5, p. 5. An interesting side benefit of the New York World's Fair was that Viktor got to know Norman Bel Geddes, who called him up asking for students who could help with the fabrication of his *Futurama* exhibition for the General Motors Highways and Horizons Building. It included a continuous train of linked chairs that took pairs of visitors on a 16-minute tour around the periphery of a two-level diorama portraying the world of the future. The diorama featured a million model trees and a half-million scaled buildings that had been attached to a plaster landscape nearly an acre in size. Some 50,000 miniature teardrop autos and streamlined motor coaches and trucks moved along the superhighways.

Viktor's friend from Sebring and art school classmate Charles Murphy also did notable work connected with the 1939 World's Fair. Perhaps the most notable work of his career was a souvenir plate of the 1939 World's Fair that he designed for Homer Laughlin.

63. Interview #2, p. 16; "Monument Near Stable Is Honor to Hugh O'Neill," *Plain Dealer* (22 October 1949).

64. According to Melvin Rose at Rose Ironworks, the project was completed in June 1955. The billing date was 17 November 1955. The sculpture was originally on the exterior of the building and was later moved inside. It is currently in storage.

65. Information from Viktor Schreckengost and letter from William G. Freytag, senior designer, Marathon Oil Company (4 August 1998).

66. Curtiss, "Many Roles of an Artist's Wife," reported: "A favorite pastime of the couple is to plan and replan the house they expect to build some day on a lot they bought just before the war."

67. "The Bird Building at The Cleveland Zoological Park," *Explorer: Cleveland Museum of Natural History* 2 (March, 1952), p. 94.

68. Nancy McCrosky, "Viktor Schreckengost's Architectural Terra Cotta," *Ceramics Monthly* (October 1997), p. 68. The passenger pigeon became extinct in 1914.

69. Doris Milavec, "New Zoo Building Gets Plaques of Extinct Birds," *Cleveland News* (18 May 1950); Kathleen Colan, "Zoo Art Worth a Look!," *Zoo News*, Cleveland Zoological Society (Summer/Fall 1993), p. 12.

70. Interview #8, p. 15.

71. Louise Bruner, "Schreckengost Designs Murals for Exterior of New Zoo Building," *Cleveland News* (25 February 1950).

72. McCrosky, "Viktor Schreckengost's Architectural Terra Cotta," p. 67.

73. "Building for Birds," *Newsweek* (12 November 1951), p. 56.

74. Doris E. Brown, "Brilliantly-Colored Ceramic Panels of Birds Completed for Midwest Zoo by County Firm," *Sunday Times* (New Brunswick, New Jersey) (no date).

75. "Building for Birds," p. 56. Viktor worked on this project for three years, from 1947 to 1950.

76. Viktor had a portfolio of early drawings for the sculpture, which explore several alternative poses and manners of treatment. He gave the drawings for the final design to Hays and they have since disappeared.

77. McCrosky, "Viktor Schreckengost's Architectural Terra Cotta," p. 68.

78. Colan, "Zoo Art Worth a Look!" p. 13.

79. McCrosky, "Viktor Schreckengost's Architectural Terra Cotta," p. 68.

80. *18th Ceramic National Exhibition* (Syracuse: Syracuse Museum of Fine Arts, 1954), unpaginated; Susan Tunick, *Terra-Cotta Skyline* (New York: Princeton Architectural Press, 1997), p. 120. Viktor's bird tower has also been featured in John B. Kenny, *Ceramic Design* (Philadelphia: Chilton Books, 1963), p. 294 (text) and 244 (illustration). His *Pachyderms* and *Early Settler* are reproduced and discussed in Richard N. Campen, *Outdoor Sculpture in Ohio* (Chagrin Falls, Ohio: West Summit Press, 1980), pp. 66, 67.

81. McCrosky, "Viktor Schreckengost's Architectural Terra Cotta," p. 68 (order of sentences shifted); Interview #7, p. 6.

82. Interview #2, p. 1; Interview #8, p. 18.

83. Interview #2, pp. 4–5, and information from labeled photographs, collection of Viktor Schreckengost.

84. Ibid., p. 2.

85. Interview #8, pp. 18–19.

86. Interview #2, p. 3.

87. Interview #8, p. 19. Viktor's terrain maps are mentioned in a *New Yorker* article on de Florez: "In addition, he has devised a novel system of taking aerial photographs, perhaps of an area to be invaded, and then making accurate models of the terrain from the pictures. The process is still mostly secret. It is expected to solve some of the problems of making safe landings with invasion craft." See Robert Lewis Taylor, "Profiles: Captain Among the Synthetics" (part two), *New Yorker* (18 November 1944), p. 41.

88. Richard Guy Wilson, "The Industrialist as Artist," in Angela Schönberger, ed., *Raymond Loewy* (Munich: Prestel, 1990), p. 72.

89. Jeffrey L. Meiklie, "From Celebrity to Anonymity," in ibid. p. 52.

90. Arthur J. Pulos, "Nothing Succeeds Like Success," in ibid., p. 75.

91. "If I happened to do a design for a stove," he said, "another manufacturer would be interested and call me in to do something quite different. So I had to learn how to adapt form to basic function. One day I may be designing a delicate handle for a fragile tea set; the next I'll be up on a scaffold working on something several feet long." See Grafly, "Viktor Schreckengost," p. 51.

92. Jane Dwyre Garton, *Pedal Cars: Chasing the Kidillac* (Atglen, Pennsylvania: Schiffer Publishing, 1999), p. 98.

93. "Youthful Cleveland Designer Inherited His Taste for Art," *Cleveland News* (2 November 1931); Interview #2, p. 11.

94. *U.S. Industrial Design, 1949–50* (New York: Studio Publications, 1949), p. 30.

95. Interview with Viktor Schreckengost for PBS documentary (12 July 2000).

96. Letter from Harriet Keyes to Viktor Schreckengost (26 July 2000), citing bicycle number 50 million made by Murray Ohio, which was given to her husband by the employees of the company.

97. Undated letter from William M. Hannon, chairman and CEO (retired) of the Murray Ohio Manufacturing Company, nominating Viktor for the National Medal of Arts.

98. For Cowan Pottery, see Mark Bassett and Victoria Naumann, *Cowan Pottery and the Cleveland School* (Atglen, Pennsylvania: Schiffer Publishing, 1997); Tim and Jamie Saloff, *The Collector's Encyclopedia of Cowan Pottery* (Paducah, Kentucky: Collectors Books, 1994).

99. Bassett and Naumann, *Cowan Pottery and the Cleveland School*, pp. 69–87.

100. Henry Hawley, "Cowan Pottery at the Cleveland Museum of Art," *CMA Bulletin* 76 (1989), pp. 255–57.

101. Interview #5, p. 8.

102. Bassett and Naumann, *Cowan Pottery and the Cleveland School*, p. 186.

103. Schreckengost's sports plates were praised as "smart"; see *Design* (January 1932), p. 207. The plates were also featured in *Ceramic Age* (November 1931), p. 251. In 1933, when Cowan joined Onandaga Pottery in Syracuse, he brought some of the Cowan Pottery molds with him and made samples of some of the various designs, including Viktor's sports plates. The sports plates, however, were never approved for production. It is not difficult to distinguish the two editions of the sports plates because the original Cowan edition was decorated in a range of cheerful colors whereas the trials produced at Syracuse were in monochrome.

104. "Under-glaze crayon, a totally new idea, was first used at Cowan Potteries, Rocky River, just a few miles west of Cleveland." See "Ceramic Sculpture, Pottery and Batik Wall Hangings by Viktor Schreckengost, Artist, and Potter Superlative, November 1 to November 30," *Akron Art Institute Bulletin* (November 1931).

105. Bassett and Naumann, *Cowan Pottery and the Cleveland School*, p. 209.

106. Unfortunately, when Cowan Pottery tried to produce another speckled batch, the ware emerged from the kiln completely smooth and unblemished. It took further experiments to establish that the crystalline brown sections only appeared when the atmosphere of the kiln was saturated with uranium in its gaseous form. By thoroughly spraying the interior surfaces of the saggers they could consistently achieve a mottled effect.

107. Viktor also tried painting a plate with reddish brown engobe and then glazing it with clear crackle. This procedure was not very satisfactory, however, since the colored slip was difficult to control.

108. Bassett and Naumann, *Cowan Pottery and the Cleveland School*, p.186.

109. Ibid.

110. Ibid., p. 189.

111. Ibid., p. 100.

112. Bassett and Naumann shape X-38.

113. Bassett and Naumann, *Cowan Pottery and the Cleveland School*, p.191.

114. The 1931 Cowan catalogue (copy in the Rocky River Public Library) reproduces the *Cocktails and Cigarettes* bowl [134] on p. 2, noting that it was available in Egyptian blue, melon green, and black. A variety of drypoint pieces appear on p. 3, including *Danse Moderne* [39], all of which could be ordered in "dark blue, green, or yellow." The yellow was guava yellow, according to the Index and Quick Reference Price List (pp. 23–24). It should be noted that the Cowan catalogue was not entirely accurate, since when Viktor sold his *Cocktails and Cigarettes* bowl, he agreed not to mass produce it. But the catalogue does suggest that Viktor's punch bowls and other forms were available in a variety of colors.

115. See "Youthful Cleveland Designer Inherited His Taste for Art"; *Plain Dealer* (7 January 1934); "Schreckengost Is New Designer for Limoges," *Crockery and Glass Journal* (December 1933).

116. By any reckoning, the number of *Jazz Bowls* that can now be located is much smaller than the number that were made. Examples of the first version exist at the Museum of Fine Arts, Boston; Cooper-Hewitt National Museum of Design, Smithsonian Institution, New York; High Museum of Art, Atlanta; and the Rowfant Club, Cleveland. Those made for Eleanor Roosevelt have disappeared and cannot be found at the White House, the Governor's Mansion in Albany, or Hyde Park. Albert Wasserman, Cleveland, owns a *Jazz Bowl* with a flared rim; there is one in a private collection in Rochester, New York; a third, with a yellow glaze, is owned by Don H. Clung, Cleveland. Examples of the *Poor Man's Bowl* in turquoise are owned by the Harvard University Art Museums, John Axelrod, Boston, and Jerry Maschino, Incline Village, Nevada. Examples in green are owned by Albert Wasserman, Cleveland, and Barbara Wamelink, Cleveland.

117. Hamann, "Ceramic Sculptures of Viktor Schreckengost," p. 18.

118. Richard Guy Wilson, Dianne H. Pilgrim, and Dikran Tashjian, *The Machine Age in America, 1918–1941* (New York: Harry N. Abrams, 1986), pp. 290–91; Bassett and Naumann, *Cowan Pottery and the Cleveland School*, p. 191.

119. See note 40; interview #4, pp. 9–10.

120. In fact, Christie's in London once labeled a *Jazz Bowl* as Viennese until set straight by Henry Hawley, the curator of decorative arts at the Cleveland Museum of Art. ("They weren't very pleased," Hawley recalls, "when I told them it was made in Cleveland.")

121. Karen Lucic, "Seeing Through Surfaces: American Craft as Material Culture," in *Craft in the Machine Age: The History of Twentieth-Century American Craft, 1920–1945*, ed. Janet Kardon (New York: Harry N. Abrams, 1995), p. 56.

122. The generational progression exhibited here in the Mather line, from the soul-searching denial of material things exhibited by the legendary exemplar of the Puritan conscience, Cotton Mather, to the capitalist wealth of his descendants, and finally to the seemingly extravagant acquisition of this punch bowl exalting cocktails and cigarettes, would make an interesting essay—or even a book—just in itself. In this case the progression has an added element of poignancy and psychological and moral interest, since Livingston Mather's much-loved wife was dying of cancer when he purchased the bowl, and he was probably not in a party-going mood. From the circumstances it appears that he purchased the object not simply because it was beautiful, but out of loyalty to the museum and to the cause of Cleveland art.

123. In 1931 Viktor also used the same shape he had employed for the large *Jazz Bowl* for a unique painted piece, a punch bowl and 12 service plates with fox hunt motifs painted by hand in underglaze colors [37]. Viktor comments: "The interesting bit about it is that you have to drink all the booze to find the fox—it's down in the bottom of the bowl." Interview #1, p. 4.

124. "Fine Craftsmanship," *London Studio* (February 1933), p. 131.

125. Over the course of his career, he designed for Cowan Pottery in Rocky River, Ohio, the American Limoges China Company in Sebring, the Atlas Globe China Company in Cambridge, Ohio, Onandaga Pottery in Syracuse, and the Salem China Company in Salem, Ohio. In addition, he designed stove radiants for the Gem Clay Forming Company in Sebring and a variety of tableware, ashtrays, and accessories for Louis Rorimer, whose decorating firm outfitted the Statler Hotels. He also designed stoves and cookware for the American Stove Company in Cleveland. Finally, as a curious outgrowth of his work with lighting systems, he designed decorative glassware for Verlys of America, based in New York, owned by the same holding company that owned Holophane of New York, a maker of prismatic lighting fixtures.

126. Garth Clark, "A Survey of Ceramic Art and Design, 1919–1939," in Karen McCready, *Art Deco and Modernist Ceramics* (London: Thames and Hudson, 1995), p. 25. This list was derived from Martin Eidelberg et al., *Eva Zeisel: Designer for Industry* (Montreal: Le Chateau Dufresne, 1984), p. 32; which in turn is derived from Helen Stiles, *Pottery in the United States* (New York: E.P. Dutton & Co., 1941), pp. 77–80, 82–83.

127. My thanks to Richard Fiorelli, who recorded and transcribed Viktor's comments during his dinnerware class, in seven sessions held in 1996.

128. Grace V. Kelly, "New American Limoges China Design by Schreckengost Is Exhibited at Coulter Gallery," *Plain Dealer* (c. spring 1935), p. 18 (Schreckengost scrapbook).

129. "Although each detail can be a pure beautiful form in itself, the whole may be held together by a graceful sweep of line or a fundamental relationship of parts. For instance in a teapot we should not be conscious of the body, spout, handle, lid and knob as separate units. A true test of this simplicity of form is to see this piece in the clay state, where not even the quality of the glaze enhances it.... Decoration should emphasize the form, not attempt to disguise it.... When it comes to decorating, it is not a matter of camouflaging. The form or mass should not be distorted, but the decoration should be used to enrich and accent, or give a textural quality to the surface." Viktor Schreckengost, "The Designer Must Know Modern's Possibilities and Limitations," *Crockery and Glass Journal* 114 (June 1934), pp. 12, 24, 26.

130. Viktor's designs, however, were patented under Cowan's name because Viktor was not an employee of the company.

131. "If you were serving in a restaurant where you wanted them to eat, drink, and get out, you opened up the cup so that the heat would leave immediately. If it was a nice place to spend the evening after dinner you made a very small cup with a small opening, and it would stay hot for almost an hour." Interview #6, p. 1. One of the Statler beer mugs is in Viktor's collection.

132. Bassett and Naumann, *Cowan Pottery and the Cleveland School*, briefly discusses Econo-Rim on p. 316 and reproduces Cowan's patent for an Econo-Rim cup on p. 317 (design patent 97,119); for an account of Econo-Rim, see Cleota Reed and Stan Skoczen, *Syracuse China* (Syracuse: Syracuse University Press, 1997), pp. 114–18.

133. Reed and Skoczen, *Syracuse China*, pp. 114–16; Interview #6, p. 1.

134. Fox, "May Show Exhibition Reveals Unusual Work."

135. Robert Bordner, "Ceramics Lead in May Show: Cleveland Potters Set New High Mark," *Cleveland Press* (30 April 1932).

136. Christina Corsiglia, "Viktor Schreckengost: Evolution of a Cleveland Ceramist," *Cleveland as a Center of Regional American Art*, symposium proceedings, Cleveland Artists Foundation (1994), p. 103. For a miscellaneous collection of items produced by American Limoges, see Raymonde Limoges, *American Limoges: Identification and Value Guide* (Paducah, Kentucky: Collectors Books, 1996).

137. Interview #6, p. 2; Interview #8, p. 8.

138. Grace V. Kelly, "Limoges China Designed by Schreckengost and Made in Sebring, at Korner & Woods," *Plain Dealer* (11 February 1934), Women's Magazine and Amusement section. In this article, Kelly noted: "During the past year he has designed all sorts of modern things for the automotive industry, glass, stoves, pen sets in chromium and bakelite, enamel, furniture, and many other lines."

139. Untitled, undated article (Schreckengost scrapbook).

140. Unidentified newspaper article, apparently roughly contemporary with the article by Kelly in note 128 (Schreckengost scrapbook).

141. Frederick H. Rhead, "Chats on Pottery," *Potter's Herald* (East Liverpool, Ohio) (17 January 1934).

142. "Limoges Ware Given Space in Cleveland Show," *Alliance* (Ohio) *Review* (10 February 1934).

143. "Pottery Show Business Is Encouraging," *Potter's Herald* (c. January 1934).

144. Kelly, "Limoges China Designed by Schreckengost."

145. Advertisement for show at the New Yorker Hotel, 29 July–4 August 1934 (Schreckengost scrapbook).

146. See Kelly, "New American Limoges China Design by Schreckengost," p. 18.

147. Ibid.

148. See note 126.

149. Kelly, "New American Limoges China Design by Schreckengost," p. 18.

150. Interview #6, p. 3.

151. Interview #8, p. 8.

152. Ibid.

153. Interview #6, p. 3. The Schreckengost scrapbook contains an ad published by the Republican Party in Sebring declaring: "The Japs steal our shapes. The Japs have stolen our decorations" and urging workers to vote Republican to get effective protective tariffs. The ad specifically mentions Viktor's Flower Shop decoration. While he had no role in creating the ad, and would not have approved of its racist language, it securely documents the piracy of Viktor's designs and also gives a sense of the anxiety that existed within the U.S. ceramic industry of the time, which was battling for its life against the flood of foreign imports. Jo Cunningham, *The Best of Collectible Dinnerware* (Atglen, Pennsylvania: Schiffer Publishing, 1995), p. 74, reproduces an imitation of Flower Shop produced by the Edwin Knowles China Co.

154. Design patent 99,052, plate or similar article, awarded 24 March 1936.

155. "The Animals Come to Town," *China, Glass and Lamps* (February 1936), p. 27.

156. Kelly, "New American Limoges China Design by Schreckengost," p. 18.

157. Claire Rosenberg, "Right Out of the Kiln," *Crockery and Glass Journal* (August 1935), p. 18; "New Designs for Mass Production," *Design* (November 1935), p. 15; Cunningham, *Best of Collectible Dinnerware*, p. 91, dates Embassy to 1940, but in fact it was released by the summer of 1935 because it was reproduced in the August issue of *Crockery and Glass Journal*.

158. "Dinnerware Lines Show Marked Advance in Design and Style," *Retailing*, Home Furnishing Edition (18 January 1937), p. 32; "The Case for Colors and Decorations on Ceramics and Glass," *Crockery and Glass Journal* (September 1937); Charles Venable et al., *China and Glass in America, 1880–1980* (Dallas: Dallas Museum of Art, 2000), pp. 303, 451–52.

159. Cunningham, *Best of Collectible Dinnerware*, p. 91.

160. "Better Business Is Noted at Pittsburgh Show," *Ceramic Industry* (February 1940), p. 22.

161. Unrecorded interview (May 2000).

162. The name, however, varied slightly from place to place—in Atlanta, for example, it became Harmony House, and in St. Louis, Homemaker's Shop.

163. "Science Takes the Guesswork Out of Home Decorating with the Regency Ensemble" (October 1940), section 2, p. 66, the source of what appears to be a full-page advertisement is unidentified (Schreckengost scrapbook).

164. "Here Are the Regency Colors," *House and Garden* (September 1940), section 11, p. 51.

165. Schreckengost, in *China and Glass* (19 August 1940).

166. Schreckengost, "Will the American Buyer Play Ball with Manufacturers?" *Ceramic Industry* 35 (December 1940), p. 37.

167. Ibid.

168. Sharon Dale, *Frederick Hurten Rhead: An English Potter in America* (Erie, Pennsylvania: Erie Art Museum, 1982); F. H. Rhead, "More About Color," *Crockery and Glass Journal* 102 (1937), p. 13.

169. William J. Hennessey, *Russell Wright, American Designer* (Cambridge, Massachusetts: MIT Press, 1983); Ann Kerr, *Russell Wright Dinnerware: Designs for the American Table* (Paducah, Kentucky: Collectors Books, 1985).

170. For a superb study of Eva Ziesel, see Eidelberg et al., *Eva Zeisel*.

171. Interview #4, pp. 3–4.

172. Grafly, "Viktor Schreckengost," p. 49.

173. Advertisements for Tempo appeared in the January 1949 issues of *Crockery, Glass and Decorative Accessories* and *Crockery and Glass Journal* (Schreckengost scrapbook). See also *U.S. Industrial Design 1949–50*, p. 30.

174. Viktor registered five patents for the Free Form shape: cup, serving bowl, sugar bowl with lid, creamer, and teapot (design patents 177,433–437, awarded 10 April 1956). Along with dinnerware, in 1953 Viktor designed frying pans, casseroles, and chicken fryers, in iron with enamel coating, for the Consolidated Iron-Steel Manufacturing Company of Cleveland. A novelty of these designs was that the bottom of the pans was divided into compartments, to allow one to cook different foods at the same time without having the flavors run together. Venable, *China and Glass in America,* pp. 400, 467.

175. Ibid., pp. 391–93, 466.

176. Interview with Don Schreckengost (29 July 1999); Cunningham, *Best of Collectible Dinnerware,* pp. 84–89.

177. Design patent 94,245, plate, awarded 1 January 1935, Frank A. Sebring Jr. and Donald Schreckengost.

178. Interview #2, p. 11; interview with Paul Schreckengost Jr. (October 1999), followed by letter and biographical account of his father (22 October 1999); Wilson, Pilgrim, Tashjian, *The Machine Age,* p. 310.

179. Interview #8, p. 10.

180. Tom Schemenauer, "The Pancake White," *Wheels of Time* (November/December 1989), p. 26.

181. An unidentified article of 15–20 October 1934 noted that the White Motor Company was showing its new truck at the Dairies Industries Exposition to be held in Cleveland, 15–20 October. "Equipped with a stream-lined tank body, this new truck is the 'hit of the show' as White discarded all conventional practices and developed new engineering ideas to achieve these new trucks—which place payload and power on a profit basis. The engine—a 12 cylinder horizontally opposed 'pancake engine' is an exclusive White design and is the only one of its kind in commercial service. This unique design was achieved by opening the angle of a 'V' type engine so that the two banks of cylinders, containing six each, are horizontally opposed."

182. Hugh Greenlee, "The Art of Car Design, a Brief CIA History," *Link* (Cleveland Institute of Art Magazine) 20 (Summer 1987), pp. 3–4. See also Carmie Armata, "The Essence of an Era," *Plain Dealer Magazine* (14 August 1983), p. 53.

183. Sakhnoffsky's most famous truck design is the White Streamliner of 1937, with a streamlined cab-over-engine tractor and matching streamlined trailer.

184. The best history of White Motors is a typescript, "The Rise and Fall of White Motors," by Christopher J. Dawson, curator of urban and industrial history, Western Reserve Historical Society. My thanks to him for giving me access to this manuscript. See also *White Trucks 1900 Through 1937: Photo Archives,* edited and with introduction by Don Bunn, Iconografix Photo Archive Series (Hudson, Wisconsin, 1998); and Brian Wheeler, "White's 81 Years as a Major Truck Builder," *Wheels of Time* (May/June 1996), pp. 26–28, and (July/August 1996), pp. 16–18.

185. Dawson, "The Rise and Fall of White Motors," pp. 8–10; Bunn, *White Trucks 1900 Through 1937,* p. 9.

186. For an account of this truck, see Schemenauer, "The Pancake White," pp. 22, 23, 26.

187. Viktor shared the patent with one of the engineers at White, Frank G. Alborn (design patent 93,960, motor vehicle cab, awarded 4 December 1934). An article in the Sebring press noted that Viktor Schreckengost "has been issued a patent on a cab design for a new type White Motor Company truck. The streamline cab designed by the local artist will be used only on the largest White trucks which will be propelled by a 12 cylinder 'pancake' motor. The new motor is flat and will be installed underneath the truck chassis." (The same article noted that Viktor's brother Don had just won a competition for a design of a carton in which to pack rubber gloves made by an Akron rubber firm. It was one of many competitions won by Don Schreckengost.)

188. Bobby Alford, *The Murray Cycle: History of Murray Ohio* (Lawrenceburg, Tennessee: Murray Ohio, 1981).

189. Garton, *Pedal Cars,* p. 92; Alford, *Murray Cycle,* p. 6. Generally speaking, Murray patented Viktor's designs just before they were shown at the annual toy fair. Once they were shown and orders placed, the company would invest in new tooling, basing their investment on the number of orders (Garton, *Pedal Cars,* p. 28).

190. Interview #8, p. 23; Interview #2, p. 7.

191. Paul B. Metzler, "Schreckengost's Designs Help Murray Ohio Co. Please Santa," *Plain Dealer* (18 December 1949).

192. Since the same clay was reused from project to project, none of Viktor's clay models survive.

193. Garton, *Pedal Cars,* p. 27.

194. Ibid.

195. George Z. Griswold, "Good Industrial Design Pays Off," reprinted from *Clevelander* (April 1948) (Schreckengost scrapbook).

196. Ibid.

197. Metzler, "Schreckengost's Designs Help Murray Ohio Co. Please Santa."

198. Ibid.

199. Griswold, "Good Industrial Design."

200. Metzler, "Schreckengost's Designs Help Murray Ohio Co. Please Santa."

201. Griswold, "Good Industrial Design."

202. Herman Millman, "Schreckengost's Toy Designs Show Artist's Vital Role in Industry," *Cleveland Press Magazine* (11 December 1948).

203. Garton, *Pedal Cars,* p. 31.

204. The Murray Champion sold for about $14 in the 1950s and now commands $500 to $1,500.

205. Metzler, "Schreckengost's Designs Help Murray Ohio Co. Please Santa."

206. Garton, *Pedal Cars,* p. 31.

207. Jack Warfel, "Toy Factories Pour Out Flood of Gifts," *Cleveland Press* (12 August 1941).

208. *U.S. Industrial Design 51* (New York: Studio Publications, Thomas Y. Crowell, 1951), p. 37.

209. Viktor's flat-face design is recorded in patents 187,992–994, awarded 24 May 1960.

210. *Murray Cycle,* p. 70.

211. Design patent 194,324, awarded 1 January 1963.

212. Design patent 202,434, awarded 28 September 1965.

213. In 1956 Viktor received a patent for the Rocket, Sky Rocket, and Atomic Missile.

214. Tractor: design patent 202,436, awarded 28 September 1965; boats: design patent 209,458, awarded 5 December 1967.

215. Judy Marcus, "Fancy Foot Work," *Chicago Tribune* (23 January 2000).

216. Patents to Viktor for riding lawn mowers include a riding-type lawn mower (design patent 215,110, awarded 2 September 1969), riding-type lawn mower frame (design patents 218,632–633, awarded 8 September 1970), and riding-type lawn mower (design patent 218,768, awarded 22 September 1970). Viktor designed his first motorized lawn mower—one of those devices that you walk behind—sometime before 1939. Grace V. Kelly mentions Viktor's skill in designing lawn mowers in a note of 1939 on art happenings in Cleveland. The article is somewhat misleadingly titled: "Museum of Art Acquire Group of 16 Rare Pieces of Ancient Silk and Velvet," *Plain Dealer* (29 October 1939), Amusement section.

217. Interview #8, p. 24.

218. Invention patent 2,798,739, awarded 9 July 1957.

219. In May 1947 he applied for a patent for this idea, in partnership with the chief engineer at Murray, Herman L. Kraeft; they were awarded a patent on 25 July 1950.

220. In November 1947, Viktor delivered a lecture, "Design of a New Three-Wheel Chain Driven Cycle." See *Silhouette* 25 (Cleveland Institute of Art) (November 1947).

221. For the company's labor difficulties, see Garton, *Pedal Cars,* p. 96.

222. Interview #2, pp. 13–14. By the time of his retirement he had flown so many miles that he had become an "Admiral" of American Airlines, their highest category of frequent flier.

223. Jay Pridmore and Jim Hurd, *The American Bicycle* (Osceola, Wisconsin: Motorbooks International, 1995), pp. 22–67.

224. Ibid., pp. 104–17.

225. For photos of these bicycles, see ibid., 104–7, 109, and 111.

226. Design patents 123,574–577, awarded 19 November 1940. The fourth patent is for the girl's version of the bicycle design.

227. Tambini, *Look of the Century,* p. 16.

228. Pridmore and Hurd, *American Bicycle,* p. 123.

229. Ibid., p. 110.

230. While ancestors of the spring fork on this model can be traced back to the 1890s, such an elaborate mechanism was clearly a novelty, which was stressed in the advertising promoting the machine. Thus, a 1949 advertisement for this bicycle included a detailed description of "How Spring Fork Works," explaining: "When front wheel strikes rut, cantilever action of front hub and special fork transfer the shock to powerful coil spring. Spring then expands upward to absorb jolt. Bi-flex action eliminated 'return shock' on recoil to give a steady 'flow-motion' ride. Patterned after 'knee-action' principle of automobile springs." See Neil S. Wood, *Evolution of the Bicycle* (Gas City, Indiana: L-W Book Sales, 1991, rev. ed. 1994), p. 97.

231. Design patent 152,437, awarded 18 January 1949.

232. *U.S. Industrial Design, 1949–50,* p. 70. It had an extra-sturdy hydrogen-brazed frame. It had a spring fork with the latest engineering features. It had twin lights in the front and inside the light was a battery for an electric horn. In the back was a real luggage carrier with a metal clamp that went over it to prevent things from falling off. It had a stop-and-go taillight, which you could turn on at night that would flash at regular intervals. It had chain and skirt guards, bumper braces, front and rear Stimsonite reflectors, and a long-lasting paint job of distinctive pearlesque enamel.

233. Throughout this period, Viktor gamely produced designs that responded to whatever new trends were hot on the market, fulfilling even the most bizarre and unusual requests with the ease with which an experienced stage designer would produce a theater set in any stylistic idiom. In 1951, for example, he produced two different sizes of cowboy bikes for small children, one with training wheels and the other slightly larger, without. The inspiration for this was surely the 1951 Gene Autry, produced by Monark, a truly hideous confection, with a saddle, horse blanket, and leather gun case, as well as a molded plastic horse's head protruding from the front fork like a figurehead, and finally, as the crowning touch, two additional such horse's heads, this time pointing backward, emerging from the two plastic grips of the front handlebars. See Pridmore and Hurd, *American Bicycle,* p. 134. Given the obvious challenges of such a commission, Viktor's bicycle for young cowpunchers is a surprisingly handsome design, with an ingenious visual interplay between the leather gun case conveniently provided for a pop gun rifle and the chain guard. A saddlebag draped over the rear wheel was complemented by a leather pouch on the handlebars. "Just the hoss a hard ridin' cowpuncher needs for round-ups and fast bandit chases," the advertising copy noted. "It's the steed every buckaroo dreams about." While hardly Viktor's greatest bicycle, it nicely demonstrates his versatility and unflinching willingness to take on a new challenge. See Wood, *Evolution of the Bicycle,* p. 109.

234. Design patent 170,169, bicycle frame, awarded 11 August 1953.

235. The frame of the Spaceliner was protected by design patent 198,827, awarded 4 August 1964.

236. Viktor's patents allow us to chart the gradual evolution of this supersonic look. On 27 April 1953, he applied to patent the idea of using twin tubes on a bicycle frame, the innovation that created a new style of ultra-streamlined design (design patent 170,169, awarded 11 August 1953.) Several additional patents continue this line of thinking, such as a patent covering the frame of a girl's bicycle based on similar principles (design patent 185,575, awarded 23 June 1959), as well as various patents for luggage carriers (design patent 185,323, awarded 26 May 1959; design patents 199,774–775, awarded 8 December 1964), and bicycle chain guards (design patent 185,101, awarded 5 May 1959), which significantly lighten these elements, to go along with the overall "weightless" look.

237. Concurrently with his work on the Fleetlines and Spaceliners, Viktor adopted this general look for tricycles as well. For example, a patent for a Z-frame tricycle employs the same sort of double-framing that Viktor had devised earlier for full-sized bikes (design patent 183,544, awarded 16 September 1958). In addition, not long after he designed a front fender and truss rod ensemble for a tricycle in a wishbone shape that made it possible for tiny tots to go supersonic, just as teenagers did (design patent 185,681, awarded 14 July 1959; the double bars on the front end of this tricycle are doing nothing useful, except to look good). This was then followed by a patent for a streamlined velocipede fender (design patent 185,909, awarded 18 August 1959).

238. Several of Viktor's patents relate to the frame, handlebars, and chain guards of kooky bikes: frame (design patent 213,347, awarded 18 February 1969); handlebar (design patent 215,987, awarded 11 November 1969), bicycle (design patent 213,753, awarded 1 April 1969); frame (design patent 217,208, awarded 14 April 1970); frame (design patent 219,087, awarded 27 October 1970).

239. Notably, in the Eliminator series, Viktor moved away from the minimal chain guards of the Spaceliner toward an exaggeratedly large surface. Thus he could use the chain guard as a billboard on which to place imagery, in a fashion somewhat similar to the flat-face pedal cars. Viktor's chain guard for the Mark II Eliminator was protected by design patent 214,979, awarded on 12 August 1969.

240. Viktor received two design patents for gear shifting consoles used on the Eliminator series (216,932 and 217,206, awarded 17 March 1970 and 14 April 1970, respectively).

241. Viktor received two design patents for the Campus Compact (221,119 and 221,120, awarded 6 July 1971).

242. Pridmore and Hurd, *American Bicycle,* p. 142.

243. This is surely the design recorded in two patents, 131,353 and 131,354, awarded to Viktor 10 February 1942. Not long afterward, he designed both a stamped metal chair for patio use (design patent 127,281, awarded 20 May 1941) and a window ventilator housing (design patent 131,270, awarded 27 January 1942).

244. Interview #8, p. 25.

245. Viktor's patents for fans include a housing for a window-mounted ventilating fan (design patent 182,931, awarded 27 May 1958), window fan (design patent 181,318, awarded 29 October 1957), mobile adjustable fan (design patent 195,944, awarded 13 August 1963), fan (design patent 205,168, awarded 28 June 1966), and adjustable appliance stand (design patent 205,252, awarded 12 July 1966).

246. *Industrial Design in America, 1954* (New York: Farrar, Straus & Young, 1954), p. 44.

247. This was not Viktor's first corporate logo. While in art school, he made a design that became the logo for the O'Keeffe and Merritt Stove Company.

248. Interview #2, p. 9.

249. Interview #8, p. 24.

250. Interview #3, p. 12.

251. Design patent 152,437, awarded 18 January 1949.

252. Interview #8, pp. 31–32.

253. Lens for lighting fixtures (design patent 190,759, awarded 27 June 1961); luminaire (design patent 189,057, awarded 18 October 1960); wall lighting fixture or similar article (design patent 190,385, awarded 23 May 1961); lens for lighting fixtures (design patent 190,386, awarded 23 May 1961); luminaire lens (design patent 190,921, awarded 18 July 1961).

254. Viktor produced sculptural forms in plaster, from that cast-iron molds were made. The molten glass was pressed into these molds and then fire-polished, hand-beveled, and polished. Etching was often employed to provide visual contrast. Those surfaces that were to remain clear were masked by hand with resin-bitumen, and the piece was given a bath in hydrofluoric acid, which produced an opaque white surface on the areas that had not been masked.

255. *U.S. Industrial Design 51,* p. 37.

256. Dietrich Neumann at Brown University is planning an exhibition, *Architecture for the Night,* on the research at Nela Park.

257. Interview #2, p. 12.

258. For Harris Corporation of Cleveland, Viktor designed printing presses and electronic gear; for the Harris-Seybold Company of Dayton, Ohio, he designed cutters and presses; for Harris Computers in Fort Lauderdale, he designed computers; for the Cottrell Company of Westerly, Rhode Island, he designed web presses; for the Intertype Corporation of Brooklyn, New York, he designed typesetting equipment; for the Macey Company of Cleveland he designed collators; for the Langston Company of Camden, New Jersey, he designed paper board presses; for the Schriber Company of Dayton, Ohio, he produced business forms presses; for the Sheridan Company of Easton, Pennsylvania, he designed collators; for the Electronics Systems Division in Melbourne, Florida, he designed composition equipment; and for the Data Communications Division in Dallas, he designed communications equipment.

259. Information from the wall labels and correspondence associated with the exhibition *Three Generations of Designers,* Cleveland Institute of Art, 23 August–6 October 1996, organized by Robert A. Meyer, president of the school. The show featured the work of Schreckengost, Greenlee-Hess, and Nottingham-Spirk.

260. *U.S. Industrial Design 51,* p. 37.

261. Interview #2, p. 13.

262. Invention patent 2,791,323, portable printing press, awarded 7 May 1957, Viktor Schreckengost and Jack E. Vandemann.

263. Interview #2, p. 13.

264. Interview #2, p. 13. Viktor's final designs for Harris show machines that are completely enclosed in sheet metal, such as a papercutting machine of 1962 (patent awarded 22 December 1964) or a typesetting machine of 1964 (patent awarded 21 September 1965). Both these machines resemble household appliances, such as a refrigerator or a stove, and they contain large and prominent control panels, on which the dials and instruments are clearly marked.

265. Interview #8, p. 22.

266. Undated interview.

267. Undated letter from Stephen Knapp, one of Viktor's students (April 2000).

268. From a lecture on automotive design by Giuseppe Delena, delivered at the Cleveland Museum of Art (1 September 1999), typescript p. 24.

269. Ibid.

270. Ibid., pp. 25–26.

271. Ibid., p. 26.

272. A complete list of Viktor's students, from 1932 to 2000, was provided by Anna Cottos, executive secretary, Cleveland Institute of Art.

273. Delena lecture typescript, p. 15.

274. Ibid., p. 15–17.

275. Ibid., p. 17.

276. Ibid., pp. 18–19.

277. Ibid., pp. 20–21; Jerry Hirshberg, *The Creative Priority: Driving Innovative Business in the Real World* (New York: HarperBusiness, 1998).

278. Wall labels and correspondence associated with the exhibition *Three Generations of Designers.*

279. John Nottingham, "Nottingham-Spirk and the Schreckengost Influence," typescript; taped interview with John Nottingham and John Spirk (19 June 2000).

280. Steve Litt, "Museum's Gift to City: Big Bicentennial Show Is the Best Imaginable," *Plain Dealer* (19 May 1996), p. 4K.

281. Ibid.

282. Grafly, "Viktor Schreckengost," p. 56.

283. Always one to see the humorous side of things, at a recent conference on art deco he produced a clipping on a golfer named Art Deko.

284. William Daley, "In Conversation: Viktor Schreckengost/William Daley," *American Craft* 57 (June–July 1997), p. 49; Interview #8, p. 25.

285. Daley, "In Conversation: Viktor Schreckengost/William Daley," p. 49.

U.S.

Checklist of the Exhibition

1. *German Soldiers,* 1915
Watercolor; 51.4 x 66 cm
Viktor Schreckengost

2. *Blue Revel,* 1931
Oil on canvas; 127 x 81.3 cm
Viktor D. Schreckengost

3. *Moroccan Lutes,* 1934
Oil on canvas; 85.5 x 70.5 cm
The Cleveland Artists Foundation, Gift of Viktor Schreckengost

4. *The Low-Down,* 1933
Watercolor; 45 x 29 cm
Viktor Schreckengost

5. *Harlem Hoofers,* 1933
Watercolor; 44.5 x 29 cm
Viktor Schreckengost

6. *Christmas (Salvation Army),* 1933
Watercolor; 44.5 x 28.5 cm
Viktor Schreckengost

7. *All Quiet,* 1946
Graphite and watercolor; 54.3 x 75 cm
Viktor Schreckengost

8. *House of Memories,* 1946
Watercolor; 53.5 x 73.5 cm
Frank A. Simoni Sr.

9. *O.H.'s Place,* 1947
Graphite and watercolor; 55.9 x 76.2 cm
The Cleveland Museum of Art, Cleveland Traveling Exhibitions Fund 1947.86

10. *Dried Fruit,* 1946
Watercolor; 53.5 x 75 cm
Viktor Schreckengost

11. *Studio Window,* 1947
Graphite and watercolor; 53.5 x 75 cm
Viktor Schreckengost

12. *First Snow, Last Flowers,* 1974
Watercolor; 53.5 x 75 cm
Viktor Schreckengost

13. *Fall Festival,* 1962
Watercolor; 53.5 x 75.5 cm
Viktor Schreckengost

14. *Floral,* 1973
Watercolor; 97.5 x 75 cm
Viktor Schreckengost

15. *Derelict,* 1947
Watercolor; 54.5 x 74.5 cm
Viktor Schreckengost

16. *Tornado's Wake,* 1956
Watercolor; 54 x 75 cm
Viktor Schreckengost

17. *Late Show,* 1964
Watercolor; 54 x 75 cm
Myron N. Krotinger

18. *Light on the River,* 1975
Watercolor; 53.5 x 75 cm
Dr. and Mrs. Douglas Nowacek

19. *Pattern of the Sea,* 1985
Watercolor; 74 x 100.5 cm
Viktor Schreckengost

Promotional photo of *Pursuit Plane (Child's Pedal Car),* first issued 1941.

20. *New York Buildings, Blue Background,* 1977
Watercolor; 98.5 x 75.5 cm
Viktor Schreckengost

21. *Big City Jazz,* 1987
Watercolor; 99 x 73.5 cm
Mr. and Mrs. Ridley Watts

22. *Stage Set Rendering for "Jim Dandy,"* 1941
Graphite and paint; 35 x 53 cm
Viktor Schreckengost

23. *Character Design for "Jim Dandy,"* 1941
Graphite and paint; 33 x 25.5 cm
Viktor Schreckengost

24. *Costume Drawing for the Akron Rubber Ball: Air (Female),* 1938–39
Gouache and graphite; 45.7 x 35.3 cm
Viktor Schreckengost

25. *Costume Drawing for the Akron Rubber Ball: Air (Male),* 1938–39
Gouache and graphite; 45.7 x 35.3 cm
Viktor Schreckengost

26. *Costume Drawing for the Akron Rubber Ball: Industry (Female),* 1938–39
Gouache and graphite; 45.7 x 35.3 cm
Viktor Schreckengost

27. *Costume Drawing for the Akron Rubber Ball: Transportation (Male),* 1938–39
Gouache and graphite; 45.7 x 35.3 cm
Viktor Schreckengost

28. *Costume Drawing for the Akron Rubber Ball: Fire (Female),* 1938–39
Gouache and graphite; 45.7 x 35.3 cm
Viktor Schreckengost

29. *Costume Drawing for the Akron Rubber Ball: Fire (Male),* 1938–39
Gouache and graphite; 45.7 x 35.3 cm
Viktor Schreckengost

30. *The Seasons Vase,* 1931–32
Glazed and painted earthenware; H. 27.3 cm, Diam. 20.4 cm
The Cleveland Museum of Art, Hinman B. Hurlbut Collection 964.1932

31. *Floral Vase,* 1931
Glazed and painted earthenware; H. 29.5 cm, Diam. 20.2 cm
Cowan Pottery Museum, Rocky River Public Library (76.1.165)

32. *Leda and the Swan,* 1931–32
Glazed earthenware with engobe, sgraffito; H. 6.8 cm, Diam. 41.8 cm
Viktor Schreckengost

33. *Pegasus Plate,* 1931
Glazed earthenware with engobe, sgraffito; Diam. 42.5 cm
The Western Reserve Historical Society (75.113.4)

34. *Baseball Plate: Pitching,* about 1930s
Glazed and painted earthenware; Diam. 27.9 cm
Viktor Schreckengost

35. *Baseball Plate: Batting,* about 1930s
Glazed and painted earthenware; Diam. 27.7 cm
Viktor Schreckengost

36. *Polo Plate,* about 1937
Glazed and painted earthenware; Diam. 24.3 cm
Viktor Schreckengost

37. *The Hunt,* 1931
Glazed and painted earthenware; bowl, H. 25.4 cm, Diam. 41.9 cm; plates, Diam. 29.2 cm
National Museum of American Art, Smithsonian Institution, Gift of the Artist (1985.92.3A–E)

38. *Neptune Plaque,* 1936
Glazed and underpainted earthenware; Diam. 38.8 cm
Viktor Schreckengost

39. *Danse Moderne,* 1931
Cowan Pottery; glazed earthenware with engobe, sgraffito; Diam. 28.5 cm
The Western Reserve Historical Society (74.170.2)

40. *Cocktails Plate,* 1931
Cowan Pottery; glazed earthenware with engobe, sgraffito; Diam. 29.2 cm
Cyd Kowit

41. *Janus Plaque,* 1936
Glazed and painted earthenware; Diam. 39 cm
Viktor Schreckengost

42. *Warrior Heads Plaque (No. 5),* 1932
Glazed and painted earthenware; Diam. 45.7 cm
The Cleveland Museum of Art, Hinman B. Hurlbut Collection 1760.1931

43. *Still-Life Plaque,* 1931–32
Glazed and painted earthenware; Diam. 41.3 cm
The Cleveland Museum of Art, Hinman B. Hurlbut Collection 963.1932

44. *Alces Americanus Shirasi,* 1948
Glazed earthenware; 44.1 x 29 x 15.5 cm
Viktor Schreckengost

45. *Brahman,* 1951
Glazed earthenware; 54.5 x 67 x 24.5 cm
Viktor Schreckengost

46. *Beauty Nap,* 1948
Glazed earthenware; 23.6 x 55.4 x 20.3 cm
The Cleveland Museum of Art, Silver Jubilee Treasure Fund 1948.59

47. *Naama,* 1939
Glazed earthenware; 44.2 x 46.7 x 15.2 cm
The Cleveland Museum of Art, The Mary Spedding Milliken Memorial Collection, Gift of William Mathewson Milliken 1939.228

48. *Mountain Sheep with Sea Green Glaze,* about 1922
Glazed earthenware; 26 x 18.3 x 14.5 cm
Viktor Schreckengost

49. *Mountain Sheep with White Glaze,* about 1922
Glazed earthenware; 26 x 18.6 x 14.2 cm
Viktor Schreckengost

50. *Fish,* 1948
Glazed earthenware with engobe; 26.7 x 73 x 13.5 cm
Viktor Schreckengost

51. *Kublai,* 1950
Glazed earthenware; 39.5 x 60 x 29 cm
Viktor Schreckengost

52. *Spring,* 1941
Glazed earthenware; 38.1 x 76.2 x 19.7 cm
Everson Museum of Art, Gift of IBM Corporation (P.C.63.44)

53. *Charger,* 1929
Glazed earthenware; 46 x 39.5 x 21 cm
Viktor Schreckengost

54. *Balashan,* 1942
Glazed earthenware; 52.5 x 42 x 17.5 cm
Viktor Schreckengost

55. *Bull,* 1948
Glazed earthenware; 30.7 x 65 x 22.1 cm
Viktor Schreckengost

56. *Leap Frog,* 1950
Glazed earthenware; 50 x 31.3 x 33 cm
Viktor Schreckengost

57. *Pachyderm,* 1951
Glazed earthenware; 61 x 68.6 x 40.7 cm
The Cleveland Museum of Art, Anonymous Gift 1959.126

58. *Samoa,* 1950
Glazed earthenware; 46 x 76.5 x 20 cm
Viktor Schreckengost

59. *Anteater,* 1950
Glazed earthenware; 29 x 75 x 14.5 cm
Viktor Schreckengost

60. *Bumptious and Toto,* 1951
Glazed earthenware; 31.6 x 80 x 39 cm
Viktor Schreckengost

61. *Bovine,* 1955
Glazed earthenware; 32.4 x 45.7 x 18.7 cm
The Cleveland Museum of Art, Silver Jubilee Treasure Fund 1955.231

62. *Three-Toed Sloth,* 1957
Glazed earthenware; 79.5 x 38.5 x 21 cm
Viktor Schreckengost

63. *Tiger,* 1951
Glazed earthenware; 26.2 x 51.8 x 14.8 cm
Viktor Schreckengost

64. *Bull #4,* 1953
Graphite and watercolor; 16 x 22 cm
Viktor Schreckengost

65. *Buffalo Sketch,* 1953
Graphite and watercolor; 18 x 23 cm
Viktor Schreckengost

66. *Camel,* 1953
Graphite and watercolor; 18 x 23.5 cm
Viktor Schreckengost

67. *Bovine #9,* 1953
Graphite and watercolor; 16 x 22 cm
Viktor Schreckengost

68. *Hand-Thrown Head Form,* 1929
Glazed earthenware; 23.7 x 14.8 x 12.5 cm
Jerry and Wynne Maschino

69. *Chinese Head,* 1930
Glazed earthenware; 34.3 x 20.4 x 23 cm
Viktor Schreckengost

70. *Keramos,* 1939
Glazed earthenware; 48.9 x 34.3 x 29.2 cm
Everson Museum of Art, Gift of the Artist (P.C.42)

71. *The Seasons: Winter,* 1938
Glazed earthenware; H. 44 cm, Diam. 26.5 cm
Viktor Schreckengost

72. *The Seasons: Spring,* 1938
Glazed earthenware; H. 43.1 cm, Diam. 24.2 cm
Viktor Schreckengost

73. *The Seasons: Summer,* 1938
Glazed earthenware; H. 45.3 cm, Diam. 24.5 cm
Viktor Schreckengost

74. *The Seasons: Fall,* 1938
Glazed earthenware; H. 45.3 cm, Diam. 27.5 cm
Viktor Schreckengost

75. *Harlem Hoofers,* 1930
Glazed earthenware; 33 x 17.8 x 12.7 cm
John P. Axelrod

76. *Harlem Melodies,* 1930
Glazed earthenware; 31.8 x 25.4 x 17.8 cm
John P. Axelrod

77. *The Abduction,* about 1940
Glazed earthenware; 34.6 x 56.4 x 18.3 cm
Viktor Schreckengost

78. *Shadrach, Meshach, and Abed Nego,* 1938
Glazed earthenware; H. 71.7 cm overall; figures, 38.7 x 27.9 x 20.3 cm; base, 33 x 27.9 x 10.3 cm
The Metropolitan Museum of Art, Purchase, Edward C. Moore Jr. Gift, 1942

79. *Mother Earth,* 1939
Glazed earthenware; 42.3 x 21.4 x 16 cm
Viktor Schreckengost

80. *The Dictator,* 1939
Glazed earthenware; 33 x 31.8 x 26.7 cm
Everson Museum of Art, Gift of the Artist (P.C.86.13)

81. *Filibuster,* 1949
Glazed earthenware; 49.5 x 20.3 x 20.3 cm
Virginia Museum of Fine Arts, Gift of John Axelrod (91.26)

82. *Apocalypse '42,* 1942
Glazed earthenware; 40.6 x 50.8 x 20.3 cm
National Museum of American Art, Smithsonian Institution, Gift of the Artist (1985.92.1)

83. *Sappan,* 1947
Glazed earthenware; H. 57.2 cm, Diam. 25.4 cm
John P. Axelrod

84. *Shell,* 1949
Glazed earthenware; 12.9 x 47.2 x 45.7 cm
Viktor Schreckengost

85. *Canoa,* 1951
Glazed earthenware; 13.5 x 77.4 x 15.1 cm
Viktor Schreckengost

86. *Cellular,* about 1950
Glazed earthenware; 41.4 x 42.9 x 22 cm
Viktor Schreckengost

87. *Butternut Vase,* 1947
Glazed earthenware; H. 45.7 cm, Diam. 13.5 cm
The Butler Institute of American Art, Museum Purchase 1950 (950-C-104)

88. *Oblongata,* 1950
Glazed earthenware; 40.6 x 48.3 x 21.6 cm
Everson Museum of Art, B. F. Drakenfeld Company Purchase Prize, 15th Ceramic National, 1950 (P.C.51.594)

89. *Crater,* about 1950
Glazed earthenware; 72 x 17.5 x 31.5 cm
Viktor Schreckengost

90. *Fusion,* about 1950
Glazed earthenware; 69.5 x 21 x 33 cm
Viktor Schreckengost

91. *Crusader Decanter,* 1931
Glazed earthenware; H. 37 cm, Diam. 9.8 cm
Viktor Schreckengost

92. *Crusader Decanter,* 1931
Glazed earthenware; H. 38.1 cm, Diam. 10.2 cm
Cowan Pottery Museum, Rocky River Public Library (76.1.423)

93. *Madonna,* 1931
Glazed earthenware; 24.6 x 19.7 x 14.3 cm
Viktor Schreckengost

94. *Colt in Egyptian Blue,* 1931
Glazed earthenware; 20.2 x 13.7 x 6.5 cm
Viktor Schreckengost

95. *Jeddu,* 1931
Painted plaster; 62.2 x 24.1 x 39.4 cm
Viktor Schreckengost

96. *Mangbettu Child,* 1933
Cast bronze; 47.3 x 21 x 14 cm
Viktor Schreckengost

97. *The Circus Group #1: Henri the Great,* 1935
Glazed earthenware; 22.8 x 15.6 x 8.8 cm
Viktor Schreckengost

98. *The Circus Group #1: Little Nell,* 1935
Glazed earthenware; 14.4 x 10.4 x 8.7 cm
Viktor Schreckengost

99. *The Circus Group #1: Jum and Jumbo,* 1935
Glazed earthenware; 25.8 x 12.2 x 9.6 cm
Viktor Schreckengost

100. *The Circus Group #1: Madame Kitty,* 1935
Glazed earthenware; 21.8 x 24.5 x 8.8 cm
Viktor Schreckengost

101. *The Circus Group #1: The Great Cellinis,* 1935
Glazed earthenware; 39.5 x 24.5 x 7.8 cm
Viktor Schreckengost

102. *Jonah,* 1937
Glazed earthenware; 29.1 x 28 x 18.8 cm
Viktor Schreckengost

103. *Samson and Delilah,* 1940
Glazed earthenware; 25.4 x 48.3 cm
John P. Axelrod

104. *Judas,* 1949
Glazed earthenware; 41 x 28.5 x 20.3 cm
Viktor Schreckengost

105. *Rhythm of the Soil,* 1947
Glazed earthenware; 28 x 14 x 47 cm
The Cleveland Museum of Art, Gift of The Cleveland Art Association 1947.78

106. *Ichabod Crane,* 1948
Glazed earthenware; 30.6 x 61.4 x 15 cm
Viktor Schreckengost

107. *Peter the Fisherman,* 1954
Glazed earthenware; 76 x 35 x 15 cm
Viktor Schreckengost

108. *Women's Flying Trophy,* 1939
Silver-plated bronze; 101.6 x 35.6 x 22.9 cm
Collection, Mitchell Wolfson Jr., Miami, Florida

109. *The Four Elements: Water,* 1939
Glazed earthenware; H. 50.5 cm, Diam. 33.5 cm
Viktor Schreckengost

110. *The Four Elements: Air,* 1939
Glazed earthenware; H. 50.5 cm,
Diam 35 cm
Viktor Schreckengost

111. *Ceramic Head for the 1939 World's Fair (The Four Elements: Fire),* 1939
Glazed earthenware; H. 51 cm; Diam. 31 cm
Robert Bullock

112. *The Hugh M. O'Neill Police Memorial Monument,* 1949
Cast and tinted plaster; 68.5 x 68 x 29 cm
Viktor Schreckengost

113. *Hesperornis,* 1950
Cast plaster; 47.2 x 72.5 x 8 cm
Viktor Schreckengost

114. *Diatryma,* 1950
Cast plaster; 48.7 x 67.5 x 8 cm
Viktor Schreckengost

115. *Dodo,* 1950
Cast plaster; 44.5 x 65.2 x 8.5 cm
Viktor Schreckengost

116. *American Bald Eagle,* 1950
Cast plaster; 45.2 x 66 x 9.2 cm
Viktor Schreckengost

117. *Sports Plate: The Hunt,* 1930–31
Glazed earthenware; Diam. 29 cm
Viktor Schreckengost

118. *Sports Plate: Tennis,* 1930–31
Glazed earthenware; Diam. 29 cm
Viktor Schreckengost

119. *Sports Plate: Polo,* 1930–31
Glazed earthenware; Diam. 29.3 cm
Cowan Pottery Museum, Rocky River Public Library (76.1.600)

120. *Vase with Abstract City Scenes,* 1930
Glazed and painted earthenware; H. 20.7 cm, Diam. 18.8 cm
Viktor Schreckengost

121. *Congo Vase,* 1931
Glazed and painted earthenware; H. 23.2 cm, Diam. 25 cm
Dr. and Mrs. Michael Dreyfuss

122. *Flora Vase,* 1931
Glazed earthenware; H. 25 cm, Diam. 18.5 cm
Viktor Schreckengost

123. *Orange Globular Vase with Ring Handles,* 1931
Cowan Pottery; glazed earthenware; H. 15.3 cm, Diam. 13.3 cm
Viktor Schreckengost

124. *Egyptian Blue Globular Vase with Ring Handles,* 1931
Cowan Pottery; glazed earthenware; H. 15.3 cm, Diam. 13.5 cm
Viktor Schreckengost

125. *Yellow Globular Vase with Ring Handles,* 1931
Cowan Pottery; glazed earthenware; H. 15.4 cm, Diam. 13.5 cm
Viktor Schreckengost

126. *Fish Vase* (Egyptian blue and black), 1931
Cowan Pottery; glazed earthenware with engobe, sgraffito; H. 14.5 cm, Diam. 16.5 cm
Mark Bassett

127. *Fish Vase* (melon green), 1931
Cowan Pottery; glazed earthenware with engobe, sgraffito; H. 24.3 cm, Diam. 17.7 cm
Cowan Pottery Museum, Rocky River Public Library (76.1.67)

128. *New Yorker* or *The Jazz Bowl,* about 1930
Cowan Pottery; glazed earthenware with engobe, sgraffito; H. 28.6, Diam. 41.3 cm
The Cleveland Museum of Art, John L. Severance Fund 2000.65

129. *New Yorker* or *The Jazz Bowl,* about 1930
Cowan Pottery; glazed earthenware with engobe, sgraffito; H. 29.2 cm, Diam. 41.3 cm
Cowan Pottery Museum, Rocky River Public Library (76.1.602)

130. *New Yorker* or *The Jazz Bowl,* about 1930
Cowan Pottery; glazed earthenware with engobe, sgraffito; H. 29.5 cm, Diam. 41 cm
The Rowfant Club

131. *Egyptian Blue Jazz Bowl with Flared Rim,* 1931
Cowan Pottery; glazed earthenware with engobe, sgraffito; H. 21.6 cm, Diam. 34.9 cm
Private collection

132. *Poor Man's Bowl, Egyptian Blue Glaze,* 1931
Cowan Pottery; glazed earthenware with engobe, sgraffito; H. 21.6 cm, Diam. 34.9 cm
John P. Axelrod

133. *Poor Man's Bowl, Melon Green Glaze,* 1931
Cowan Pottery; glazed earthenware with engobe, sgraffito; H. 21.6 cm, Diam. 34.9 cm
Private collection

134. *Cocktails and Cigarettes Punch Bowl (Party Bowl),* 1931
Cowan Pottery; glazed earthenware with engobe, sgraffito; H. 23.5 cm, Diam. 42.8 cm
Elizabeth Mather McMillan

135. *Charger with Jazz Design,* 1930
Cowan Pottery; glazed earthenware with engobe, sgraffito; Diam. 29.3 cm
Donn W. Kirschenbaum

136. *American Limoges Peasant Ware Dinnerware,* 1932
Glazed earthenware
Bowl, H. 15.8 cm, Diam. 30 cm; two 9-inch plates, Diam. 24.6 cm; two saucers, Diam. 16.7 cm; two cups, 5.4 x 13.1 x 10.7 cm; bread and butter plate, Diam. 18.5 cm; teapot and lid, 14.7 x 24.2 x 16.4 cm; sugar bowl and lid, 10.5 x 16.8 x 12.5 cm; creamer, 16.5 x 16 x 11.5 cm
Viktor Schreckengost

137. *American Limoges Manhattan Shape Meerschaum Pattern Dinnerware* (working model), 1935
Glazed earthenware
15-inch chop plate, Diam. 39.4 cm; 9-inch plate, Diam. 23.4 cm; cup, 5.2 x 11.7 x 9.5 cm, and saucer, Diam. 14.9 cm; teapot and lid, 11.9 x 23 x 16.1 cm; sugar bowl and lid, 9 x 15.5 x 11.8 cm; creamer with lid, 8 x 14.8 x 10.5 cm; muffin dish with cover, 8.5 x 21.4 x 18.6 cm; bowl, H. 6.2 cm, Diam. 22.5 cm
Viktor Schreckengost
Coffee pot with lid, 16.7 x 21.2 x 14 cm
Mark Bassett

138. *American Limoges Manhattan Shape Plates,* 1935
Glazed earthenware
Flower Shop F pattern, Diam. 23.7 cm; Red Sails H pattern, Diam. 23.6 cm; Metropolis pattern, Diam. 23.5 cm; Garden of Eden Blue pattern, Diam. 23.8 cm; unmarked pattern (flowers with red trim), Diam. 23.9 cm; Port pattern, Diam. 25.5 cm; Blue-(illegible) pattern, Diam. 23.7 cm; Zenith H pattern, Diam. 23.5 cm; Eclipse pattern, Diam. 23.5 cm
Viktor Schreckengost

139. *American Limoges Manhattan Shape Animal Kingdom Pattern Ashtrays,* 1935
Glazed earthenware
Cow, Diam. 11.8 cm; rooster, Diam. 11.8 cm; ram, Diam. 11.8 cm; elephant, Diam. 11.8 cm; squirrel, Diam. 11.8 cm; donkey, Diam. 11.8 cm; fish, Diam. 11.8 cm; pig, Diam. 11.8 cm
Viktor Schreckengost

140. *American Limoges Snowflake Shape Blue Plate,* 1935
Glazed earthenware; Diam. 28 cm
Viktor Schreckengost

141. *Animal Kingdom Pattern Uncut Decal Sheet,* 1935
57.5 x 75 cm
Viktor Schreckengost

142. *American Limoges Triumph Shape Plates,* 1937
Glazed earthenware
Twinkle Twinkle T pattern, Diam. 23.5 cm; Tone T Pink-Royalty Blue pattern, Diam. 23.6 cm; Tone Yellow pattern Diam. 23.5 cm
Viktor Schreckengost

143. *American Limoges Jiffy Ware Space-Saving Design,* 1942
Glazed earthenware
Refrigerator dish and lid, 10.3 x 24 x 16 cm; butter dish and lid, 9.5 x 18 x 11.4 cm; pitcher and lid, 16.8 x 18.9 x 10 cm; salt and pepper set, 12.5 x 8.5 x 6.5 cm (each); salt and pepper set with handles, 10.8 x 4.4 x 4.4 cm (each)
Viktor Schreckengost

144. *American Limoges and Salem China Coffee Pots and Lids,* 1937–38 and 1951
Glazed earthenware
American Limoges Triumph shape, 1937: Bermuda T pattern, 21.8 x 18.6 x 13 cm; Flower Shop TW pattern, 21.8 x 18.7 x 13 cm. Salem China Victory shape, 1938: Basket Petit Point pattern: 23.3 x 22.3 x 13 cm; Godey Ladies pattern, 23 x 22.2 x 13 cm
Mark Bassett
Salem China, 1951: Ranch pattern, charcoal matte glaze, 20.7 x 15 x 12 cm; Ranch pattern, constellation glaze, 21.3 x 16.5 x 14.5 cm
Viktor Schreckengost

145. *Salem China Ranch Pattern Dinnerware,* 1951
Glazed earthenware
Charcoal matte glaze: 6-inch plate, Diam. 15.9 cm; creamer, 9.9 x 16.4 x 18.4 cm; sugar bowl with constellation glaze lid, 8.3 x 10.8 x 10.8 cm; dish with handle and constellation glaze lid with flare, 6.5 x 17.6 x 11.9 cm. Constellation glaze: casserole dish with lid, 8.7 x 32.7 x 23.3 cm; casserole dish with lid, 9 x 32.5 x 23.3 cm; creamer, 9.2 x 17.9 x 9.5 cm; dish with two compartments, 6.3 x 23.5 x 19 cm; creamer with lid, 13.1 x 10.5 x 8.2 cm; cup, 5 x 12.5 x 10 cm. Metal casserole holder, 8.5 x 20.7 x 20.3 cm
Viktor Schreckengost

146. *Salem China Plates,* 1950s
Glazed earthenware
Parsley pattern, Diam. 25.4 cm; Strawberry Patch pattern, Diam. 25.4 cm; Garden pattern, Diam. 25.6 cm; Windblown pattern, Diam. 25.4 cm; Flair Fantasy pattern platter, Diam. 26.3 cm
Viktor Schreckengost

147. *Salem China Free Form Shape Primitive Pattern Dinnerware,* 1955
Glazed earthenware
Four 10½-inch plates, Diam. 25.7 cm; 10-inch bowl with spout, 10.3 x 25.5 x 15.5 cm; 6½-inch bowl with spout, 8.5 x 14.2 x 16.5 cm; 10-inch platter-bowl, Diam. 25.5 cm; 11-inch pitcher with lid, 15.2 x 26.8 x 13.2 cm; two cups, 5.7 x 12.7 x 10 cm; three 6-inch saucers, Diam. 15.8 cm; 9½-inch dish (holds salt and pepper set as well as oil and vinegar), 2 x 24.3 x 20.3 cm; salt and pepper set: salt, H. 9 cm, Diam. 5.6 cm; pepper, H. 6.5 cm, Diam. 5.6 cm; oil and vinegar vessels with stoppers: oil, H. 12 cm, Diam. 8.5 cm; vinegar, H. 17 cm, Diam. 8.5 cm; 6-inch bowl, 6 x 15.5 x 14.2 cm; 7½-inch plate, Diam. 18.6 cm
Viktor Schreckengost

148. *Royal Crest Dinnerware,* about 1950
Glazed earthenware
Cup, 6 x 12 x 9 cm; cup, 4.5 x 9.2 x 6.9 cm, and 5-inch saucer, Diam. 12.5 cm; square 5-inch saucer, Diam. 12.2 cm; 4-inch sugar bowl with white lid, 9.9 x 11.1 x 6.2 cm; teapot with lid, 16.5 x 20 x 8.3 cm
Viktor Schreckengost

149. Don Schreckengost (born 1910)
Salem China Tricorne Shape Dinnerware, 1933
Glazed earthenware
Two nut dishes, Diam. 9.8; four bowls, 2.8 x 14.1 x 14.1 cm; two cups, 6 x 12.8 x 10 cm; two saucers, Diam. 15.7 cm; two bread and butter plates, Diam. 16.1 cm; creamer, 5.7 x 14.7 x 10.1 cm; sugar bowl (no lid),: 5.5 x 17.8 x 13.8 cm; two dinner plates, Diam. 23 cm
Dr. and Mrs. Stephen A. Ockner

150. Paul Shreckengost (1908–1983)
Gem Clay Forming Company Teapot, about 1938
Glazed earthenware; 19.1 x 29.2 x 10.2 cm
Paul and Renee Schreckengost

151. *Fire Chief Car (Child's Pedal Car),* first issued about 1965
Murray Ohio; steel; 45 x 82.5 x 42 cm
Nicole L. S. Prenevost

152. *Pursuit Plane (Child's Pedal Car),* first issued 1941
Murray Ohio; metal, rubber, plastic; 64 x 105.5 x 89 cm
Paul and Renee Schreckengost

153. *Pursuit Plane (Child's Pedal Car),* first issued 1941
Murray Ohio; metal, rubber, plastic; 64 x 105.5 x 89 cm
Mark Michalek

154. *Super De Luxe 4-Ball Bearing Wagon,* first issued 1961
Murray Ohio; metal, rubber, plastic; 40.1 x 91.5 x 41.3 cm
Viktor Schreckengost

155. *Champion Pedal Car,* first issued 1938
Murray Ohio; metal, rubber, plastic; 51 x 86 x 38 cm
Edward J. Karee

156. *Speedway Pace Car (Child's Pedal Car),* first issued 1959
Murray Ohio; metal, rubber, plastic; 36 x 88.5 x 38 cm
Viktor Schreckengost

157. *Tricycle,* first issued 1964
Murray Ohio; metal, rubber, plastic; 78 x 89 x 56 cm
Joe and Elaine Kisvardi

158. *Murray Mercury Bicycle* (World's Fair model), first issued 1939
Murray Ohio; aluminum alloy fenders, chrome-plated tank; 175.3 cm from front to rear tires
Leon Dixon/National Bicycle History Archive of America

159. *J.C. Higgins Bicycle,* first issued 1948
Murray Ohio; aluminum alloy fenders, chrome-plated tank; 175.3 cm from front to rear tires
Leon Dixon/National Bicycle History Archive of America

160. *Sears Spaceliner Bicycle,* first issued 1965
Murray Ohio, for Sears, Roebuck; metal, rubber, plastic; 97 x 180 x 66 cm
The Bicycle Museum of America

161. *Mark II Eliminator Bicycle,* first issued 1968
Murray Ohio; metal, rubber, plastic; 175.3 cm from front to rear tires
Private collection

162. *Campus Compact Bicycle,* first issued 1968
Murray Ohio; metal, rubber, plastic; 101.6 x 147.3 x 58.4 cm
The Western Reserve Historical Society

163. *Lawn Chair, Beverly Hills Model,* first issued 1941
Murray Ohio, for Sears, Roebuck; metal; 83 x 63 x 56 cm
Viktor Schreckengost

164. *Mobile Adjustable Fan,* first issued 1963
Murray Ohio, for Sears, Roebuck; metal and plastic; 81 x 67 x 33 cm
Viktor Schreckengost

165. *Toys*
Die-cast metal
Steelcraft Spitfire Airplane, first issued 1941, replica released 1994; Murray Ohio, for Hallmark Kiddie Car Classics; 11 x 19.5 x 15 cm. Pontiac, first issued 1948, replica released 1995; Murray Ohio, for Hallmark Kiddie Car Classics; 9.5 x 15 x 8 cm. Steelcraft Junior Service Truck, first issued 1941, replica released 1996; Murray Ohio, for Hallmark Kiddie Car Classics; 10 x 20 x 7.5 cm. General, first issued 1950 (numbered edition), replica released 1999; Murray Ohio, for Hallmark Kiddie Car Classics; 11 x 16 x 7.5 cm. Torpedo, first issued 1950, replica released 1994; Murray Ohio, for Hallmark Kiddie Car Classics; 8.5 x 15 x 7.5 cm. Tractor and Trailer, first issued 1950, replica released 1991; Murray Ohio, for Hallmark Kiddie Car Classics; tractor 11 x 17 x 9.3 cm; trailer 8 x 4.5 x 5.2 cm. Royal Deluxe Automobile, first issued 1955, replica released 1995; Murray Ohio, for Hallmark Kiddie Car Classics; 9.5 x 17 x 8 cm. Atomic Missile, first issued 1958, replica released 1994; Murray Ohio, for Hallmark Kiddie Car Classics; 11 x 19.5 x 11 cm. Police Cycle, first issued 1958 (limited edition), replica released 1995; Murray Ohio, for Hallmark Kiddie Car Classics; 9.7 x 14.5 x 7.5 cm. Circus Car, first issued 1961, replica released 1984; Murray Ohio, for Hallmark Kiddie Car Classics; 8.5 x 18.5 x 8 cm. Super Deluxe Fire Truck, with Two Ladders, first issued 1962, replica released 1995; Murray Ohio, for Hallmark Kiddie Car Classics; 9.5 x 19.5 x 8 cm. Airplane, replica released 1991; Murray Ohio, for Hallmark Kiddie Car Classics; 11.5 x 20 x 15 cm. Champion, replica released 1991; Murray Ohio, for Hallmark Kiddie Car Classics; 10 x 15 x 7.5 cm. Fire Truck, with Two Ladders, replica released 1991; Murray Ohio, for Hallmark Kiddie Car Classics; 11 x 20 x 7.5 cm. Dump Truck, replica released 1992; Murray Ohio, for Hallmark Kiddie Car Classics; 11 x 20 x 7.5 cm. Pedal Boat with Flag and Motor, replica released 1996; Xonex, Cleveland, for Kiddie Kraft; 1:3 scale model; 12.5 x 33.5 x 13.5 cm
Viktor Schreckengost

Chronology

Born 26 June 1906 in Sebring, Ohio.
Father: Warren G. Schreckengost, potter; mother: Ada Noulton Schrecengost; brothers: Don and Paul, designers, potters; uncles: potters

Education

Lincoln Elementary School in Sebring, 1912–20

McKinley High School in Sebring, 1920–24

Cleveland Institute of Art, 1925–29, diploma. Major in design, Julius Mihalik; minor in ceramics, R. Guy Cowan and Arthur Baggs; Henry G. Keller, Paul B. Travis, Frank Wilcox, drawing; Dr. Wyngate Todd, special classes in anatomy, Western Reserve University; Otto F. Ege, calligraphy

Kunstgewerbeschule, Vienna, 1929–30, postgraduate study, certificate of completion. Michael Powolny, ceramics; critiques from Josef Hoffmann (Wiener Werkbund) and Franz Cizek

Travel

1930
Austria, Czechoslovakia, France, Germany, Hungary, Poland, Russia, Switzerland

1932
Algeria, Austria, England, France, French Morocco, Germany, Hungary, Italy, Spain, Spanish Morocco

1937
Austria, Czechoslovakia, Denmark, France, Germany, Holland, Norway, Sweden, Switzerland

Teaching Positions

Cleveland Institute of Art, 1930–present: chairman, industrial design department, 1936–76; named Lindseth Professor, 1991; Viktor Schreckengost Teaching Award inaugurated, 2000

Western Reserve University, 1934–42: school of education, design and theater design

Publications

Ceramic section, *Encyclopedia of the Arts* (New York: Runes & Scrickel, 1946)

Numerous articles for trade magazines and other trade publications

World's Fairs

1933–34, *Century of Progress Exposition*, Chicago

1937, *Paris International Exposition*

1939–40, *New York World's Fair*

1939–40, *San Francisco World's Fair*

Awards

Accademia Bedriacense, Calvatone, Italy
1984, Diploma di Maestro

Accademia Italia delle Arti e del Lavoro, Salsomaggiore Terme, Italy
1980, Member

American Ceramic Society, Westerville, Ohio
1962, Design Division Award, Outstanding Contribution to the Ceramic Arts
1982, Honorary Life Membership

American Institute of Architects, New York
1958, Gold Medal, Ceramic Architectural Sculpture

American Institute of Graphic Arts, New York
1950, Certificate of Excellence

American Watercolor Society, New York
1955, Grumbacher Purchase Prize
1962, 1964, Rudolf Lesch Purchase Prize
1963, Lena Newcastle Purchase Prize

Architectural League of New York
1955, Architectural Sculpture Award

Butler Institute of American Art, Youngstown, Ohio, *Annual Exhibition*
1948, First Award and Purchase (sculpture)
1950, First Award and Purchase (pottery)
1966, Purchase (watercolor)

Cleveland Museum of Art, *May Show*
1929, Third Prize (batik)
1931, First (pottery)
1932, Special Award, Outstanding Excellence (pottery); Third (sculpture)
1934, First (pottery); Honorable Mention (mural and decorative painting)
1936, First (pottery)
1937, Special Award (pottery); First (sculpture)
1938, Special Award (sculpture); First (pottery)
1939, First (sculpture)
1940, Second (sculpture)
1941, Third (sculpture)
1942, Second (sculpture)
1943, First (sculpture)
1946, Honorable Mention (watercolor)
1947, First (sculpture); First (pottery); Third (watercolor)
1948, Special Award (sculpture); Special Award (pottery); Honorable Mention (watercolor)
1949, First (sculpture); Third (watercolor)
1950; Special Award (sculpture); Special Award (watercolor); Third (pottery)
1951, First (pottery); Second (sculpture); Honorable Mention (watercolor)
1952, Special Award (pottery); First (sculpture); Third (watercolor, mural and decorative painting)
1953, Third (pottery); Honorable Mention (watercolor)
1954, Honorable Mention (pottery, sculpture, watercolor)
1955, Special Award (sculpture); First (pottery); Honorable Mention (watercolor)
1956, Third (pottery); Honorable Mention (watercolor); Honorable Mention (sculpture)
1957, Honorable Mention (watercolor)
1958, Honorable Mention (freehand drawing)

International Institute of Arts and Letters, Lindau, Germany
1958, Fellow

McKinley High School, Sebring
1993, Distinguished Alumni Award

New York State College of Ceramics, Alfred University; American Ceramic Society
1939, Charles Fergus Binns Medal, Outstanding Contribution to the Ceramics Field

Pennsylvania Academy of the Fine Arts, Philadelphia
1938, Award of Merit (sculpture), *Annual Exhibition*

Philadelphia Art Alliance
1940, Certificate of Honor, Finest Piece of Sculpture, *Contemporary Handcraft Exhibition*

State of Ohio
2000, Governor's Award for the Arts

Syracuse Museum of Fine Arts, *Ceramic National Exhibition*
1938, First (sculpture)
1941, Honorable Mention (sculpture)
1947, Hall Award (ceramics)
1948, Vitro Award (ceramics)
1950, Drakenfield Award (ceramics)
1951, IBM Award (sculpture)
1951, First (architectural sculpture)
1951, Citation, Syracuse Museum and American Ceramic Society
1954, First, Syracuse Museum and American Ceramic Society; Third (architectural and ceramic sculpture)

United States Navy
1962, Companion of the Order

Universitá dell'Arti, Salsomaggiore Terme, Italy
1982, Diploma di Merito

Women's City Club, Cleveland
1973, Fine Arts Award (visual arts)

Exhibitions, Solo and Group

Abilene (Texas) Fine Arts Museum, 1948, 1950, 1954

Akron Art Institute, 1931, 1938, 1950, 1951, 1953

Albany (New York) Art Institute, 1952

Albright-Knox Art Gallery, Buffalo, 1940, 1951

Alfred (New York) University, 1936

All Ohio Invitational, Marietta, 1971

Allen Memorial Art Museum, Oberlin, Ohio, 1932, 1935, 1940

American Watercolor Society, New York, 1954, 1955, 1957, 1959, 1962, 1963, 1964, 1965, 1966, 1969, 1974

American Artists Group, Inc., New York, 1960, 1961, 1962, 1963, 1964, 1965, 1966, 1967, 1968, 1969, 1970, 1971, 1972, 1973, 1974, 1975, 1976

Amherst (Massachusetts) College, 1953

Art Colony Gallery, Cleveland, 1952, 1953

Art Institute of Chicago, 1933, 1934, 1942

Ashtabula (Ohio) Arts Center, 1967

Associated American Artists, New York, 1950

Baldwin Museum of Art, Massillon, Ohio, 1935, 1939

Baltimore Museum of Art, 1941, 1948

Blossom Music Center, Akron, Ohio, 1968

Boston Museum of Fine Arts, 1949

Bonfoey Gallery, Cleveland, 1969, 1970, 1971, 1972, 1973, 1974, 1975, 1976

Bradley University Gallery, Peoria, Illinois, 1951

Brooklyn Museum of Art, 1953

Brooks Memorial Art Gallery, Memphis, 1935, 1938, 1949, 1950, 1953

Bratenahl (Ohio) Invitational, 1974, 1975, 1976

Butler Institute of American Art, Youngstown, Ohio, 1938, 1943, 1948, 1949, 1950, 1951, 1952, 1953, 1954, 1955, 1956, 1963, 1964, 1965, 1966, 1969

Canton (Ohio) Art Institute, 1950, 1951, 1952, 1962

Carnegie Library, Steubenville, Ohio, 1951

Carnegie Museum of Art, Pittsburgh, 1950

Chattanooga Art Association, 1936

Christ the King Exhibit, Birmingham, Michigan, 1959

Church of the Savior, Cleveland Heights, Ohio, 1965

Circle Gallery, Cleveland, 1963, 1964, 1965

Cleveland Athletic Club, 1971, 1973, 1974, 1975

Cleveland College, Western Reserve University, 1932, 1934

Cleveland Museum of Art, 1929, 1931, 1932, 1933, 1934, 1935, 1936, 1937, 1938, 1939, 1940, 1941, 1942, 1943, 1946, 1947, 1948, 1949, 1950, 1951, 1952, 1953, 1954, 1955, 1956, 1957, 1958, 1959, 1960, 1961, 1962

Cleveland Institute of Art Gallery, 1935, 1936, 1937, 1938, 1939, 1949, 1950, 1951, 1952, 1953, 1954, 1955, 1956, 1957, 1958, 1959, 1960, 1961, 1962, 1963, 1964, 1965, 1966, 1967, 1968, 1969, 1970, 1971, 1972, 1973, 1974, 1975, 1976

Cleveland Society of Artists Gallery, 1932, 1938, 1949, 1950, 1954

Cleveland State University, 1972

Colorado Springs Fine Arts Center, 1947

Columbus (Ohio) Gallery of Fine Art, 1939, 1947, 1948, 1949, 1950, 1951, 1952, 1954, 1956

Corcoran Gallery of Art, Washington, D.C., 1942, 1952

Cornell University Gallery, Ithaca, New York, 1936, 1946

Corvoisier Gallery of Art, San Francisco, 1938

Cranbrook Academy of Art, Bloomfield Hills, Michigan, 1941, 1949, 1953

Currier Gallery of Art, Manchester, New Hampshire, 1939, 1940, 1947, 1949, 1950, 1951

Dallas Museum of Art, 1950, 1954

Dartmouth College Gallery, Hanover, New Hampshire, 1951

Davenport (Iowa) Municipal Art Gallery, 1948, 1950, 1952, 1954

David Strawn Art Gallery, Jacksonville, Florida, 1936

Dayton Art Institute, 1952, 1956

Dayton Museum of Art, 1941, 1947, 1949, 1950

Demonstration Art Gallery, Greenville, Raleigh, and Winston-Salem, North Carolina, 1936

Denver Art Museum, 1939, 1947

Des Moines Art Center, 1950

Detroit Institute of Arts, 1948

Eastman School of Music, Rochester, New York, 1947, 1948, 1950

Easton (Pennsylvania) School of Music, 1936

Ecumenical Art Exhibit, Cleveland, 1963

Erie (Pennsylvania) Art Museum, 1947

Everhart Museum, Scranton, Pennsylvania, 1935

Flint (Michigan) Institute of Fine Arts, 1941

Florida State College, Tallahassee, 1936

Fort Wayne (Indiana) Museum of Art, 1936, 1949

Foyer Eastman Gallery, Rochester, New York, 1950

George Walter Vincent Smith Art Museum, Springfield, Massachusetts, 1937

Hanley Museum, Stoke-on-Trent, England, 1937

Higbee Gallery, Cleveland, 1950

Indiana State Teachers College, Terra Haute, 1950

Indiana University Gallery, Bloomington, 1940, 1950, 1953

Institute of Contemporary Art, Washington, D.C., 1951

Intown Club, Cleveland, 1952, 1953, 1961, 1963, 1964, 1967, 1969, 1973

Iowa University, 1955

Irvin and Co. Invitational, Shaker Heights, Ohio, 1970, 1971, 1972

Isaac Delgado Museum, New Orleans, 1952

Jacques Seligman Gallery, New York, 1950

J. B. Speed Art Museum, Louisville, 1935, 1950

Jewish Community Center, Canton, Ohio, 1971

Jewish Community Center, Cleveland, 1975

John Herron Art Institute, Indianapolis, 1940, 1949

Joslyn Memorial Art Museum, Omaha, 1948

Kalamazoo (Michigan) Institute of Art, 1948

Kansas City Art Institute, 1940

Kansas State Teachers College, Emporia, 1947, 1949, 1952, 1953

Kent (Ohio) State University, 1947, 1949, 1959

Konstall, Hellingsfor, Finland, 1937

Kunstindustrimuseet, Copenhagen, 1937

Lake Erie College Gallery, Painesville, Ohio, 1950

Lakewood (Ohio) Civic Auditorium, 1963, 1966

Lehigh University, Bethlehem, Pennsylvania, 1972

Little Gallery, Birmingham, Michigan, 1951, 1952

Lyman Allyn Museum, New London, Connecticut, 1947

Los Angeles County Museum of Art, 1937, 1947, 1950

Louisiana Art Commission, Baton Rouge, 1952

Grover M. Herman Fine Arts Center, Marietta (Ohio) College, 1971, 1972, 1973

Malvina Freedson Gallery, Lakewood, Ohio, 1966, 1967, 1968, 1969, 1970, 1971, 1972, 1973, 1974, 1975, 1976

Mansfield (Ohio) Art Center, 1960, 1972

Marshall Field Gallery, Chicago, 1951

Metropolitan Museum of Art, New York, 1931, 1935, 1940, 1946, 1951, 1952

Minneapolis Institute of Art, 1950

Minnesota University Art Gallery, Minneapolis, 1938, 1941, 1951, 1952

Mint Museum, Charlotte, North Carolina, 1941

Mount Holyoke College, South Hadley, Massachusetts 1948

Munson-Williams-Proctor Institute Museum of Art, Utica, New York, 1940, 1952

Museum of Contemporary Crafts, New York, 1962

Museum of Fine Arts, Houston, 1941, 1950

National Academy of Design, New York, 1957, 1962, 1963, 1965, 1967, 1969, 1973

Nationalmuseet, Stockholm, 1937

National Museum of American Art, Smithsonian Institution, Washington, D.C., 1948, 1950, 1951, 1955, 1960

National Religious Art, Detroit, 1964

Nebraska University Gallery, Lincoln, 1951

Newark (New Jersey) Museum of Art, 1937

New Britain (Connecticut) Institute Art Museum, 1951

Newcomb College Gallery, New Orleans, 1938

New Jersey State Museum, Trenton, 1936

Northern Illinois State Tech College, De Kalb, 1948

Oberlin (Ohio) College Gallery, 1939

Oglebay Institute, Wheeling, West Virginia, 1941, 1948, 1954

Ohio State University, Columbus, 1958

Ohio University, Athens, 1949, 1950, 1951

Ohio Wesleyan University, Delaware, 1954

Oregon University Gallery, Eugene, 1947

Park Synagogue, Cleveland, 1962, 1963, 1964, 1965, 1966

Parma (Ohio) Fine Arts Council, 1968

Pennsylvania Academy of the Fine Arts, Philadelphia, 1931, 1932, 1933, 1934

Pennsylvania State College, State College, 1949

Philadelphia Art Alliance, 1937, 1940, 1942, 1946, 1949, 1953

Pittsburgh University Gallery, 1937, 1939, 1940, 1947, 1949

Portland (Oregon) Art Museum, 1940, 1947

Purdue University, Lafayette, Indiana, 1951

Rhode Island League Arts and Crafts, Providence, 1951

Riverside Museum, New York, 1949

Robert Hull Fleming Museum, Burlington, Vermont, 1949

Rochester (New York) Memorial Art Gallery, 1937, 1939, 1940, 1946, 1949, 1951, 1952

Rockford (Illinois) Art Museum, 1948

Rohsska Konstojdmuseet, Gothenberg, Sweden, 1937

Rundel Gallery, Rochester, New York, 1952

Russell Art Gallery, Bloomington, Illinois, 1952

Saint Lawrence University, Canton, New York, 1953

Saint Paul (Minnesota) Gallery, 1953

San Antonio Museum of Art, 1941

San Diego Museum of Art, 1937, 1940, 1947

Sandusky (Ohio) Cultural Art Center, 1976

San Francisco Museum of Art, 1937, 1947, 1950

Scarab Club Gallery, Detroit, 1952

Scarborough on the Hudson, New York, 1964

Scripps College, Claremont, California, 1947

Seattle Art Museum, 1937, 1940, 1947

Sheldon Swope Art Gallery, Terra Haute, Indiana, 1950, 1952

Slater Memorial Museum, Norwich, Connecticut, 1949

Smith College Gallery of Art, Northampton, Massachusetts, 1949

South Bend (Indiana) Art Association, 1957

Springfield (Massachusetts) Art Association, 1947

State Teacher's College, Edinboro, Pennsylvania, 1958

Syracuse Museum of Fine Arts, New York, 1931, 1933, 1935, 1936, 1937, 1938, 1939, 1940, 1941, 1946, 1947, 1948, 1949, 1950, 1951, 1952, 1956

Ten-Thirty Gallery, Cleveland, 1948, 1949

Texas Technical College Art Association, Lubbock, 1948, 1950, 1952

Toledo Museum of Art, 1938, 1939, 1940, 1948

University of Georgia, Athens, 1951

University of Illinois Gallery, Urbana, 1952

University of Wisconsin, Madison, 1952

Utah State University, Logan, 1958

Valley Art Center, Chagrin Falls, Ohio, 1974, 1975, 1976

Virginia Museum of Fine Arts, Richmond, 1951

Wakefield Marine Museum, Vermilion, Ohio, 1961

Walker Art Center, Minneapolis, 1948

Watercolor, U.S.A., Springfield, Missouri, 1969

Westfield (Massachusetts) Athenaeum, 1947

West Virginia Wesleyan College, Buchannon, 1962

Wheaton (Illinois) College, 1972

Whitney Museum of American Art, New York, 1937

Wichita Art Association, 1948, 1949

William Rockhill Nelson Gallery of Art, Kansas City, 1948, 1949, 1950

Wooster (Ohio) College, 1951, 1952, 1966

Women's City Club, Cleveland, 1965, 1973

Worcester (Massachusetts) Art Museum, 1936, 1951

American Limoges China Company, Sebring, Ohio: dinnerware

American Stove Company, Cleveland: stoves, accessories

Atlas Globe China Company, Cambridge, Ohio: dinnerware

Chandler Price, Cleveland: printing presses

Cottrell Company, Westerly, Rhode Island: web printing presses

Cowan Pottery, Rocky River, Ohio: pottery, sculpture

Data Communications Division, Dallas: communications

Delta Electric Company, Marion, Indiana: portable lighting equipment

Electronic Systems Division, Melbourne, Florida: composition equipment

Gates Radio Corporation, Quincy, Illinois: broadcast equipment

General Electric Company: major and small appliances, lighting concepts

Harris Computers, Ft. Lauderdale, Florida: computers

Harris Corporation, Cleveland: printing presses, electronic gear

Harris-Seybold Co., Dayton, Ohio: cutters, printing presses

Holophane Company, Newark, Ohio: lighting units

Intertype Corporation, Brooklyn, New York: typesetting equipment

Langston Company, Camden, New Jersey: paper board

Macey Company, Cleveland: collaters

Murray Ohio Manufacturing Company, Nashville: bicycles, mowers, juvenile vehicles

R.F. Communications, Rochester, New York: marine and mobile communications

Salem China Company, Salem, Ohio: dinnerware, cookingware

Schriber Company, Dayton, Ohio: business forms presses

Sears, Roebuck & Company, Chicago: fans, mowers, bicycles, vehicles

Sheridan Company, Easton, Pennsylvania: collaters

Syracuse China, Syracuse, New York: dinnerware, hotelware

Verlys of America, New York: ornamental glass

Warner & Swasey, Cleveland: machine tools

White Motor Company, Cleveland: truck cabs, buses

Patents

The patents that follow are all design patents, unless noted otherwise.

No. 93,960, motor vehicle cab, awarded 4 December 1934, Frank G. Alborn and Viktor Schreckengost

No. 93,997, motor vehicle cab, awarded 4 December 1934, Frank G. Alborn and Viktor Schreckengost

No. 93,998, motor vehicle cab, awarded 4 December 1934, Frank G. Alborn and Viktor Schreckengost

No. 95,152, cream pitcher, awarded 9 April 1935, Viktor Schreckengost

No. 99,052, plate or similar article, awarded 24 March 1936, Viktor Schreckengost

No. 122,004, chair seat, awarded 20 August 1940, Viktor Schreckengost

No. 122,005, chair back, awarded 20 August 1940, Viktor Schreckengost

No. 123,574, bicycle, awarded 19 November 1940, Viktor Schreckengost

No. 123,575, bicycle, awarded 19 November 1940, Viktor Schreckengost

No. 123,576, bicycle, awarded 19 November 1940, Viktor Schreckengost

No. 123,577, bicycle, awarded 19 November 1940, Viktor Schreckengost

No. 127,281, chair back, awarded 20 May 1941, Viktor Schreckengost

No. 131,270, window ventilator housing, awarded 27 January 1942, Viktor Schreckengost

No. 131, 353, cabinet, awarded 10 February 1942, Viktor Schreckengost

No. 131, 354, cabinet, awarded 10 February 1942, Viktor Schreckengost

No. 132,601, plate or similar article, awarded 2 June 1942, Viktor Schreckengost

No. 152,437, headlight cluster for bicycle, awarded 18 January 1949, Viktor Schreckengost

No. 2,516,705, tricycle frame structure, awarded 25 July 1950, Herman L. Kraeft and Viktor Schreckengost

No. 162,347, printing press, awarded 6 March 1951, Viktor Schreckengost

No. 163,827, baby walker, awarded 3 July 1951, Viktor Schreckengost

No. 163,828, baby walker, awarded 3 July 1951, Viktor Schreckengost

No. 167,864, lighting fixture bowl, awarded 30 September 1952, Viktor Schreckengost

No. 168,904, paper cutter case, awarded 24 February 1953, Richard C. O'Brien and Viktor Schreckengost

No. 169,639, juvenile tractor, awarded 19 May 1953, Viktor Schreckengost

No. 169,640, juvenile tractor vehicle, awarded 19 May 1953, Viktor Schreckengost

No. 170,169, bicycle frame, awarded 11 August 1953, Viktor Schreckengost

No. 171,866, lighting fixture lens, awarded 30 March 1954, Viktor Schreckengost

No. 171,867, lighting fixture lens, awarded 30 March 1954, Viktor Schreckengost

No. 173,092, frying pan, awarded 21 September 1954, Viktor Schreckengost

No. 173,093, casserole, awarded 21 September 1954, Viktor Schreckengost

No. 173,094, casserole, awarded 21 September 1954, Viktor Schreckengost

No. 173,131, chicken fryer, awarded 28 September 1954, Viktor Schreckengost

No. 174,837, lighting fixture bowl, awarded 24 May 1955, Viktor Schreckengost

No. 175,745, pedal-type juvenile vehicle, awarded 4 October 1955, Viktor Schreckengost

No. 175,746, pedal-driven juvenile vehicle, awarded 4 October 1955, Viktor Schreckengost

No. 177,433, cup, 10 April 1956, Viktor Schreckengost

No. 177,434, serving bowl, 10 April 1956, Viktor Schreckengost

No. 177,435, sugar bowl with lid, 10 April 1956, Viktor Schreckengost

No. 177,436, creamer, awarded 10 April 1956, Viktor Schreckengost

No. 177,437, teapot, awarded 10 April 1956, Viktor Schreckengost

No. 178,212, surface-attached direct lighting, awarded 3 July 1956, Viktor Schreckengost

Invention patent no. 2,791,323, portable printing equipment, awarded 7 May 1957, Viktor Schreckengost

Invention patent no. 2,798,739, knockdown bicycle construction, awarded July 9 1957, Viktor Schreckengost

No. 181,318, window fan, awarded 29 October 1957, Viktor Schreckengost

No. 182,931, housing for a window-mounted fan, awarded 27 May 1958, Viktor Schreckengost

No. 183,544, tricycle frame, awarded 16 September 1958, Viktor Schreckengost

No. 185,101, bicycle chain guard, awarded 5 May 1959, Viktor Schreckengost

No. 185,323, bicycle luggage carrier, awarded 26 May 1959, Viktor Schreckengost

No. 185,575, girl's bicycle frame, awarded 23 June 1959, Viktor Schreckengost

No. 185,681, velocipede front fender and truss, awarded 14 July 1959, Viktor Schreckengost

No. 185,830, bicycle accessory tank, awarded 4 August 1959, Viktor Schreckengost

No. 185,909, velocipede fender, awarded 18 August 1959, Viktor Schreckengost

No. 187,992, juvenile vehicle, awarded 24 May 1960, Viktor Schreckengost

No. 187,993, juvenile vehicle, awarded 24 May 1960, Viktor Schreckengost

No. 187,994, juvenile vehicle, awarded 24 May 1960, Viktor Schreckengost

No. 189,057, luminaire, awarded 18 October 1960, Viktor Schreckengost

No. 189,385, sheet delivery apparatus, awarded 29 November 1960, Viktor Schreckengost

No. 189,674, velocipede, awarded 31 January 1961, Viktor Schreckengost

No. 189,675, velocipede, awarded 31 January 1961, Viktor Schreckengost

No. 189,676, velocipede, awarded 31 January 1961, Viktor Schreckengost

No. 189,677, velocipede, awarded 31 January 1961, Viktor Schreckengost

No. 190,385, wall lighting fixture or similar, awarded 23 May 1961, Viktor Schreckengost

No. 190,386, lens for lighting features, awarded 23 May 1961, Viktor Schreckengost

No. 190,759, lens for lighting fixtures, awarded 27 June 1961, Viktor Schreckengost

No. 190,921, luminaire lens, awarded 18 July 1961, Viktor Schreckengost

No. 194,324, juvenile vehicle, awarded 1 January 1963, Viktor Schreckengost

No. 195,019, bicycle, awarded 9 April 1963, Viktor Schreckengost

No. 195,944, mobile adjustable stand for fans, awarded 13 August 1963, Viktor Schreckengost

No. 196,522, velocipede, awarded 8 October 1963, Viktor Schreckengost

No. 196,523, velocipede, awarded 8 October 1963, Viktor Schreckengost

No. 197,569, velocipede, awarded 25 February 1964, Viktor Schreckengost

No. 198,827, bicycle, awarded 4 August 1964, Viktor Schreckengost

No. 199,130, chain-drive velocipede, awarded 15 September 1964, Viktor Schreckengost

No. 199,774, bicycle luggage carrier, awarded 8 December 1964, Viktor Schreckengost

No. 199,775, bicycle luggage carrier, awarded 8 December 1964, Viktor Schreckengost

No. 199,864, paper-cutting machine, awarded 22 December 1964, Viktor Schreckengost and Russell I. Haywood

No. 202,018, bicycle accessory tank, awarded 17 August 1965, Viktor Schreckengost

No. 202,388, console for a typesetting machine, awarded 21 September 1965, Viktor Schreckengost

No. 202,389, typesetting machine, awarded 21 September 1965, Viktor Schreckengost

No. 202,434, chain-drive juvenile vehicle, awarded 28 September 1965, Viktor Schreckengost

No. 202,436, juvenile tractor, awarded 28 September 1965, Viktor Schreckengost

No. 203,064, bicycle light, awarded 30 November 1965, Viktor Schreckengost

Index

Published on the occasion of the exhibition *Viktor Schreckengost and 20th-Century Design*, 12 November 2000–4 February 2001.

Published by
The Cleveland Museum of Art
11150 East Blvd.
Cleveland, Ohio 44106

Distributed by the
University of Washington Press
P.O. Box 50096
Seattle, WA 98145

Library of Congress Card Number: 00-107762

ISBN: 0-940717-62-X (softbound)

Produced by the publications department of the Cleveland Museum of Art.

Editing: Barbara J. Bradley and Kathleen Mills

Design: Thomas H. Barnard III

Production: Charles Szabla and Carolyn K. Lewis

Printing: Great Lakes Lithograph, Cleveland, on 100-pound Vintage gloss text

Composed in Bitstream Futura Light

Figures in brackets [ ] indicate catalogue numbers for works in the exhibition.

Front cover: *Pursuit Plane (Child's Pedal Car)* [152]; *Jazz Bowl* (detail) [128]

Back cover: Viktor Schreckengost; drawing for cab-over-engine truck

Endsheets: *Animal Kingdom Pattern Uncut Decal Sheet* [141]

Title page: *Sears Spaceliner Bicycle* [160]

PHOTOGRAPHY CREDITS

Photography by Gary Kirchenbauer and digital scanning by Janet Burke, photographic and digitial imaging services, Cleveland Museum of Art. Other photographers: pp. 24, 25 (bottom), 134, 142 (bottom left and center), 143: Robert C. Hoffner; p. 25 (top): Larry Kean; p. 39: (bottom left) Colburn Ball; p. 67 (bottom right and left): after Richard J. Powell and David A. Baily, *Rhapsodies in Black: Art of the Harlem Renaissance* (London/Berkeley: Hayward Gallery/University of California Press, 1997), 26, 27; p. 71: Peter Harholdt, courtesy the Wolfsonian-Florida International University, Miami Beach, Florida; p. 98: after *Crockery and Glass Journal* (June 1934); p. 105: after *Design* (November 1935), 15; p. 153: Cornelius.